Also by David Meltzer

Reading Jazz

WRiTING JAZZ

edited by David Meltzer

Mercury House
San Francisco

Published in the United States by Mercury House, San Francisco, California,
a nonprofit publishing company devoted to the free exchange of
ideas and guided by a dedication to literary values.

United States Constitution, First Amendment: Congress shall make no law respecting an
establishment of religion, or prohibiting the free exercise thereof; or abridging the
freedom of speech, or of the press; or the right of the people peaceably to
assemble, and to petition the Government for a redress of grievances.

Cover art and design and interior handlettering by Ward Shumaker
(www.warddraw.com).

Designed and typeset
by Kirsten Janene-Nelson after the design by David Peattie for *Reading Jazz.*
Editorial and production work by K. Janene-Nelson and Justin Edgar, with grateful
thanks to the numerous interns who graced this book with editorial and
administrative assistance. Printed on 55" Glatfelter Natural paper
by Bang Printing, Brainerd, Minnesota.

Mercury House and colophon are registered trademarks of
Mercury House, Incorporated.
www.wenet.net/~mercury

Library of Congress Cataloguing in Publication Data
Writing jazz / edited by David Meltzer.
p.   cm.
Includes bibliographic references (p. 298) and index (p. 314).
ISBN 1-56279-096-X (acid-free paper)
1. Jazz—History and criticism.   I. Meltzer, David.
ML3507.W75   1999
781.65 DC21   99-30298
CIP

This book has been made possible by generous support from the Reva and David Logan Foundation and the Lannan Foundation.

For the fallen and the arising

CONTENTS

*The real work of making this anthology possible begins
when the editor hands it over to the interns and editors of Mercury House.
The labyrinthian grunt work of negotiating permissions was patiently and tactfully
managed by Kirsten Edmondson and Jennifer Llacera. Kirsten Janene-Nelson
again saved the day with astute and attentive copyediting,
proofreading, creative suggestions, and input.*

Pre-text

We used to look out at you all and say,
'What are they staring at? Why are they all here?'

—*Lil Hardin Armstrong*

I

*R*eading *Jazz* (1994) was a negative critique of white culture's shimmy with black jazz. Its texts were written in the main by white American and European writers, presenting in a collaged fashion the cultural colonization and reinvention of jazz as a white discourse. By describing, defining, naming, and containing jazz, absorbing its creative energies, jazz became a discourse of a predominantly middle- to upper-class educated cadre of males, at the high end of the white supremacist totem pole. (On the other hand, many white jazz musicians came from underprivileged immigrant working-class backgrounds.) White fan-based fabricators of jazz history were also often jazz entrepreneurs who produced and manufactured recordings of the music. Whites wrote the liner notes, biographies, histories, criticism; edited specialist magazines, catalogs; ran night clubs, concert halls, booking agencies, record companies, pressing plants; white culture served as the interlocutors for a post-slavery art form.

Reading Jazz wanted to demonstrate the reception and construction of jazz as a white fascination. The anthology was stridently polemic in its choice of texts. While it was favorably reviewed, I was surprised at how many reviewers missed or avoided the polemical challenge I let loose. I saw the anthology as a historical sourcebook of intentional and unintentional racism; of purposeful and accidental racialism. It was clear that American culture operates as a white supremacist invisible empire. (The un-intentionality of racism or racialism can always be debated. Closer readings unveil layers of social imprinting, naturalized and automatic practices, tics of unexamined habit reinforced by white power structures and infrastructures.)

Writing Jazz represents African-American perceptions of jazz as a subject and practice. Didactically and dialectically, the two anthologies should be read together, ideally at the same time.

There are many differences between the two anthologies. In *Writing Jazz* there's more emphasis on oral transcripts of musicians talking to interviewers, folklorists, autobiographers than in the first anthology. Speech turned into the silence of type, into "writing," is a genre in its own right. I'm cognizant that many of the scribes, like those of the nine-teenth-century slave narratives, were white—though often it's hard to discern who is master and who's the slave in these encounters. (I'm also aware of the ambiguities of an oral historian's interrogative techniques of editing and shaping the spoken into a script corresponding to the inter-viewer's narrative needs.[1]) As in any theme-driven anthology there will be many omissions, some strategic, others accidental, unavoidable, or un-negotiable. Like *Reading Jazz*, this gathering is a sourcebook to be scanned, shuffled, and surfed in riffing bibliomantic passes, or read sequentially as a polyphonic telling and retelling of jazz as myth, fact, and process, as cultural history, and as a spiritual domain.

Unlike for *Reading Jazz*, my assumptions were challenged by the mater-ial I gathered. One premise I began with was to show that jazz was sub-jected to similar forms of resistance, moral panic, and mythomania in black culture as in white culture. I did locate some editorials in African-American newspapers of the teens and twenties by black bourgeois crit-ics perceiving jazz as modernist minstrelsy, stating jazz and blues were undignified and unrepresentative of Negro aspirations, which should strive for a "higher" Fine Arts cultural level. Yet over all, there was much more acceptance and cultural pride in the music, its heroic figures, and its incorporation into the social matrix of urban black culture. In com-parison with white culture's forays into scintillating and racially exotic jazz realms—a vortex of urban life elaborately detailed by its tourists as Dante itemized the Inferno's damned[2]—jazz was a presence and force in African-American urban life, linked to African memory and social prac-tice. (Jazz was a condition some African-Americans fled from to seek, like W.E.B. DuBois, higher ground in European high culture, meeting at the crossroads the latest influx of white tourists drawn to its syncopated promises.)

This anthology follows an uneven historic spread, concentrating more on blues, the Jazz Age, the small and big bands that typified the thirties and forties, and bebop. There's a noticeable paucity of texts from post-bop through Free Jazz into fusion, jazz Muzak, and neo-con's return to yesteryear.

Anthologists have a right to sing the blues. The commerce and con-catenation of permissions-gathering is a dunning experience. Often un-pleasant encounters with the shadow side of authors, agents, estates, remote-control confidential clerks in the bowels of multiproduct con-glomerates; frazzled interns flustered and clueless, answering machines whose inner oracles can only be reached through kabbalistical number

games; editors and their subordinates who apparently have short shelf
lives with whatever publisher they are employed by. The publishing biz
(like show biz) seems to manufacture a networking platoon of nomads
whose perks are ultimately more satisfying than those of pond-scum
temps who take or mis-take dictation. Some of this confounding process
was the ultimate editor of *Writing Jazz,* and should receive full credit at
the end of the book, as at the end of a movie names scroll down the
screen while the audience abandons the theater.

In cutting and pasting, mixing these texts together into a fractured narrative, I'm aware of what's left out, of what works were unobtainable or
simply unaffordable, and I carry the anthologist's "what-if" burden of
knowing how they would have made for a richer work. *Anthology* is from
the Greek and means "flower-gathering," and this is a sparse bouquet.
Books are inevitably apologies for what they could have been.

Key presences in *Writing Jazz* are the blues, Ma Rainey, Duke Ellington
(whose grand protean body of work never forgot the blues), Lester
Young, Billie Holiday, Charlie Parker, Thelonius Monk, John Coltrane.
Core leitmotifs are Black and Blue and White, i.e., racism and its momentary creative transcendence through music making. Frantz Fanon is
another trope in the most apparently discordant or chaotic jazz muta-
tions. Dignity, anger, tolerance, rage ride alongside spirit's everpresent
given; a deeply connected spiritual continuum embodied and expressed
in the creative process as a unifying moment.

Jazz is paradox, certainty and uncertainty, stability and flux, fixed and
fluid, the hidden revealed in an instant, a sequence of instances words
fail to translate but that remain memorable nevertheless, and whose performances are told, re-told, and then written into works that become a
kind of folklore. The greatest jazz is both conservative and radical, reactionary and revolutionary at the same time.

Alain Locke and Langston Hughes initiate the African-American response to jazz and blues as art forms challenging the Euro-American
"classical" musics. Locke, like DuBois, often frames his appreciations of
black culture in relation to white high culture terms of approval. Hughes
provides a more radical stance as does LeRoi Jones/Amiri Baraka.
Baraka proclaims (and celebrates) black music and performance styles as
modernist and ancient earthquakes that crack apart white empires built
on the backs of slaves. A ruling class secretly desires and fears rebellion's
fusion and confusion, the elevated energy of a crowd surging forth and,

rage's fury, leveling all distinctions. Baraka, my contemporary, the unac-
knowledged maestro of postwar poetry and paterfamilas of the Black
Arts movement, has produced the most compelling and engaged writing
on jazz. His *Blues People*, published in 1963, was the first full-length study
and history of jazz written by an African-American.

Jazz illustrates the dynamic movement of art as a socializing energy.
Starting as a social music for pleasure and ritual, via technologies of
recording and radio it became a pop music networking through the
States and out into Europe, the Middle East, and the so-called Orient.
Through the Jazz Age and Swing Era, jazz moved the bodies of dancers
in service to its rhythms and romantic celebrations. Its major movements
of exploration and revolt occurred in cultural spaces opened up by world
wars; or, in the case of Free Jazz, in the turbulence of the Vietnam War
polarizing the nation. As with any pop music, it's synthesized and re-
shaped out of an influx of regional and phonographic musics; it's a hybrid of pilfered licks, riffs, and vocalisms from hillbilly music, Tin Pan
Alley[3], vaudeville, gospel, blues, tango, mariachi, hula … it's made and
remade from whatever's in the air. Growing out of antebellum African-
American musics whose roots were in Africa, it was also intercultural, a
product of crosscultural pollination, constantly modern and egalitarian.
It was a trade, a job, a vocation, a hobby, sometimes a career. Musicians
are thieves like poets and have big ears to latch onto sounds and rhythms
for their enterprise.

Starting in the twenties, attempts to legitimate jazz in Western high
art musical terms were mostly unwieldy vivisections, curios liminal to
both high art and durable jazz. (Jazz, like any elitist or pop art, divides
along lines of High/Low culture disputes with counter histories rein-
forcing its positions to in-house battles between "purists" and "dilutors,"
"artists" versus "sell-outs," "innovators" versus "imitators," "moldy figs"
versus "hipsters.")

Jazz, divided in its own mythologies and histories, is becoming academic Astro-turf that sweep-up crews fuss into something completely
other. Faux-gold plastic marble trophies and statuary revered by boojy
(bourgeoisie) elites seeking rapprochement with anti-establishment arts
they hate and envy yet wish to embrace before their walkers melt down.
Watch out for the embrace. The paradox of denying and desiring acceptance; a yearning for legitimacy percolates in jazz/pop culture. Today's
postmortem museum mentality about jazz is the incorporation of de-

fiance into compliancy. Curators of jazz in highly visible cultural institutions and bureaucracies regard jazz and modernism (which were once synonymous) as played-out silences that large ensembles and chamber groups can reactivate through careful reconstruction of what was once instantaneous. One can look back at jazz from a renewable distance. Its brief history of being is encased in vinyl ambergris like prehistoric bees.

2

Rush-hour gridlock: talking jazz with a professional musician who's stretching out into record producing and soundtrack composing. The sad sack status of jazz is our inevitable subject. Record companies make more money on jazz reissues, more profit with less overhead, and usually no need to pay the musicians because they were already paid for the original session. Younger players have less and less opportunity to gig and record. Cultivation and marketing of "young lions" by major labels creates market-driven boundaries around who's let into the big leagues. A form of corporate ageism excludes seasoned players from possible exposure, favoring players who look young and cool enough to be iconized on romantic album covers. Conglomerate culture factories relegate jazz to similar low profit margins as Classical Music; the distribution (and potential sales) of records further challenged by the decline of radio stations devoted to jazz and by the rise of "soft jazz" stations playing facile faceless "mood" music featuring soaring bluesy saxophonists rising above thick synthesizer lush oceanic string simulacra. Usual rancor about Kenny G., but he's returning jazz into pop music as it was decades ago. (Major amounts of hot selling recorded "jazz" in the Jazz Age was hokum, novelty bands, not "the real thing," whose fans knew the unknowing masses would never buy; swing band chart-busters of the forties were more mostly novelty songs, hit-seeking love songs, or clunky instrumental rewrites of classical music themes.) The fan, the collector, the connoisseur, "keeper of the flame," holds to a rigid cosmology kerneled with luminous presences and moments signifying the Real Thing. But in a mass culture amassing pyramids of product pouring unrelentingly out of a manic global cornucopia, everything and nothing is the Real Thing. Collectors are everywhere who see value in almost anything, who create and sustain hierarchies of value, and who value hierarchy. Driven to reclaim an imagined past made emblematic by their retrieved objects, they become conservators. Whatever freedom music made them realize is now a static historical monument, an unreal thing of something once defining great possibility.

Rush-hour gridlock redefines the postindustrial, our talk continues (between Altoids) about the miniaturization of studio technology, the displacement of one kind of musician by another computer-enhanced one, conflicting traditions and practices dichotomizing old (authentic) versus new (inauthentic) as a form of explanation. He's sour, a jazz musician who missed the moment that pulled him into jazz as devotion. He says he's a realist: jazz isn't dead, it's over. He's into free-lance TV and film scoring, video game music, commercials, and producing. Works hard; lives in the East Bay and maintains a place in L.A. that he commutes to almost weekly looking for assignments, projects, contacts, networking. A graduate of the Berkeley High School jazz program, a Julliard student, he's paid his dues: played in theater pit-bands, supperclubs, weddings, bar mitzvahs, the long unrolled dues. But jazz is over, he says, it's said all it's had to say. The new musicians, the young lions, are saying what was said. Wynton and his minions preserve what was, not what is. Jazz isn't present tense anymore. It's past tense like Palestrina or Scarlatti. Trad jazz, bebop, postbop, free and fusion are all rut-stuck in archaic moldy figdom. The jazz tradition was, like philosophy, a practice unfolding out of its past, continually renewed, reframed, and reinvented in the present, but it's all over. It's reached its end and can only return to where it's been.

Traffic's turned into a photograph of traffic. Jazz has been turned into a classical music the way Mozart and Beethoven and Bach are fixed moments and won't go away. You've got big bands in tuxes at Lincoln Center or Carnegie Hall scrupulously doing Ellington and Mingus charts, or small chamber ensembles performing Monk and Joplin.

Local FM jazz station is on low volume as traffic grinds inches ahead.

It's business, he says. What sells is what people want to buy and what people want to buy is what sells. It's that simple; it's that impossible. Gargantuan conglomerates spend megabucks every second to figure out what makes product sell; they shell out big bread to market analysts, motivational researchers, psychologists, Christ, who knows?

It goes back and forth without the desire of resolve. A poet friend writes me about heart going out of the art, and how the once-upon-a-time free zone of poetry has become institutionalized, professionalized, simonized, lanolized, gone static, inert, run by poetry CPAs, anal bureaucrats turned into banal autocrats. Wanting to defuse his blues, I tell him it's always been that way; our shared histories of poetry and music have seen cyclic showdowns, collapses, relapses, uprisings. The future's always present. Our problem's the past. Hope's ghost stuck in salt freeze like Lot's wife looking back when she should've been moving ahead.

————

In the Sunday paper Kenny G. says, "I don't mind being the butt of a joke—if it's a funny joke." Forty million (and counting) albums sold. The article goes on: "He's got a wife (Lyndie), a three-year-old son (Max), and a brand-new seaplane he bought himself for his fortieth birthday." In *JazzTimes,* Tony Williams says, "I think that a lot of the guys who are being touted now as the new breed are told by record companies and managers, look, if you give us stuff that we can recognize, that's malleable, then you don't have to pay dues. You can have a nice apartment, nice clothes, cars, stuff like that, and just do this." The Faustian bargain is no longer a dilemma, an ethical crisis, it's the pact of choice for artists on the make. "That machinery wasn't around when I was twenty. It wasn't around for a lot of the guys who came before me. Those guys had to pay dues. They had to dig down deep inside themselves and play something that came from deep inside."[4]

Anyway, he says, trying to cross over into another lane, sooner or later computers'll do it all. That's the way it rolls. Clavichord's replaced by harpsichord and dumped for the pianoforte. All those medieval and renaissance instruments cast off in favor of new improved ones that promised and provided greater ease of playing, better (hipper, more modern) sound. Lute, orpharion, bandora, theorbo were given the heave-ho for the guitar, which got warehoused in the museum of the past because of the electric guitar, which is Now, at least for a while.

Darwinian consumerism gets me edgy; the instability of goods, their incessant rapid-fire appearance and disappearance, provokes short-term memory and chronically unresolved relationships to meaningfulness.

Music moves; sounds, vibrations, rhythms that never stay still on the oscilloscope; always moving, going somewhere, never arriving, having been there and gone. All of music sampled in a handful of microchips, some diskettes, and program folders. What's done is ready to be undone, ready to reconfigure, reinvent, through new combinations and modulations through the MIDI. Drum machine can be fed samples of any imaginable percussion instrument from kettledrum to finger cymbals, tune and tone their pitch to your chart. The new samples sound as real as the instruments they're replacing. One guy can sit in a room at home with his synthesizer, computer, keyboard and write, score, and playback his own versions of Mahler, Prokoviev, Gil Evans; can compose his own symphony in digital audio the printer will print out in hard copy, putting copyists out of business, or the computer will punch out your tone poem, concerto, string quartet, jazz band, or trio into a CD or multiple CDs. You can sample all the great solos of recorded jazz into a massive masterpiece of phantoms, an angel choir dismantled into bits and pieces, reassembled into a sonic boom collage, spectral homage of digitalized breath woven into a skein of binary numbers.

———

"The noise of postmodern culture is relentless. Endless screams and howls exclaim the necessity of consumption, of work, and of inhibited desire. There is no place to hide—not on the street, not in the workplace, not even in the home. Everywhere, blasts of electronic information from appliances of convenience reverberate out to the horizons of perception enveloping the compliant and the resistant. Even in moments of natural silence, logos, trademarks, and other visual markers conspire with involuntary memory to maintain the noise with internalized and inescapable slogans and jingles. Like a prisoner whose brain functions have been disrupted by exposure to loud unceasing noise, the contemporary cultural participant is subject to neuroses that ever increase and intensify."[5]

———

A car finally makes space to let us turn into the exit lane.

It's always been that way, every new techno gizmo that appears on the scene people anticipate as either utopian or demonic. Heaven and hell wrapped up in one glittery gizmo. You always have a choice. The media is neutral; it's what you or they do with it that gives it power. And power's neutral too.

Only if you have it.

It's how you use it. Or abuse it.

Or refuse it. Most people don't have a choice; you buy from a predetermined flow of stuff representing the mutating moment-to-moment myth stock slapped onto global supermarket shelves or on-line shimmering in virtual Sear's & Roebuck's catalogues.

Any instrument is a technology, enters sonic combat toe-to-toe to make its new sound "normal" and dispose of the reigning regent, making what was the standard into a nostalgia for what's past. And each new technology has its own limit, its standardized "sound" you have to live within and personalize, like Fender Rhodes, or B-3 Hammond Organ. Some don't cut it or last too long, becoming exotic or kitschy or both like the Theremin or saxophone Veritone box. New sounds are released, realized, and restricted to the mechanical peculiarity of each new instrument; yet the MIDI and computer encompass the sounds of any instrument current or long gone.

Then anyone who can afford the equipment can create their own music and circulate their CDs through a counter economy and find a cultural niche outside of global pop cult hegemony. Right?

Get with the program.

3

What trumpets American uniqueness to itself and the world is the singular presence, impact, and embeddedness of African-American artists in almost all facets, genres, subcults of popular music, literature, lingo, dance, and style. Moves and grooves are watched and learned, circulated across neighborhoods, cities, states, oceans, and airways through CDs, cassettes, LPs, videos, recombined by musicians and audiences globally, fused, grafted, reworked, and recirculated back to World Music sectors in record megastores where white mavens of exotica buy music from Africa pushed by James Brown beats with kora counterpoint, mbira rainfall plunking inside Funkadelic ensemble voicings, or talking drum-machine unrelenting back beat for Algerian rappers out of a Paris 'hood. The music works in circles, loops, spirals, links (not chains) in tidal constancy, despite a corrupt and corrupting global economy. The music works and retains its utopian germ, its dream of possibility, of forgetting impossibility. But back in the States the dividing rope still exists, whether it's goldchain gangsta wrapped or platinum discs behind glass framed in teakwood. The borders are drawn, or, paraphrasing Bush's voice-over for the Gulf War info-mercial, the line is drawn in the sand between white and black; implanted implacably as the Great Wall, divided, apart, where whites and blacks face each other tiptoeing to the ledge of a deep Grand Canyon whose bottom can't be fathomed. Only the musics arise.

Definitions, Myths

*The roots of jazz are in suffering. Jazz is linked inti-
mately with the blues and the blues with the spirituals. Jazz comes out of a religious place, very long ago,
but it begins on the plantations with the spirituals.*

—*Richard Wright, 1960*

Eileen Southern

From the fusion of blues and ragtime with brass-band music and syncopated dance music came jazz, a music that developed its own characteristics. There are numerous theories about the origin of the word *jazz*. One
to which several authorities subscribe is that the word is somehow related to an itinerant black musician named Jazbo Brown, who was well
known in the Mississippi River Valley country. It was said that when
Brown played in the honky-tonk cafés, the patrons would shout, "More,
Jazbo! More, Jaz, more!" Another theory is that the word can be traced
to a sign painter in Chicago who, in about 1910, produced a sign for the
black musician Boisey James stating that MUSIC WILL BE FURNISHED BY
JAS.' BAND. James, a purveyor of hot music and particularly of the blues,
became known as "Old Jas," and the music he played, "Jas's music."
Eventually the word was simply called jazz.

Many varied theories have been advanced over the years. James Europe
denied, for example, having given an explanation that was attributed to
him in the press—that the word *jazz* represented a corruption of "razz,"
the name of a Negro band active in New Orleans about 1905. It is note-
worthy, however, that all of the theories suggest that the word is to be associated in one way or another with the folk mores of black men, either
in the United States or Africa.

—1971

J.L. Dillard

Since it is obvious that Blacks were not always singing and playing
music—for the same reason that it is obvious that they were not always
eating possum and watermelon—it follows quite logically that jazzmen
(most of the genuine ones having been Black) used the vocabulary of
their dialect from other domains when talking about music or composing lyrics. There are, however, some expressions that are centrally
musical ...

Swing, when it first came to American linguistic consciousness, meant
"that undefinable something that makes a jazz performance a good one
rather than a routine or mediocre one." To define the term was virtually
tantamount to delimiting what made a performance good, and many
jazzmen are on record as saying, "If you gotta ask, you'll never know."
Whatever it was, "swinging" was not a technical proficiency that could
be tested on an exam, like conservatory learning, and even the adepts

might fail to swing at some times. (Or at the very best, one solo by a jazz idol might be less swinging than his performance on another occasion, even when the musical number to be "swung" did not change.)

—1977

Julian "Cannonball" Adderley

I wish I could say who I am. I've been trying to find out for some time. I imagine most of us have. We are victimized by things like identity, which means we have a niche, a category, something to do, a place, and an expected behavior follow-through situation. Actually, that's one of my big problems. It's very difficult for me to accept what has been done to this music. We have allowed it to become categorized and placed in niches, numbered, detailed, and put into little things. We've come up with a departmentalized Black-oriented music. I imagine that the only reason there should be any emphasis on Black music is because there has been a concerted effort to be sure there hasn't been any information regarding the music that is of, from, by, and—largely—oriented *to* Black people. Consequently, some of us have taken an interest in trying to cancel those lines of demarcation that say this is jazz, this bop, this is funky jazz, this is modern jazz, this is avant-garde, this gospel, this is spiritual, this blues—well, blues may be another thing altogether—but I resent saying this is soul or rock and roll, or whatever you want to call it. From a pragmatic viewpoint, these are the realities we have to deal with in this society. Since I'm going to be a jazz chauvinist, I'll have to go along with these terms to an extent.

—1973

Faruq Z. Bey

Having a kind of passing acquaintance with the Arabic language, I came to find out that *jazz* itself is an Arabic word. And it seems that scholars and pundits here, for various reasons, a lot of which are social-political, tend to want to bury the etymology of the word under a lot of nonsense and myths, and they usually come up saying that they don't know where it came from. But it's obvious where it came from. The question is: How did it come to be here? It's obviously an Arabic word, and the Arabic meaning of the word *jazz* means to cut a thing short. Now applied to music, it means "to syncopate." The problem is socially, politically, you raise serious questions when you start asking: How was a music that was generated by black people come to be identified by an Arabic term, unless these people spoke Arabic rather fluently, and if so, then what does that mean? To me it means that a lot of people who were brought here as slaves (so-called) were Muslims, and that has its own implications and ramifications.

—1982

Richard Abrams

I think we should strike the word *jazz*, not in hostility, but because most terms for Black music were given by Whites. If we check their decisions in light of the time the terms were assigned, we would find social and spiritual considerations which influenced these words.

As far as this country is concerned, Black music is revolution: social, spiritual, and physical revolution. When you say "United States," you are saying "revolution." When you say "Black music," you are saying "nature," which is parallel with what you call balance. It's not the only balance in the land, but it's on the bottom rung of the ladder, and the natural tendency is that this balance is much greater. There has never been a name given this music by its major innovators, so when we're talking about the social role of jazz, we're talking about the social role of music. [...]

Let us go back to the blues and before the blues, before that word existed, back to the cotton fields. Survival was laid out right there. Check the means of survival the slave used: sending messages through songs, tapping his foot, putting his head in the laughing barrel when the massah stumbled on the sidewalk and almost broke his neck. That's how he survived: being himself. The way to survive is to stop trying to be like other people and just follow the thought of who you are. You receive the things you need through the process of thought. These experiences and ideas come from inside and that's why they are humanizing.

QUESTION: But you don't mean you have to go back to the roots, back to something related to slavery times, to survive?

No. Taking over our own destiny and entertaining thoughts of self-realization is an advanced idea of the laughing barrel. That's what I was saying. You have to take care of yourself. And if you get money from what you do and feel you should go and pray then, go do it. Do all of it. Do everything that has to do with keeping you within who you are. [...]

It's true that we are manipulated in various ways, including economically, by this word [*jazz*]. Some time back, someone asked, "Is jazz dead?" Right then, that question was destroying incomes, mostly of Black people. The same thing has happened to rhythm and blues but, if you tell your agent you've got a good rock group (not a rhythm-and-blues group), you're in. It's not just words I'm talking about. What do I care about a word? You can say "jazz" all day; it's all right with me. But it's not all right with me in my projection. All of us in Black music realize that the purpose of this whole revolution is to bring everything together, and the implications of the word *jazz* won't do that.

—1973

Alfred B. Pasteur and Ivory L. Toldson

Rhythm, the fundamental principle in human behavior, reigns as the basic ingredient of black expressiveness. It is most easily transmitted in aesthetic forms that become tangible enclosures for the waves of force (rhythm) that are nourished by that which is "spiritual" in the universe. Clearly a human characteristic, rhythm's vibratory nature pulsates throughout the universe. In human behavior it is expressed sensually, through lines, surfaces, colors, language, music, and movements in dance and other motor responses. Blacks walk, talk, dance, prance, look, cook, play, and pray in marvelous harmony to, and with, the rhythm of the universe.

—1982

Willie "The Lion" Smith

I've played it all, barrel house, ragtime, blues, Dixieland, boogie-woogie, swing, bebop, bop—even the classics. It doesn't make any difference what names the writers and music critics want to paste on—it's all music and it's all an expression from the soul of a human being.

What they call jazz is just the music of people's emotions. It comes from wherever there have been colored people gathered together during the last hundred years. You'd think from reading the jazz books, most of them written by non-playing, so-called critics, that all the jazz and all the musicians came from New Orleans. They'd have you believing that if a musician had not been born down in those swamps, down in the Delta country, he had no business trying to play jazz.

Well, I'll tell you. All the different forms can be traced back to Negro church music, and the Negroes have worshiped God for centuries, whether they lived in Africa, the southern United States, or in the New York City area. You can still hear some of the older styles of jazz playing, the old rocks, stomps, and ring shouts in the churches of Harlem today.

Sure it made a difference where a musician was born. Various parts of the country had their own particular styles. When those of us around New York, Baltimore, and down as far as Georgia got a good romp-down going, we call it a slow-drag. We'd tell each other, "Now I'm really going to get in the alley." This meant we were going to tell the folks what it was all about, just like a blood and thunder Baptist preacher sounding off. What they called a carving contest was when we would try to see who could decorate a well-known melody with the best variations. . . .

Those of us who played in the old-fashioned saloons before Prohibition had to be two-fisted ticklers. We had to be because those saloon owners wanted to hear that piano going all night long. I learned to move the piano with my left, so I could handle the drinks (bought for me by customers) with my right hand without missing a note.

Yes sir, you can take my word for it, there was a lot of jazz played and sung in other places besides New Orleans in the early days. I first heard the blues sung while I was still a barefoot boy out of New Jersey. It was up around Haverstraw, New York, where they had around thirty-five brickyards. The yards employed Negroes to load and unload the millions of bricks, and when you got anywhere near to that town, you could hear the workers chanting and singing. Many of the songs you heard had things in them you read about in the Bible, or were familiar melodies from the church songs. They sang them in the style that is known as spirituals, or blues, today.

Another thing—all the jazz bands on river boats were not making it up and down the Mississippi, either. There were jazz bands on the boats going up and down the Hudson River. I can recall, as a boy, seeing and hearing bands on the boats with white and Negro musicians playing together. That was something you didn't see on the Mississippi!

The other jazz books? They all have to mention Willie the Lion, because when they came here, they didn't know what street they lived on.

It all goes to prove that music does not stem from any single race, creed, or locality. It comes from a mixture of all these things. As does the Lion.

—1964

Jonah Jones

A melody and swing outswing everything, if everybody gets together. It's like what we used to call a "groove," where everybody felt the same thing. Cozy (Cole) will tell you that. We'd get into that thing and play an hour, because everyone was swinging. That was why little bands always swung better than big ones, because you could never get everybody feeling good in a whole big band of twelve pieces or more. But four or five pieces could swing you into bad health!

—1970

J. A. Rogers

Jazz is a marvel of paradox: too fundamentally human, at least as modern humanity goes, to be typically racial, too international to be characteristically national, too much abroad in the world to have a special home. And yet jazz in spite of it all is one part American and three parts American Negro, and was originally the nobody's child of the levee and the city slum. Transplanted exotic—a rather hardy one, we admit—of the mundane world capitals, sport of the sophisticated, it is really at home in its humble native soil wherever the modern unsophisticated Negro feels happy and sings and dances to his mood. It follows that jazz is more at home in Harlem than in Paris, though from the look and sound of certain quarters of Paris one would hardly think so. It is just the epidemic contagiousness of jazz that makes it, like the measles, sweep the block. But somebody had to have it first: that was the Negro.

What after all is this taking new thing, that, condemned in certain quarters, enthusiastically welcomed in others, has nonchalantly gone on until it ranks with the movie and the dollar as the foremost exponent of modern Americanism? Jazz isn't music merely, it is a spirit that can express itself in almost anything. The true spirit of jazz is joyous revolt from convention, custom, authority, boredom, even sorrow—from everything that would confine the soul of man and hinder its riding free in the air. The Negroes who invented it called their songs the "Blues," and they weren't capable of satire or deception. Jazz was their explosive attempt to cast off the blues and sorrow. And that is why it has been such a balm for modern ennui, and has become a safety valve for modern machine-ridden and convention-bound society. It is the revolt of emotions against repression.

In its elementals, jazz had always existed. It is in the Indian war dance, the Highland fling, the Irish jig, the Cossack dance, the Spanish fandango, the Brazilian *maxixe,* the dance of the whirling dervish, the hula hula of the South Seas, the *danse du ventre* of the Orient, the *carmagnole* of the French Revolution, the strains of the Gypsy music, and the ragtime of the Negro. Jazz proper, however, is something more than all these. It is a release of all the suppressed emotions at once, a blowing off of the lid, as it were. It is hilarity expressing itself through pandemonium; musical fireworks.

The direct predecessor of jazz is ragtime. That both are atavistically African there is little doubt, but to what extent it is difficult to determine. In its barbaric rhythm and exuberance there is something of the bamboula, a wild, abandoned dance of the West African and the Haytian Negro, so stirringly described by the anonymous author of *Untrodden Fields of Anthropology,* or of the *ganza* ceremony so brilliantly depicted in Maran's *Batouala.* But jazz time is faster and more complex than African music. With its cowbells, auto horns, calliopes, rattles, dinner gongs, kitchen utensils, cymbals, screams, crashes, clankings, and monotonous rhythm it bears all the marks of a nerve-strung, strident, mechanized civilization. It is a thing of the jungles—modern man-made jungles.

The earliest jazz-makers were the itinerant piano players who would wander up and down the Mississippi from saloon to saloon, from dive to dive. Seated at the piano with a carefree air that a king might envy, their box-back coats flowing over the stool, their Stetsons pulled well over their eyes, and cigars at an angle of forty-five degrees, they would "whip the ivories" to marvelous chords and hidden racy, joyous meanings, evoking the intense delight of their hearers who would smother them at the close with huzzas and whiskey. Often wholly illiterate, these humble troubadours knowing nothing of written music or composition, but with minds like cameras, would listen to the rude improvisation of the dock laborers and the railroad gangs and reproduce them, reflecting perfectly the sentiments and the longings of these humble folk. The improvised bands at Negro dances in the South or the little boys with their harmonicas and Jews' harps, each one putting his own individuality into the air, played also no inconsiderable part in its evolution. "Poverty," says J.A. Jackson of *Billboard,* "compelled improvised instruments. Bones, tambourines, make-shift string instruments, tin can and hollow wood effects, all now utilized as musical novelties, were among early Negroes the product of necessity. When these were not available 'patting juba' prevailed. Present-day 'Charleston' is but a variation of this. Its early expression was the 'patting' for the buck dance."

———

[It's] difficult to say whether jazz is more characteristic of the Negro or of contemporary America. As was shown, it is of Negro origin plus the influence of the American environment. It is Negro-American. Jazz proper, however, is in idiom—rhythmic, musical, and pantomimic— thoroughly American Negro; it is his spiritual picture on that lighter comedy side, just as the spirituals are the picture on the tragedy side. The two are poles apart, but the former is by no means to be despised and it is just as characteristically the product of the peculiar and unique experience of the Negro in this country. The African Negro hasn't it, and the Caucasian never could have invented it. Once achieved, it is common property, and jazz had absorbed the nation's spirit, that tremendous spirit of go, the nervousness, lack of conventionality, and boisterous good-nature characteristic of the American, white or black, as compared with the more rigid formal natures of the Englishman or German.

But there still remains something elusive about jazz that few, if any, of the white artists have been able to capture. The Negro is admittedly its best expositor. That elusive something, for lack of a better name, I'll call Negro rhythm. The average Negro, particularly of the lower classes, puts rhythm into whatever he does, whether it be shining shoes or carrying a basket on the head to market as the Jamaican women do. Some years ago while wandering in Cincinnati I happened upon a Negro revival meeting at its height. The majority present were women, a goodly few of whom were white. Under the influence of the "spirit" the sisters would come forward and strut—much of jazz enters where it would be least expected. The Negro women had the perfect jazz abandon, while the white ones moved lamely and woodenly. This same lack of spontaneity is evident to a degree in the cultivated and inhibited Negro.

In its playing technique, jazz is similarly original and spontaneous. The performance of the Negro musicians is much imitated, but seldom equaled. Lieutenant Europe, leader of the famous band of the "Fifteenth New York Regiment," said that the bandmaster of the Garde Republicaine, amazed at his jazz effects, could not believe without demonstration that his band had not used special instruments. Jazz has a virtuoso technique all its own: its best performers, singers, and players lift it far above the level of mere "trick" or mechanical effects. Abbie Mitchell, Ethel Waters, and Florence Mills; the blues singers, Clara, Mamie, and Bessie Smith; Eubie Blake, the pianist; "Buddy" Gilmore, the drummer, and "Bill" Robinson, the pantomimic dancer—to mention merely an illustrative few—are inimitable artists, with an inventive, improvising skill that defies imitation. And those who know their work most intimately trace its uniqueness without exception to the folk-roots of their artistry.

Musically jazz has a great future. It is rapidly being sublimated. In the more famous jazz orchestras like those of Will Marion Cook, Fletcher Henderson, Vincent Lopez and the Clef Club units, there are none of the vulgarities and crudities of the lowly origin or the only too prevalent cheap imitations. The pioneer work in the artistic development of jazz was done by Negro artists; it was the lead of the so-called "syncopated orchestras" of Tyers and Will Marion Cook, the former playing for the Castles of dancing fame, and the latter touring as a concertizing orchestra in the great American centers and abroad. Because of the difficulties of financial backing, these expert combinations which have had to yield ground to white orchestras of the type of the Paul Whiteman and Vincent Lopez organizations are now demonstrating the finer possibilities of jazz music. "Jazz," says Serge Koussevitsky, the new conductor of the Boston Symphony, "is an important contribution to modern musical literature. It has an epochal significance—it is not superficial, it is fundamental. Jazz comes from the soil, where all music has its beginning." [...]

Whatever the ultimate result of the attempt to raise jazz from the mob-level upon which it originated, its true home is still its original cradle, the none too respectable cabaret. And here we have the seamy side to the story. Here we have some of the charm of Bohemia, but much more of the demoralization of vice. Its rash spirit is in Grey's popular song, "Runnin' Wild":

> Runnin' wild; lost control
> Runnin' wild; mighty bold
> Feelin' gay and reckless too
> Carefree all the time; never blue
> Always goin' I don't know where
> Always shown' that I don't care
> Don' love nobody, it ain't worth while
> All alone; runnin' wild.

Jazz reached the height of its vogue at a time when minds were reacting to the horrors and strain of war. Humanity welcomed it because in its fresh joyousness men found a temporary forgetfulness, infinitely less harmful than drugs or alcohol. It is partly for some such reasons that it dominates the amusement life of America to-day. No one can sensibly condone its excesses or minimize its social danger if uncontrolled; all culture is built upon inhibitions and control. But it is doubtful whether the "jazz hounds" of high and low estate would use their time to better advantage. In all probability their tastes would find some equally morbid, mischievous vent. Jazz, it is needless to say, will remain a recreation for the industrious and a dissipater of energy for the frivolous, a tonic for the strong and a poison for the weak.

For the Negro himself, jazz is both more and less dangerous than for the white—less, in that he is nervously more in tune with it; more, in that at his average level of economic development his amusement life is more open to the forces of social vice. The cabaret or better type provides a certain Bohemianism for the Negro intellectual, the artist, and the well-to-do. But the average thing is too much the substitute for the saloon and the wayside inn. The tired longshoreman, the porter, the housemaid, and the poor elevator boy in search of recreation, seeking in jazz the tonic for weary nerves and muscles, are only too apt to find the bootlegger, the gambler, and the demi-monde who have come there for victims and to escape the eyes of the police.

Yet in spite of its present vices and vulgarizations, its sex informalities, its morally anarchic spirit, jazz has a popular mission to perform. Joy, after all, has a physical basis. Those who laugh and dance and sing are better off even in their vices than those who do not. Moreover, jazz with its mocking disregard for formality is a leveler and makes for democracy. The jazz spirit, being primitive, demands more frankness and sincerity. Just as it already has done in art and music, so eventually in human relations and social manners, it will no doubt have the effect of putting more reality in life by taking some of the needless artificiality out.... Naturalness finds the artificial in conduct ridiculous. "Cervantes smiled Spain's chivalry away," said Byron. And so this new spirit of joy and spontaneity may itself play the role of reformer. Where at present it vulgarizes, with more wholesome growth in the future, it may on the contrary truly democratize. At all events, jazz is rejuvenation, a recharging of the batteries of civilization with primitive new vigor. It has come to stay, and they are wise who, instead of protesting against it, try to lift and divert it into nobler channels.

—1925

E. Simms Campbell

In the late eighties and early nineties, the era of tinsel and gilt, heavy furniture and mustache cups, swing was born. Where it was born is particularly important, because this may account for its irrelevance and utter rowdyism, its very elemental nature. Memphis, St. Louis, and a host of Southern towns claim credit although New Orleans seems logically to have the preference because of the great number of ragtime Negro musicians gathered there.

At this time—New Orleans was steeped in wickedness, bawdy houses running full blast, faro games on most street corners, and voluptuous creole beauties soliciting trade among the welter of gamblers, steamboat men, and hustlers of every nationality. New Orleans was not unique in this respect, as most American cities had their proscribed redlight district, but New Orleans was more colorful. Spaniards, Italians, Germans, French and French Negro, Swedish, and a great spattering of Portuguese—and all of them speaking Creole, the handy bastard French, the patois French which even today has not changed one iota from its original form.

Here in this port of all nationalities, this western hemisphere Marseilles, came a conglomerate group of itinerant musicians—Coon shouters, honky-tonks, black butt players (Negro musicians who could not read music)—all of them seeking their pot of gold in this paradise of pleasure. Most of them had little or no training in their respective instruments but they had a rhythm and a timing that appealed to the catholic tastes of this segment of America. The sky was the limit in "hot" ballads and there was no such thing as controlled music. New York was too far away and New Orleans was the mecca of entertainment to these Southern minstrels.

True, respectable New Orleans as well as respectable America sang and played Irish ditties or saccharine sentimental tear jerkers—"Whisper Your Mother's Name"—the Curse of Saloons and Little Nellie's Gone Astray creations. All America cried in its beer over them, but the gulf was too wide for pleasure-loving America to span, from Stephen Foster's "Old Folks at Home" to the sedate piano music (song and chorus) of the horsehair parlor days.

Barbershop chords were all right too, but New Orleans had gone on a bender—and when a man or a city goes pleasure-made they want music with "umph"—something that's on the naughty side, that tickles the senses, that starts them bunnyhugging. Ragtime filled this bill perfectly.

Possibly the first ragtime number originated in a bagnio and I know of more than a score that were actually created in them, having traced them back to the musicians who wrote them, tracing others through musicians who had played in bands with the original composer—although I must confess that nothing is harder actually to track down than a musical score. It is stolen from so many sources—the so-called Classics are dipped in and musicians are as jealous and touchy about giving credits to their fellows as prima donnas. A few of the numbers I actually saw created, written all over the backs of envelopes and policy number slips in all-night joints in St. Louis (pardon my misspent youth), and I have heard these same numbers, fifteen years later, presented for the edification of swing enthusiasts on the concert stage. Without mentioning names, many of our greatest song artists have played, at some time or another, in these dens of iniquity or halls of learning—according to your aesthetic tastes.

One thing, you may be certain they were never created in a classroom where harmony and composition were taught. It is sometimes sad to contemplate, but few lasting contributions to popular music have ever been born in cloistered surroundings.

"Ta-Ra-Ra-Boom-Dee-A" was written in the house of Babe Connors, one of the more colorful Negro madams, in 1894. It was essentially ragtime—in 4/4 time, the name "rag" being given because the playing was ragged—one played between the beats, not on them, just as swing today is irregular but is played in a faster tempo—a stepped-up version. If you have ever seen Negroes dancing, that is, dancing two-steps and one-steps and waltzes, you will notice that they do not dance exactly in time with the music. They dance to the rhythm of the number and are usually in step. It's this "feel" of the dance that's important and once one has the rhythm, there is no need to wonder or worry if you are exactly in time to the music. It was as natural for Negroes to create ragtime as it was for the rest of America to fall in step with them.

But coming back to the madams, these house-mothers of wayward America, they were continually on the lookout for added attractions to their establishments. With the rise of vaudeville, they now hoped to please their patrons with special music as well as other forms of special entertainment. Every house with any pretentions to class had a beautiful mahogany upright piano strewn with the usual bric-a-brac, cupid, Daphne and Apollo, and ornate throws and the ever-present mandolin attachment. It added tone. A friend of mine who used to play the piano in the famous Everleigh Club of Chicago mentioned that they had a gold piano—where he composed many a piece—and where his tips were the highest he had ever received then or since. These madams were ever on the hunt for good musicians but particularly good piano players, as a piano could be toned down and the less noise in the wee hours of the morning, the better. Possibly a tired Romeo could be coaxed into spending just a little more if the music fitted in with his mood.

The usual procedure would be to invite the chosen entertainer to stay at the house while he was in the city—and musicians at that time were not getting any hundred a week for their playing—and his cakes and coffee were free, with of course all the liquor he wished to hold. He could play any way he wanted to as long as he was good, and he could improvise all he wanted—just so long as he didn't stop. No matter how often he played certain numbers, the audience was continually changing. Here, when liquor, used to fight off exhaustion, had befogged the brain, many of the discordant and eerie chords were born. I have talked with many a swing musician who has admitted that he has improvised these weird minor chords in these houses, and one of them used to chew calabash to keep him going. Because of the tremendous amount of energy needed to play four to six shows a day, and then doubling every night to augment their meager wages, many musicians fell into this pernicious habit.

Negro musicians were paid next to nothing, the finer white dance halls barring them, and their greater revenue came from playing "gigs" (outside jobs—special groups of three or four who were especially hired to play for wealthy white patrons at private house parties) and in playing in the finest sporting houses. Many of them have played the Redlight Circuit from New Orleans to Seattle.

You must remember that at that time Negroes had no union of their own, were not admitted to white unions, and it was impossible for them to market their songs unless they sold them outright to white publishers—and the top price was fifteen dollars, with ten being about the average. These smart publishers would keep the scores of songs stowed away in drawers, much as a man keeps gilt-edged bonds, and at a propitious time they would revise here and there, change the title, and lo!—a popular hit tune was often launched on the market in New York. It often made a song writer who never would have reached the top, unless he had the ideas of these Negroes to fall back on.

True, many a white musician shared the same fate, but he was not continually relegated to the bottom as were these early-day Negro pioneers.

This shunting aside naturally made the Negro draw into himself.

With no outlet to exchange ideas on music other than with members of his own race, he became more and more essentially Negroid in musical feeling and in interpretation. Jam sessions are as old as the hills among them—it was their only medium of expressing themselves, of learning—and it was the training school for the colored boy who hoped some day to become an accomplished musician. None of them had enough money to study their instruments, learning everything they knew from these early jam sessions, improvising and going ahead purely on natural ability. All of them patterned their playing after some musical giant who was the legendary John Henry of his day, some powerful cornetist or piano-playing fool whose exploits on his chosen instrument were known throughout colored America. Camp meetings, funerals, and lodge dances gave the embryo musician his first chance, and much later, about 1908 I believe, when the T.O.B.A. (Theatrical Owners Booking Agency) was formed, these musicians as well as entertainers had an opportunity to play before small theaters in the colored sections of various cities.

Before that time, minstrels and itinerant peddlers of tunes would go from town to town, but because of the precarious way in which they made a living, many towns never had the opportunity to hear them. Now this was all changed. Bessie Smith, Mamie Smith, Ma Rainey, Ida Cox, Clarence Williams, Butterbeans and Susie, all great names in the "blues" constellation of Negroes throughout the United States, were swinging and playing the blues years before white American recognized them. Tom Turpin of St. Louis, Scott Joplin, Jellyroll Morton were the early great swing pianists, and by great I mean that their pieces were as intricate as Bach. They wrote trick arrangements, exciting tempos, difficult passages, and at this time the great Handy was writing "Atlanta Blues," "St. Louis Blues," "New Orleans Blues," "Memphis Blues," "Beale Street Blues," "Rampart Blues," "Market Street Blues"—all these were written before 1912—just about the time Benny Goodman was six years old. And later— the great flood of records, records that are now collector's items to the swing enthusiast. A respectable family of the 1920s would not be found dead with any of these abominable discs in their homes. The old Decca records, Columbia, Okeh, but particularly the Paramount and Black Swan or Race records as they were called. This meant especially made for the Negro race, as few white people would ever buy them. I quote from old catalogues of mine, and the names are authentic. "Red Hot Mommas" and "Drunk Man's Strut," "Lonnie Johnson's Blues," "Salty Dog Blues" (which had particularly low-down lines), "Mr. Freddie's Blues," "Barrel-house Blues," "Toad Frog Blues," "Ride Jockey Ride," "Death Letter Blues," "Mean Man Blues," "Lemon Jefferson's Blues," "The Woman Ain't Born," "Grave Yard Bound," "Long Gone Blues," "Black Hand Blues"—the list is endless . . .

All through the 1920s, this endless stream of blues records—and who bought them? Dealers did not and the chances are ten thousand to one that you haven't five of them in your collection. They were a solace to Negro domestics, who after working for hours over laundry tubs, mopping floors and shining brass, would go to the dingy comfort of a one-room flat in the Negro tenements and there put these records on their victrolas. It was a release from things white—they could hum—pat their feet—and be all colored. "Blues blues—jes' as blue as ah can be—No-good man done lef'—and lef' po' me."

These were true expressions, expressed as illiterates would talk, and they were sung husky and plaintively. Even Negroes often tire of Spirituals, no matter how good they are. They wanted something earthy and salty, something that touched their lives intimately—they wanted to hear a Negro man moan on his guitar and cut loose on a piano—they KNEW this man—he was probably just like Joe or Tom or Ed who ran off with some no good gal in Memphis and left her stranded here in this flat. True, "Japanese Sandman" and "Avalon" and the others were nice but none of them meant anything to a Negro domestic—all salvation and happiness and roses and cottages were for whites—but the blues. "Lawd, lawd—they's cullud—and cain't nobody take that away fum us."

Sporting houses were possibly the next best bets for these records, and they bought them by the armful. The records sold for fifty cents with a top price of seventy-five and they were continually needing replacement, as the patrons would play certain favorites over and over again until the grooves in the discs were worn down. Every joint from New Orleans all through the Delta, up to St. Louis, Kansas City, Chicago, Detroit, on out to the coast had stacks of these records. Dim lights—and the blues—the low-down gutbucket blues—heady music as intoxicating as any of the wares for sale.

Perhaps Jellyroll Morton, so named for his famous blues, "The Jelly-roll Blues," was the first Negro and the first man, black or white, to play blues with an orchestra and to devote his whole life to perfecting them. He along with, though much later, Charlie Creath, Bennie Moton, Fletcher Henderson, and a host of creative geniuses played St. Louis and turned out records by the score that were decidedly frowned upon by many white musicians. This was my first actual contact with these men. St. Louis, being a river town, was one of the main points touched by this small band of pathfinders.

They streamed up from New Orleans and Memphis and played jazz the length and breadth of the Mississippi and many was the hot sticky summer night when I, along with many of my friends, listened breathless as these masters of weird melodies shot their golden notes out over a muddy river. Perhaps we were the first jitterbugs—but we had no white companions then—just a bunch of colored kids who loved to listen to these masters.

During the summer, on Monday nights, the Negroes of St. Louis were privileged to use the older of two paddle-wheel steamers for their boat excursions. I remember the names of both of them—the *J.S.* and the *St. Paul*—the *St. Paul* was the one we used. Lodges and fraternal orders of all sorts would get together and have a benefit—to this day I never have found out what the benefits were for—but they always meant plenty of ice cream and cake for us, and above all—music, the blues. Music that was decidedly frowned upon by respectable Negro and white families, but we kids loved it. These boat rides usually ended up in fist fights, knife fights, and bottle throwing contests. Drinking St. Louis corn, packed on the boat like cattle, bunnyhugging to the tunes of Jelly-roll Morton, some too ardent boy friend would cut in on another's girl—then fireworks! I can still see an excited crew, red-faced and panting among a sea of black faces, trying to restore order—and then the clear strains of Charlie Creath's trumpet drowning out the noise and the scuffling. Charlie Creath of the one lung (he had literally blown his other lung out in New Orleans proving his superiority over other trumpet players)—Charlie had cut loose on the "St. Louis Blues."

Fights and even gun play meant nothing to these musicians who had seen it all too often—Charlie was playing a monumental solo ... The trumpet was in the clear now, it would not be denied—sweet and hot, the staccato notes splintered among the crowd and even the boy wielding the knife was transfixed. Someone bellowed out, "Oh, play it, Mr. Charlie, play that thing!" There was laughter and the tenseness disappeared—that trumpet was laughing now—"What's a few cuts—doctor below deck'll fix 'em up and BOY—does you realize we on'y got a half-hour t'dance?"

The crowd that had formed a semicircle to watch the men fight surged forward and blended together—they were one—Charlie had won another fight.

Then and there I decided I would quit drawing and become a trumpet player or anyway a jazz pianist. Drawing was a silent art—a lonely one—but a musician, why he could work wonders before a crowd and everybody could SEE him while he worked. I remember practicing diligently by the hour on my piano lessons. True they were such exciting things as barcaroles, but in some unfathomable way I knew that sooner or later they would lead me to the "Beale Street Blues" and I would burst forth like Athens, a finished jazz pianist.

—1941

David N. Baker

The first music that Blacks made in this country was African. One is then obligated to understand those traditions within the context of slavery, but the essence of African musical culture is a prerequisite. Music is the center of African culture, in all its manifestations. Three basic divisions of African music might be made. Secular music is the common property of all the people, regardless of cult or affiliation. When a new "composition" is created, the elders judge its acceptability. Second is the ceremonial music, employed for festivals and ceremonies. The third category is esoteric music, which comprises the bulk of African music and usually belongs to a particular cult. Only members of that cult use this music. It is true that master drummers might change from one cult to another, but they do not divulge the secrets of any cult.

Music is the functioning part of all aspects of the culture, and this is a factor we will find retained throughout Black music history. It will appear for political, social, economic, religious, and historical purposes. In a political framework, music serves most obviously in songs of praise for a leader. You will find instances of drums regarded as symbols of political power, owned by the royal family. And you will find music playing an important part in the settling of legal disputes. Music is used for social reasons (such as births, rites of passage, marriage, and death), and as Hugh Tracey has indicated, these social reasons might relate to protest. [...]

In economics, music serves principally as an aid to cooperative labor. When a rhythmic pattern of the work song is established, the work is easier. The combined strength of many men, using rhythmic coordination, is far more effective that it would be if they were acting as individuals.

The role of music in religion is varied. Music is so important in the ceremonies and rites that the event will be postponed if the right music is not available. This is not just a matter of the sounds. The instruments themselves can become objects of worship, or they may serve other important functions within the religious context. The elaborate symbolism for certain instruments we will find carried over into rural Black-American music.

Music functions within history through those songs which relate important events in the history of a tribe or lineage: battle songs, epics, stories of family history. The singer thus becomes a keeper of records, one who memorizes the history and has immediate access to that information, who relates it to others by song. [...]

Ante-bellum music consisted of spirituals, shouts, gospel tunes, hollers, and work songs. You find three categories of spirituals. The first is syncretic: the adaption of African ritual to Christian liturgy, the attempt to find similarities between the two. It was not difficult for the guy one generation from Africa to see a relationship between baptism and his river gods, between spirit possessions and the holy Ghost, or between West African gods and the Trinity. Second was the spirituals spontaneously created by the preacher and his congregation, with its interlocutions and exclamations. You can hear this at any Black church now, with the preacher doing his thing on Sunday morning. The third variety consisted of variations on White tunes. The first thing the Black man had to do was take care of the rhythm, so he introduced syncopation to the tune. Then he had to change the words, so that the massah he's talking about was the one up there in the front house. And then he brought in the blue notes to personalize the music, giving the melodies flat threes and fives and sevens, or making the tunes pentatonic. [...]

Let's see briefly [what was preserved]. We lost the African songs and dances when they served no function, but we kept those which could be adapted or fitted to the new economic patterns: work songs, love songs, lullabies, play songs, song games, wedding and funeral songs, and some magic songs. We lost the epic songs and battle songs about our African heroes. Whereas Western languages take pride on being exact and to the point (technology and clocks had a lot to do with this), Africans enjoy indirect statements and find direct expressions unimaginative, if not crude. Even though we find contemporary ghetto language being appropriated by our presidents, it is still ours. You talk about a pair of shoes being your pair of kicks, about your girl being your rib. That's colorful. Our educational systems don't like this kind of talk because it ain't good English, you dig? But it is important in Black music that it can translate itself from one period to another, still veiled in ever-changing para-phrase. The minute Whites cop one part of the language, it changes. We change it. It's gone before you can even get hold of it. Unless you're right there in the middle of it, you're going to be a year or two behind the times. I'm talking about music and language both, you know!

The roots of the whole American pop music scene rest in the min-strels. If pop music were divested of those things which came about be-cause of Black people, it would cease to exist. Minstrelsy was originally social, born in the slave quarters of the South. In an environment in which the slave was viewed as subhuman, music had to fulfill an outlet. Music in Africa had been propelled by social motivations. It had been conceived as a participative music which was meaningful to the entire community. When we talk to the Black composers today, you will find many of them still think in these terms. No popular music has escaped the Black influence. Those people who say jazz is influenced by rock and roll (White rhythm-and-blues) are just naive, or misinformed. The flow continues to be as it always was: from Black to White, as in the route from minstrelsy to the Broadway musical, from rhythm and blues to rock, from jazz to pop.

—1973

Wole Soyinka

No, few recognize their ghosts.
Few recognize the time-hatched chickens
"Stomping" home to roost. With every plunge,
With every wombward rip and its unanswered
Scream, remember Bessie Smith. Remember
Muddy Waters, Leadbelly, Sojourner Truth,
Recall that other Railroad Underground,
Remember why the Lady Sang the Blues,
Remember, yes, the Scottsborough Boys,
The sweet-sad death-knell of Joe Hill,
John Brown, and oh, the much-abused,
Misunderstood, sly Uncle Tom.
I saw his patriarch face, at peace,
    Reflected in a subway flash. Beside him
    An old disguise, snatched at knife point,
    From the museum of history's stereotypes.

—1988

Dominique-Rene de Lerma

What is Black? There is certainly little difficulty in such an identification if the person speaks ghetto and sings blues, if his skin is dark. White America has already established definitions of Blacks and has liberally included those with only one drop of Black blood. In doing this, they have been forced to include their own progeny many times. If it is a matter of skin color, there is no trouble about including most who embrace the culture. And we know they don't all speak ghetto. I have heard Blacks in London with Oxford accents, Blacks in Paris whose French is beautiful, and Blacks in the Caribbean who might say, "Mahn, I love to beat de pahn."

If the definition cannot be restricted by one kind of speech, by skin or hair, what are its limits? The more non-Black in one's veins makes one less Black? Doubtful. If we find someone (and we can) whose ancestry includes Irish, Spanish, and Indian blood, could the music of that person be cited within an Irish Music Center, a Spanish Music Center, and an Indian Music Center? If we find a person without any African ancestry who is darker than a major Black leader, how might this affect our definition?

Perhaps it is a matter of culture, then. If you can really sing the blues, e.g., you are Black. That won't work. It ignores acculturation, such as is manifest in the neo-Delta singer, John Hammond, Jr. It would also sidestep Louise Parker, who can sing German art songs as wonderfully as any German can.

The result of this quandary could put us in a state of nondecision, but we are suggesting that the manifestations of the culture are to be acknowledged after the work in documentation has been done, thus throwing us back to the sometimes superficial matter of skin color. But we do not measure Blackness this way; we measure it as we were taught to do by the White racists and find few instances of confusion or indecision. Some of us, the fruit of miscegenation, might have identity problems, but that is also part of the story: to be White or Black, to be forced by social and cultural traditions into electing a side.... Perhaps wholesale miscegenation is the answer. [...]

Our survey ... suggests the presence of certain qualities which might be unique, in context, to Black music. These are certainly generalizations, and they are not offered as standards by any means. Perhaps they might serve as points of discussion.

1. Black music often relates directly to social functions. It is a part of

life, not a superimposition on it. It is the agent for social communication, not just social commentary. [This can be seen] in Coltrane, and it can be found in protest songs, in freedom songs, in work songs, in satirical music.

2. There is a blurred distinction between the audience and the performer, the composer, and arranger, the music and the dance. This is music for everyone.... The almost ubiquitous element of improvisation ... suggests that roles in Black music are not as neatly assigned to individuals as they are in White-American music (which has become so structured that performers are wedded to the printed page in every detail—if, indeed, an electronic work has not dismissed the performer altogether). In the Black church, it is often impossible to separate the congregation from the choir, and this encourages all the more the element of improvisation.

3. The "blues" scale is one element of a specific technical musical nature. The persistence of this distinct scale in so much of Black music immediately gives harmonic and melodic flavors not found elsewhere: in jazz, in the blues, in the spiritual.

4. Rhythm is not confined to a supportive role. At its most minimal, it is coequal with melody and harmony. Its vitality and emotional range can be easily seen in African music as well as in the drumming of Elvin Jones and in the performances of Charlie Parker or John Coltrane.

5. Singing is the mother tongue, and Black voices often have special characteristics. In imitation or allegiance, instruments in Black hands do not forget the inflection and sonorities of the voice. As the African has talking drums, Louis Armstrong had a talking trumpet.

6. The Black man is at peace with the earth, and he is bound to it. It is not part of his culture to fly from the earth in extended ballet leaps. In his barefeet, he can feel the soil and caress it. In his life style, he can swing with the realities of life (even if he laments them in his blues) because he has not accepted abstractions and idealizations which religious and social dogma have imposed on the White man. There is then an earthiness which produces a special kind of sophistication, of resiliency, of buoyancy, of naturalness, and this—with his deeply ingrained respect for the oral tradition—has helped to keep the essentials of his age-old culture alive and vital.

7. He has style. He takes pleasure in his individuality, and it is respected. It is not just a matter of economics that stimulates the Black man to dress in other than flannel suits and tuxedos. Conformity and the absence of individual expression have less merit in Black culture. This, as

well as White exploitation, accounts for the ability of the Black musician to move on into new ideas, to retain his individuality. This accounts for the lesser degree of inhibition which the Black man feels and for the joy he has in doing his thing his way, no matter if his football talents are less than Gayle Sayers, his musical imagination less than Sun Ra, his oratorical delivery less eloquent than Ralph Abernathy.

8. There is a matter of "inspired intensity." . . . This relates to the fact that, no matter what obstacles are in the way, the Black musician will manage. If he lacks an instrument, he will build one or use materials readily at hand. If he does not understand the principles of fingering, how to hold an instrument, or the idea of embouchure development (these according to traditional approaches), he'll find a way—and may even start a new school. What he has to express will find expression, even with the blessing of academic discipline. And this very frequently relates to several points cited above: to the social function of music, to the lack of separation between the performer and audience, to the imitation of Black vocal sonorities, to the Black man's unity with the earth, and to the style and freedom of his individuality.

—1973

Clinton M. Jean

Bias, I understood very well, was not just something that was directed against me personally. It sprung from an assumption that liberal formula—*Eurocentric* formulas, period—were the universal benchmark by which to judge the worth of all cultural practices. It was always surprising when white friends, even those from the hip left, said they thought the Stones were more danceable than James Brown, or that Miles Davis derived from Chet Baker. That had no feeling for Celia Cruz and Sonora Matancera, Tito Puente, and Willie Bobo. Very few seemed to know who Charlie Parker was. How could they call Paul Whiteman the king of jazz when Louis Armstrong was on the scene? And if they thought Dave Brubeck's "Take Five" was so original, why didn't they feel the same way about Max Roach and Sonny Rollins's "Valse Hot"? Without the slightest apparent twitch of conscience Europeans had destroyed entire peoples—there was not a single Tasmanian left alive on the planet. All this in the name of Western progress—materialistic frenzy; the use of human energy, knowledge, and science in a progressive and unyielding dismemberment of human beings and the natural order; a toxic narcissism; and the divorce of action from humane morality.

—1991

Bob Kaufman

O-JAZZ-O-WAR MEMOIR: JAZZ, DON'T LISTEN TO IT AT YOUR
OWN RISK

In the beginning, in the wet
Warm dark place,
Straining to break out, clawing at strange cables
Hearing her screams, laughing
"Later we forgave ourselves, we didn't know"
Some secret jazz
Shouted, *wait, don't go.*
Impatient, we came running, innocent
Laughing blobs of blood & faith.
To this mother, father world
Where laughter seems out of place
So we learned to cry, pleased
They pronounce human.
The secret Jazz blew a sigh
Some familiar sound shouted *wait*
Some are evil, some will hate.
"Just Jazz blowing its top again"
So we rushed & laughed.
As we pushed & grabbed
While jazz blew in the night
Suddenly they were too busy to hear a simple sound
They were busy shoving mud in men's mouths,
Who were busy dying on the living ground
Busy earning medals, for killing children on deserted street corners
Occupying their fathers, raping their mothers, busy humans we
Busy burning Japanese in atomicolorcinemascope
With stereophonic screams,
What one hundred percent red blooded savage, would waste precious
           time
Listening to jazz, with so many important things going on
But even the fittest murderers must rest
So they sat down in our blood soaked garments,
and listened to jazz
           lost, steeped in all our death dreams
They were shocked at the sound of life, long gone from our own

They were indignant at the whistling, thinking, singing, beating,
    swinging,
They wept for it, hugged, kissed it, loved it, joined it, we drank it,
Smoked it, ate with it, slept with it
They made our girls wear it for lovemaking
Instead of silly lace gowns,
Now in those terrible moments, when the dark memories come
The secret moments to which we admit no one
When guiltily we crawl back in time, reaching away from ourselves
They hear a familiar sound,
Jazz, scratching, digging, blueing, swinging jazz,
And listen,
And feel, & die.

—1967

Duke Ellington

A Negro musician, or a Negro who was not a professional musician, decided to do what he though he could do on a musical instrument, just to see what he sounded like. For personal kicks, he tried banjo, guitar, violin, cornet, clarinet, trombone, saxophone, and other instruments to hand. He was strongly influenced by the type of music of his time, and the black beat was his foundation. The soul of his brothers, sisters, and neighbors broke through to reassure him of their sympathy. The music of his time—and sound devices—were always parallel to the progress of science, medicine, and labor. When you pick the jazz musician of any period, if he happens to be one of the many unique performers, you may be sure he always reflects what's happening in his time. "What's happening" is the name of the game.

Jazz became popular in one way and unpopular in another. Some people enjoy listening to jazz because somebody told them that they should. Others have more valid reasons: 1. to dance to; 2. to give one's sitting stance the flash and swank that match a ringside old-fashioned (of course, one must never tilt on the beat as one pats one's foot); 3. it's an art form, discovered by the neo-intellectuals, and some find it something to listen *down*, like taking the ear slumming; 4. others use it for social advancement in that world of hipsters who believe everything in their lives must swing; 5. those who enjoy monetary participation; 6. professional courtesy; 7. those who genuinely get torn up emotionally when listening to an extraordinary rendition; and 8. some young people like to dig it because it is not associated with juvenile delinquency, which brings us now to those who prefer *not* to listen to jazz.

There are many romantic and colorful stories about jazz and its upbringing in New Orleans whorehouses. Whoever started that story, of course, had to be in the whorehouse, to see and hear the musicians of the band, or else it's just hearsay, or a lie. Even if they were working in a New Orleans whorehouse, I like to point out, they did not learn their instruments there, and they obviously were not patrons of the joint. It's easy to visualize jazzmen in the whorehouses: sitting rather inanimately at first with or at their instruments, from which came sounds that were compatible with whatever social activity was going on. As the sound grew more attractive, the customers began to realize that the players were *people*, sitting or standing there by their instruments. Soon they realized that since they *were* people, they must have names. So they set about finding out the names of the musicians.

Later, when they were at a social gathering of the more respectable climate, and engaged in conversation, one would take the floor—or spotlight—by talking about what he had heard, by this *great* and *Negro* player of jazz, as though he were speaking about an adventurous lion hunt with a master hunter in some strange and exotic land. At the end of his speech, the speaker would be accepted as more traveled and experienced, as the true sophisticate of the day. The name "jazz," accepted as referring to a great land of adventure, accordingly spread out and, as I have said before, many romantic and colorful stories about it were invented.

But one continuing story is that what's happening is happening. It was happening then and will continue in its happening until the happiest happening will be to be what's happening.

—1973

Langston Hughes

They must have been pretty good, those African drummers who, as slaves in New Orleans long before the War Between the States, drew crowds of people to Congo Square on Sundays to listen to their syncopated rhythms, played for their own amusement. The rhythms must have been unusually tantalizing and powerful because they are still echoing in the widely popular music of today—jazz—a music that has gone around the world. The old slave songs, shouts and field hollers, the blues and spirituals musicologists now acknowledge as having possessed great intensity and beauty. And there are living people who still remember—

and still play—the lively New Orleans music of the turn of the century that became Dixieland jazz. The trumpeter, Louis Armstrong, is on these people, as are the trombonist, Kid Ory, the drummer, Baby Dodds, and the clarinetist, Sidney Bechet. These are famous contemporary musicians whose lives began back in those old days when ragtime was new and jazz was just being born.

The word *jazz* itself is only about forty years old, as applied to music, and at first it was spelled "jass." Its origins are obscure, but some say it came from the fact that there was a Spasm Band player once in old New Orleans named Jasper—Jas for short. Others say his name was Charles, which he wrote "Chas.," and the illiterate, who couldn't read very well, called this "Chass," which got changed to "jass." Another theory is that a little band around 1909 called Razz's Band somehow got twisted into Jazz Band. Still others say the word has an African origin. However that may be, by the time Dixieland music reached Chicago in the early 1920s, people were calling it jazz. Now it is a word that is the same in every language in the world.

The first jazz band to be recorded was the Original Dixieland Jass Band, in 1917, a white group from New Orleans that had learned their music from Negroes. Jelly Roll Morton's Red Hot Peppers, Bessie Smith's blues, and Louis Armstrong's first records with various groups were among the early best-sellers of Negro jazz. Since jazz began being recorded it has made a fortune for recording companies and juke box combines, and has been the main contributor to the vast incomes of radio chains. Today it supports thousands of disc jockeys. It has become the mainstay of the dance band and night club business. Jazz contributed its rhythms to most Hollywood musicals. It nourishes Tin Pan Alley. Billions of dollars have been made from jazz. Not much of this money went to the musicians themselves, and very little indeed to its pioneer creators. Except for a handful of outstanding stars like Louis Armstrong, the old-timers of jazz are not well off. Juke boxes reap nickels, dimes, and quarters, but nothing of this harvest goes to the music makers. Current copyright laws, sadly in need of amending, have not protected recorded performances in the past from being used *solely* for the profit of juke box owners. Once the performers have been paid for the original recording session, that is usually the end for them, no matter how big a hit a record may become on the mechanical machines—and there are hundreds of thousands of juke boxes in the world.

Since the days of the troubadours, musicians of whatever race have seemingly never known how to gather gold and songs at the same time. Bland, who wrote "Oh, Dem Golden Slippers," died a pauper, and Stephen Foster of "Swanee River" fame passed away in the charity ward of Bellevue Hospital. Most musicians remain poor. But the music that they make, even if it does not bring them millions, gives millions of people happiness. The jazz musicians and composers of the United States have contributed to the delight of the whole world, and America's own music—of Negro origin—has gone everywhere. Negro music has been one of our great cultural contributions, and Negro musicians have been among the most joyous of our ambassadors.

—1955

Rudolph Fisher

Willingly would I be an outsider in this if I could know that I read aright—that out of this change in the old familiar ways some finer things may come. Is this interest akin to that of the Virginians on the veranda of the plantation's big house—sitting genuinely spellbound as they hear the lugubrious strains floating up from the Negro quarters? Is it akin to that of the African explorer, Stanley, leaving a village far behind, but halting in spite of himself to catch the boom of its distant drum? Is it significant of basic human responses, the effect of which, once admitted, will extend far beyond cabarets? Maybe these Nordics at last have tuned in on our wavelength. Maybe they are at least learning to speak our language.

—1927

W. E. B. DuBois

"Well," says I, after we had gotten nicely settled for our first real meeting, "what is the first thing that's gone to making America and who did it?" I had my own mind on music and painting and I know that Birdie is daft on architecture; but before either of us could speak, Bill Graves grinned and said, "hard work."

The chairman nodded and said, "Quite true, labor."

I didn't know just what to say but I whispered to Birdie that it seemed to me that we ought to stress some of the higher things. The chairman must have heard me because he said that all higher things rested on the foundation of human toil.

"But, whose labor?" asked the editor. "Since we are all descended from working people, isn't labor a sort of common contribution which, as it comes from everybody, need not be counted?"

"I should hardly consent to that statement," said Mrs. Cadwalader Lee, who is said to be descended from a governor and a lord.

"At any rate," said the chairman, "the Negroes were America's first great work force."

"Negroes!" shrilled Birdie, "but we can't have them!"

"I should think," said Mrs. Cadwalader Lee, softly, "that we might have a very interesting dark scene. Negroes hoeing cotton and that sort of thing." We all were thankful to Mrs. Lee and immediately saw that that would be rather good; Mrs. Lee again said she would consult her cook, a very intelligent and exemplary person.

"Next," I said firmly, "comes music."

"Folk songs," said the Methodist preacher.

"Yes," I continued. "There would be Italian and German and—"

"But I thought this was to be American," said the chairman.

"Sure," I answered, "German-American and Italian-American and so forth."

"There ain't no such animal," said Birdie, but Mrs. Cadwalader Lee reminded us of Foster's work and thought we might have a chorus to sing "Old Folks at Home," "Old Kentucky Home," and "Nelly Was a Lady." Here the editor pulled out a book on American folk songs by Krehbiel or some such German name and read an extract. (I had to cop it for the minutes.) It said:

The only considerable body of songs which has come into existence in the territory now compassed by the United States, I might even say in North America, excepting the primitive songs of the Indians (which present an entirely different aspect), are the songs of the former black slaves. In Canada the songs of the people, or that portion of the people that can be said still to sing from impulse, are predominantly French, not only in language but in subject. They were for the greater part transferred to this continent with the bodily integrity they now possess. Only a small portion show an admixture of Indian elements; but the songs of the black slaves of the South are original and native products. They contain idioms which were transplanted from Africa, but as songs they are the product of American institutions; of the social, political, and geographical environment within which their creators were placed in America; of the influences to which they were subjected in America; of the joys, sorrows, and experiences which fell to their lot in America.

Nowhere save on the plantations of the South could the emotional life which is essential to the development of true folksong be developed; nowhere else was there the necessary meeting of the spiritual cause and the simple agent and vehicle. The white inhabitants of the continent have never been in the state of cultural ingenuousness which prompts spontaneous utterances in music.

This rather took our breath and the chairman suggested that the auxiliary colored committee might attend to this. Mrs. Cadwalader Lee was very nice about it. (She has such lovely manners and gets her dresses direct from New York.) She said that she was sure it could all work out satisfactorily. We would need a number of servants and helpers. Well, under the leadership of that gifted cook, we'd have a cotton-hoeing scene to represent labor and while hoeing they would sing Negro ditties; afterward they could serve the food and clean up.

—1925

Ted Vincent

Let us always remember that African-American music, from the blues through jazz and all its evolving forms, is symbolic of fundamental and provocative changes that society is experiencing. It is, as Leopold Stokowski notes, the results, efforts, and expression of musicians who are "pathfinders into new realms." And so we can rest assured that the music will continue to be an integral part of the historical process of the African-American struggle: a source of inspiration, an articulator of purpose and a definition of existence. Moreover, from a global perspective, we know that it will simultaneously help our world to heal and understand itself.

—1995

C. L. R. James

In the early days [jazz] was a genuinely popular music. To America being whipped into a remorseless discipline by mechanization, its strong recurrent rhythm and its abandon within that rhythm offered a relief that matched the strains of modern life. But early jazz was essentially music

for the *new dancing*. One of the old band leaders speaking recently compares the modern bands and listeners to the old. "We," he said, "played
for folks to dance to. And how they danced in the old days." And then he
added what in the writer's opinion is the most remarkable statement ever
made about modern jazz. In a big hall, he said, a sensitive leader *caught the
rhythm for the evening from the dancers*. And when he had caught it, he told his
band to hold it. The crowd of dancers therefore expressed their particular feeling for that evening and it was transferred to the musicians. Today,
with the commercialization of jazz, that is gone. [...] The great popular
tunes, the famous blues, were all the work of composers who did their
best work before the Depression.

—1949

Ralph Ellison

There is ... a cruel contradiction implicit in the art form itself. For true
jazz is an art of individual assertion within and against the group. Each
true jazz moment (as distinct from the uninspired commercial performance) springs from a contest in which each artist challenges all the rest;
each solo flight, or improvisation, represents (like the successive canvases
of a painter) a definition of his identity: as an individual, as a member of
the collectivity, and as a link to the chain of tradition. Thus, because jazz
finds its very life in an endless improvisation upon traditional materials,
the jazzman must lose his identity even as he finds it—how often do we
see even the most famous of jazz artists being devoured alive by their imitators and, shamelessly, in the public spotlight?

—1958

hattie gossett with carolyn johnson

women and jazz? what? women's jazz festival? tv specials and films about
jazzwomen? why? who cares? they've been overlooked by history? they
should have been—what have they done that's worthwhile? everybody
knows can't no woman blow no saxophone or beat no drums. somebody
just gave them a gig knowing there's always a sucker ready to give up
some money to see some broads, no matter what they doing. hell! i never
heard of a men's jazz festival. hmmmmph! ain't that reverse discrimination? hmmmmph! what about that? huh?
     women. jazz.

most jazz lovers hearing those 2 words if asked to put a name to the first image that comes to mind would probably say singer—bessie, billie, sarah, dinah, betty, carmen, ella. or singer/pianist—nina simone, hazel scott, amina meyers. pressed for instrumentalists, most will come up with keyboard players like shirley scott, lil armstrong, marylou williams, alice coltrane. a few might mention trombonist/ arranger melba liston, alto saxophonist/vocalist vi redd or trombonist janice robinson. a middleaged hipster or jazz scholar would mention the all girl (so called) orchestras and bands of the '40s. like the international sweethearts of rhythm. mostly though it's singers and piano players. only a horn player or two. hardly any drummers.

this is not about the singers and piano players and their magnificent contributions. not because these women don't deserve more attention, honor, gigs, and money. anyone who has attempted the simplest research about women jazz performers will attest to the embarrassing shortage of material—no booklength biographies except for billie and bessie, few magazine articles, no films or tv shows, little radio. there is much work to be done.

but i want to shine my light on *this* question: why are there so few female names in the great roll call of jazz saxophonists, drummers, trumpeters, arrangers, composers, orchestra leaders? did god make women physically unfit to play certain instruments? are women mentally incapable of dealing with the ups and downs of jazz life? is all this stuff about women and jazz another media hype? a subversive plot to take over jazz being put out here by some mad feminists? are women musicians trying to get over by using their sex to cover up for their lack of musical ability? how come there's most singers and piano players, only a horn player or two, hardly any drummers?

herstory: how it was

actually it goes back as far and as deep as the music's roots, this practice of women playing hardly any of the major solo instruments. power instruments.

as an afroamerican art form, jazz is rooted in west african culture, with certain ties to euro-american culture as well. the african connection began with the drum on the mother continent and made its way across the atlantic along with kidnapped africans whose fate it was to lay the foundations for the new world. not only was the drum a major power symbol in music, drama, literature, medicine, and religion but also in communications. talking drums broadcast news over vast areas in an amazingly brief time. in the new world, the euro-american contribution consisted of additional instruments and a system of harmony based on a 7-tone scale. blues and jazz musicians soon subverted 3 of these 7 tones to blue tones or blue notes. the european power instruments were orchestra, piano, and violin. in west africa women did not play drums. the idea was so highly taboo that the suggestion could elicit bales of laughter or fierce anger. some cultures even forbade women touching drums. women sang, chanted, danced. men were master drummers. this tradition was continued in the new world as was the european tradition of women not being major piano or violin soloists or orchestra leaders. both of these age-old traditions combined in the new world to lay a firm basis for excluding women from power instruments in any form of music, including jazz.

by the dawn of the 20th century secular afroamerican musical expression increasingly had an economic motive—the music had become a valuable commercial entity, musical creations had to be marketable or the creators couldn't eat. show business. entertainment. due to some queer notions equating black musical creativity with low life animal impulses and promiscuous sex, this highly inventive music energy was confined to the red light districts of the newly industrialized cities. the term "hot" when applied to the music by its creators had one meaning, which was soon distorted. only the most "daring" whites and middle class blacks would venture to the red light districts to hear this "hot music." it's a good thing the recording process was invented and perfected around the same time the music was getting itself together. furthermore, at the time when the music was developing there was a severe social prohibition against women being involved in any kind of commercial endeavor. women performers were thought to be harlots by most decent people. even high-class opera singers and big-time actresses (white) were often regarded as somewhat less than ladylike. so you know what was said about jazzwomen.

with all this, it's not surprising that most parents didn't (and still don't) want their sons to be jazz musicians or any other kind of artist, let alone their daughters. it's a rough life, a dangerous life. even for men. wild, fast, uncontrollable. alcohol. drugs. loose women. loose men. seediness. unsteady income. all that traveling. cooking beans on a hotplate in a tiny hotel room. all these images have been perpetrated by a hostile and racist media system. so lots of parents think it's better for their kid to have something steady. lots of parents didn't (won't) want their daughters to even date a musician. musicians are full of stories about being told—sometimes at gunpoint or knifepoint—by parents to stay away from their houses cuz they are raising their daughter to be decent and don't want to see her with any wild man.

---

in polite conversation, the girl singer was called names like sparrow, wren, warbler, chirp. regardless of her talent she first had to fill the bill as a beautiful, charming, gracious, delicate, softspoken ornament. in fact, if you wanted to be a singer or instrumentalist, you had better be beautiful, charming, gracious, soft-spoken, and ornamental. and then you had better be ready for the outright propositions, sly pinches, fast feels, leering eyes and mouths, direct hits, attempted rapes from bandleaders, sidemen, club owners, promoters, record company execs, customers, waiters. many times you had to wear some kind of weird gaudy costume which showed more than it covered. you often had to be nice to the customers—get them to spend more money. and sometimes if the customer or the boss wanted to take you home with him you had to go if you wanted to keep your gig. and if you weren't thin with long flowing hair, you had to be ready for the names like can-o-lard, hamhocks hips, greasy gertie, bit butt bertha. and if you had a big loud voice and not a sexy sweet voice it was even worse. your talent was somehow secondary. no wonder there was a steady stream of minimally or notalented women who got over on their looks while less attractive gifted women often languished in the shadows.

the road has taken the weight for the breakup of miles of love affairs and marriages. but when we think of this situation most of us think of the husband as traveling musician and the wife as keeper of the homefront. no one expected a jazzman to rearrange his schedule so that he could be with his wife at the time when a child was born for instance or at other critical times in a family's life. some did, of course, but mostly they didn't. this is even more peculiar when you remember that one of the attractions of the artistic life is freedom of schedule. and what is it like when the woman travels and the man stays home? traditionally this has not happened. in the past most women traveled with their husbands or some family member because this was a good way to avoid leering mouths and creeping hands and also because the road can be lonely. then too the husbands or family members weren't too thrilled about their wives, sisters, daughters being out on the road alone seeing, being seen, free. so then we have the phenomenon of the husband as manager or bandleader, often incompetent, jealous and possessive, sometimes better at squandering his wife's money and ruining her career than anything else. in contrast, jazzwomen often took leave from their careers to have babies and to raise families. in fact, many jazz women worked less frequently than they might have in order to spend more time with their families. after all, it's expected for a woman to do this. right? as for jazzwomen who decided to go on the road alone, to hang out, get high, have a succession of lovers and husbands? well, we know what was said about them—right?

and then there's the question of physical fitness. are women physically capable of maintaining the rigorous condition needed to perform the physical act of playing a set of drums or blowing into a saxophone all night long night after night year after year? doesn't it take a big strong muscular body? and won't your lips and mouth get deformed from all that blowing? or your chest? and what about the muscles in your arms and legs if you're a drummer? won't they be too big? and if you're not a drummer or a piano player, who at least get to sit down, will your legs and back be strong enough to stand up all night? and what about when you have your time of the month or you're pregnant? doesn't all this add up to another big deterrent? well, if any of that's true, it sure doesn't show up in the women instrumentalist's photographs or in their living selves. if you saw a woman saxophone player or drummer without her instrument, you would see no standout or hidden physical features or distortions that would set her apart from any other woman. besides, if women have stood on their feet as waitresses, factory workers, and household workers, etc., throughout history, isn't standing on a bandstand for 40 minutes out of every 60 for 4 or 5 hours a night kinda lightweight?

<hr>

we have seen that traditionally jazzwomen had to be acceptable first as ornament/objects. as if this is not already bad enough, if we take a careful look at official jazzhistory (or american history or the history of western civilization), we will see that the most desirable ornament/objects have been those with flowing hair, blue eyes, and white skin.

oldtimers knew that ma rainey and bessie, clara, and mamie smith were the baddest new orleans shouters, but sophie tucker got the shot in the movies and in the standard history books. and she assuredly got more money and better contracts and working conditions, too. she was the acceptable version. and then there was that whole generation of white women singers who got over by copying note for note the recordings made originally by black women singers. these copies or covers as they were known were then boosted to the top of the top 40, while the original black product was restricted to the chitlin circuit. actually, all women end up losing in this game. the white woman lost and still loses because she is forced to squash whatever creative ability she has in the slavish effort to imitate someone else. though her white skin can give her an illusion of having more creative ability and power than darker women, she pays for this shallow, hollow privilege by having to sacrifice her ability to develop along her own line.

the black woman's situation is even worse. not only can she never hope to successfully compete for the empty title of ornament/object; in order to even be in the game at all she is pressured to become ultimately a poor and sad imitation—several times removed—of herself.

but there is an even deeper irony to the situation. the playing of jazz has been not only a black prerogative but a black male prerogative. jazz has been one of the few pieces of turf held almost unquestionably by black males. like boxing, every now and then a new great white hope emerges, but it ain't no sweat cuz the hometeam knows that a joe louis or a charlie parker will emerge from the corner and reclaim the crown.

conversely, it seems that once jazz (like boxing) became a profitable and big business, white men have not brooked any serious challengers to their hold on the various commercial enterprises that reap profits from jazz.

black culture is a natural resource over which its creators have a diminishing amount of control. the african and other oppressed third world kinspeople of black americans are still connected to their land in varying degrees and therefore have some access to and control over their natural resources (oil, gold, labor power) and various cultural resources. although they too have suffered the ripoff of their cultural resources as part of the process of colonialism and imperialism. how else do you think the european and american museums got to be full of african and other third world art and artifacts? in fact, it is only through the process of political struggle for liberation and nationalization that third world peoples have regained meaningful control over any of their resources.

the process of black american cultural disenfranchisement is often as subtle as it unscrupulous. the current attack on sexism in jazz appears to be a liberating force because women's abilities as instrumentalists are now being recognized. but a deeper look at this "feminizing" process shows us that the trickbag of cultural ripoff is deeper yet because white women

are still being promoted over black women. the first trick out of the bag
was the promotion of white men over black men for racist reasons. the
next trick has been white women's promotion over black women for sex-
ist *and* racist reasons. no matter how many tricks come out of the bag
though, it is clear they are all designed to keep afroamericans from controlling our cultural resources. the same way we are not allowed to control another, even more important resource—our labor power.

—1980

Danny Barker and Jack V. Buerkle

It takes a lot of ability, ambition, and ingenuity to be a musician. Just
anybody can't be a musician, because a man has to be an advanced
thinker to be one. In other words, you're readin' the notes over there, and
you're playin' it way back here! So, if you can't see the note over there,
and hear the note before it comes outa the instrument, you're in trouble!
You don't just play. You read a note. You see the note. But, your eyes notice only a sign that shows you the degree and pitch the note has to be
played in, and the time. It's a silent sign. So, you see the sign with your
eye, and you know from practice where the note should be played on the
instrument. But, you've read this thing way over there, and you're playin'
it over here! And, if you can't think that fast, you can't play music! A slow
thinker can't make it playin' music! Then, another thing. You have millions of people in this world that can't memorize anything. And, you
have other people who can memorize a book of stuff like this. So, they's
no comparison between the two sets of people. And to play music, you
gotta know how to memorize. Lots of the music I play, I just look and
see what key the thing's written in, and put it in my pocket and go ahead
and play!

—1973

Harold Cruse

Despite the grievous lack of a classical culture in America, however, this
country always has at its disposal a reserve cultural weapon and that is
jazz music, the Afro-American cultural contribution to the national soul.
In 1955, the *New York Times* carried a headline on its front page to the
effect: "United States Has a Secret Sonic Weapon—Jazz." The article
went on to say: "All Europe now seems to find American jazz as necessary as the seasons ... American jazz has now become a universal lan-

guage. It knows no national boundaries ..." etc. The State Department is quite willing to use jazz as a cultural weapon because it hasn't got much else. The problem posed here is that jazz, in the view of America's white cultural elite, is a "popular" mode of cultural expression and does not make up for the serious lack of American "classical" cultural arts. The question then is why was jazz music never cultivated by musical America into an American school of classical music in the same fashion that European folk music was incorporated into the European classical music tradition? The answer to this question is also the answer to the question: Why does America have no real culture? American jazz was never seriously developed into an American classical school of musical creation because American composers and critics never really desire it. For to elevate jazz into a serious classical school would have demanded that the whole body of Afro-American folk music also be elevated and glorified. This would also mean that the Afro-American ethnic minority which originally created this music would have to be culturally glorified and elevated socially, economically, and politically. It would mean that the black composer would have to be accepted on this social, cultural, economic, and political level. But this the white American cultural ego would never permit. The inescapable conclusion is this: At the bottom of the whole question of the backward cultural development of America, the cultural banality, the cultural decadence, the cultural debasement of the entire American social scene, lies the reality of racism—racial exclusion, racial exploitation, racial segregation, and all the manifestations of the ideology of white superiority.

—1963

Duke Ellington

WHAT IS MUSIC?

What is music to you?
What would you be without music?

Music is everything.
Nature is music (cicadas in the tropical night).

The sea is music,
The wind is music,
Primitive elements are music, agreeable or discordant.

The rain drumming on the roof,
And the storm raging in the sky are music.

Every country in the world has its own music,
And the music becomes an ambassador;
The tango in Argentina and calypso in Antilles.

Music is the oldest entity.

A baby is born, and music puts him to sleep.
He can't read, he can't understand a picture,
But he will listen to music.

Music is marriage.

Music is death.

The scope of music is immense and infinite.
It is the "esperanto" of the world.

Music arouses courage and leads you to war.
The Romans used to have drums rolling before they attacked.
We have the bugle to sound reveille and pay homage to the brave
warrior.
The Marseillaise has led many generations to victories or revolutions;
It is a chant of wild excitement, and delirium, and pride.

Music is eternal,
Music is divine.

You pray to your God with music.

Music can dictate moods,
It can ennerve or subdue,
Subjugate, exhaust, astound the heart.

Music is a cedar,
An evergreen tree of fragrant, durable wood.

Music is like honor and pride,
Free from defect, damage, or decay.

Without music I may feel blind, atrophied, incomplete, *inexistent.*

—1973

Blues, Roots

Thomas A. Dorsey

Blues notes are on the piano; been on the piano just like opera and its trills and things. A blue note? There's no such thing as a blue note. Blues don't own no notes. The world of music owns the notes and sounds on the piano. You're talking about the old blue seventh. We gave the blues that seventh. But it can be in anything. It's up to the individual to know how and when to bring it out.

Music is a universal something. It was here when we come here and it was here when other generations came. [There] is not a people or a race or a nation or anything in creation that is human that doesn't have its song. I may not know it. I may not like it. I may not be able to sing it. But everything, everybody, I'm talking about every nation, every human being that came across the earth had a song and sang in some way to their god. They could sing some way in their power.

—1976–77

James H. Cone

The origin and definition of the blues cannot be understood independent of the suffering that black people endured in the context of white racism and hate. Therefore, the question that gave shape and purpose to the blues was: How could black people keep themselves together, preserving a measure of their cultural being, and not lose their physical lives? Responding to the significance of that question for the black community, blues people sang:

> Times is so tough, can't even get a dime,
> Yes times is so tough, can't even get a dime,
> Times don't get better, I'm going to lose my mind.

The blues tells us about black people's attempt to carve out a significant existence in a very trying situation. The purpose of the blues is to give structure to black existence in a context where color means rejection and humiliation.

Suffering and its relation to blackness is inseparable from the meaning of the blues. Without pain and suffering, and what that meant for black people in Mississippi, Tennessee, and Arkansas, there would have been no blues. The blue mood means sorrow, frustration, despair, and black people's attempt to takes these existential realities upon themselves and not lose their sanity. The blues are not art for art's sake, music for music's sake. They are a way of life, a life-style of the black community; and they came into being to give expression to black identity and the will for survival. Thus to seek to understand the blues apart from the suffering that created them is to misinterpret them and distort the very creativity that defines them. This is what Clarence Williams, a New York publisher who has written many blues, meant when he said:

> Why, I'd never have written blues if I had been white. You don't study to write the blues, you *feel* them. It's the mood you're in—sometimes it's a rainy day ... just like the time I lay for hours in a swamp in Louisiana. Spanish moss dripping everywhere ... White men were looking for me with guns—I wasn't scared, just sorry I didn't have a gun. I began to hum a tune—a little sighing kinda tune—you know like this ... "Jes as blue as a tree—an old willow tree—nobody 'round here, jes nobody but me."

Because we know that we have survived, that we have not been destroyed, and that we are more than stripes on our backs, we can sing as a way of celebrating our being. Indeed, for black people, existence is a form of celebration. It is joy, love, and sex. It is hugging, kissing, and feeling. People cannot love physically and spiritually (the two cannot be separated!) until they have been up against the edge of life, experiencing the hurt and pain of existence. They cannot appreciate the feel and touch of life nor express the beauty of giving themselves to each other in community, in love, and in sex until they know and experience the brokenness of existence as disclosed in human oppression. People who have not been oppressed physically cannot know the power inherent in bodily expressions of love. That is why white Western culture makes a sharp distinction between the spirit and the body, the divine and the human, the sacred and the secular. White oppressors do not know how to come to terms with the essential *spiritual* function of the human body. But for black people the body is sacred, and they know how to use it in the expression of love.

Most interpreters agree that the dominant and most expressive theme in the blues is sex. Whatever else is said about them, the blues cannot be understood if this important theme is omitted. As blues man Furry Lewis puts it: "The blues come from a woman wanting to see her a man, and a man wanting to see his woman." Or, as Henry Townsend says:

"You know, that's the major thing in life. Please believe me. What you love the best is what can hurt you the most." Ma Rainey also puts it well:

> People have different blues and think they're mighty sad,
> But blues about a man the worst I ever had ...

And another says:

> You know my woman left me,
> Left me cold in hand.
> I wouldn't had it so bad,
> But she left with another man.

The blues are the songs of men and women who have been hurt and disappointed and who feel the confusion and isolation of human love.

> 'Gwine lay my head on de railroad track,
> 'Gwine lay my head on de railroad track,
> Cause my baby, she won't take me back.

The blue mood is about black men and women—their lament, grief, and disillusionment. In a world where a people possess little that is their own, human relationships are placed at a high premium. The love between men and women becomes immediate and real. Black people live in that kind of world; and they express the pain of separation and loneliness.

> Did you ever wake up in the morning, find your man had gone?
> Did you ever wake up in the morning, find your man had gone?
> You will wring your hands, you will cry the whole day long.

But the blues were not just sad feelings about separation, the loss of a man or woman. There was also humor about sexuality.

> Good lookin' woman make a bull dog break his chain,
> Good lookin' woman make a bull dog break his chain,
> Good lookin' woman makes a snail catch a passenger train.

> Yaller gal make a preacher lay his Bible down,
> Yaller gal make a preacher lay his Bible down,
> Good lookin' high brown make him run from town to town.

> Good lookin' woman make a mule kick his stable down,
> Good lookin' woman make a mule kick his stable down,
> Good lookin' woman make a rabbit move his family to town.

Woman without a man like a ship without a sail,
Woman without a man like a ship without a sail,
Ship without a sail like a dog without a tail.

There is seriousness, too, when a man appeals to his woman to make up her mind.

If you didn't want me girlie what made you say you do,
If you didn't want me girlie what made you say you do,
Take your time little girl, nobody's rushin' you.

The blues are honest music. They describe every aspect of a woman's feelings about a man, and what a man thinks about a woman. Through the blues, black people express their views about infidelity and sex. The blues woman said:

You can cheat on me, you can steal on me,
you can fool me all along.
You can cheat on me, you can steal on me,
you can fool me all along.
All I ask you, daddy, please don't let me catch you wrong.

And her man answered:

I'm a hard-working man and, baby, I don't mind dying,
I'm a hard-working man and, baby, I don't mind dying,
I catch you cheating on me, then, baby, you don't mind dying.

It has been the vivid descriptions of sex that caused many church people to reject the blues as vulgar or dirty. The Christian tradition has always been ambiguous about sexual intercourse, holding it to be divinely ordained yet the paradigm of rebellious passion. Perhaps this accounts for the absence of sex in the black spirituals and other black church music. But most blacks only verbalized the distinction between the "sacred" and "profane" and found themselves unable to follow white Christianity's rejection of the body. And those who did not experience the free acceptance of sexual love on Saturday nights, expressed it indirectly on Sunday mornings through song and sermon.

In the blues there is an open acceptance of sexual love, and it is described in most vivid terms: "She moves it just right," "I'm going to have it now," "It hurts me so good," "Do it a long time," "Warm it up to me," "Drive it down," "Slow driving."

Peach Orchard Mama, you swore nobody'd pick your fruit but me,
Peach Orchard Mama, you swore nobody's pick your fruit but me,
I found three kid men shaking down your peaches free.

What are we to make of such blatant descriptions of sexual love? Theologically, the blues reject the Greek distinction between the soul and the body, the physical and the spiritual. They tell us that there is no wholeness without sex, no authentic love without the feel and touch of the physical body. The blues affirm the authenticity of sex as the bodily expression of black soul.

The blues are not profane in any negative sense and neither are they immoral. They deal with the truth of human existence and the kinds of difficulties black people experience trying to hold themselves together. They tell us about their strengths and weaknesses, their joys and sorrows, their love and hate. And because they expressed their most intimate and precious feelings openly, they were able to survive as a community amid very difficult circumstances. They sang together, prayed together, and slept together. It was sometimes sweet and sometimes bitter; but they could make it because they tried; they "kept on pushing," looking for that new black humanity.

White people obviously cannot understand the love that black people have for each other. People who enslave humanity cannot understand the meaning of human freedom; freedom comes only to those who struggle for it in the context of the community of the enslaved. People who destroy physical bodies with guns, whips, and napalm cannot know the power of physical love. Only those who have been hurt can appreciate the warmth of love that proceeds when persons touch, feel, and embrace each other. The blues are openness to feeling and the emotions of physical love.

—1972

Daphne Duval Harrison

The blues ... are a means of articulating experience and demonstrating a toughness of spirit by creating and recreating that experience. Two qualities highly valued in the black community, articulateness and toughness, are thus brought together in this art form. Fluency in language is considered a powerful tool for establishing and maintaining status in the black community. Thus a man or woman who has mastered the art of signifying, rapping, or orating can subdue any challenger without striking a blow and is held in high esteem. (The present-day phenomenon of the grand masters of rap music demonstrates the continuation of this value among blacks in cities.) The resilience developed by black folks in the face of slavery and post-Reconstruction violence armed them with a will to survive against seemingly insurmountable odds. Those who did were the heroes and heroines of the black world—Frederick Douglass, Sojourner Truth, Harriet Tubman, Mary McLeod Bethune, John Henry, Marcus Garvey, and so on. To summarize, the blues are paradoxical in that they contain the expression of the agony and pain of life as experienced by blacks in America; yet, the very act and mode of articulation demonstrates a toughness that releases, exhilarates, and renews.

The blues singer evokes, matches, and intensifies the "blue" feeling of the listener in the act of singing the blues ... Neither the intent or the result is escape but, instead, the artistic expression of reality. According to Roosevelt Sykes, blues pianist,

> Blues is like a doctor. A blues player ... plays for the worried people ...
> See, they enjoy it. Like the doctor works from the outside of the body to
> the inside of the body. But the blues works on the inside of the inside.

The aesthetic quality depends upon the singer's ability to express deep feelings.

> You got to sing the blues with your soul. It looks like you hurt in the
> deep-down part of your heart. You really hurt when you sing the blues.

—1988

Julian "Cannonball" Adderley

I've always felt that the blues idiom is a feeling. Duke Ellington has said that some people like to travel and that a traveling man who has to leave his wife at home sometimes has need for another woman. If he has left his woman too long, she may find she needs the attention of another man. Duke has said that these feelings and reasons give rise to situations which lay the foundation for a blues expression. He said that sometimes the man is happy his woman found another man, because he didn't want her. Under these circumstances you can have happy blues, rather than sad blues. You know Count Basie's "I Know My Baby Gonna Jump and Shout?" That's the blues. But I don't know what the blues is, I just know how it feels to me. Definitions and rhetoric can't say in finite terms what the blues is all about. People just know.

—1973

Julio Finn

The Hoodoo Church was gone, sacrificed in the hope that if its followers shed their African identity they would become acceptable in the society in which they lived. Possibly it was one of the most expensive sell-
outs in the history of the world, and, since the rulers of that society held
all the trumps, it was a highly unlikely gamble. How this pitiably loaded
game turned out is too well-known for details to be necessary. The
blacks' bartering of their true Church for acceptance proved to be the
height of folly. There is an African song which aptly describes the Afro-
Americans' ordeal of their lost homeland:

> Marassaelo, I have no mother here who can speak for me;
> Marassaelo, I have left my mother in Africa

Luckily for them, blacks were still in possession of the "invisible" side of
their religion: folklore, slang, dances, cuisine, and above all, music; in
short, a *black* way of viewing and interpreting the world. But unlike their
Haitian cousins they were no longer prepared from earliest youth to be
receptive to things African; they were no longer sure if the tales of worship and power, of magic and healing, were true or false, miracles or su-
perstitions. Were they to give credence to Hoodoo when they had never
seen anyone possessed by a *loa?* Everything in their upbringing, their
whole environment, denied its possibility; their Christian backgrounds
told them that all those old stories were but stuff and nonsense, tricks
used by the wily to overawe the gullible. But from whence, then, came
those vague but all too real visions which assailed their minds during
solitude? From whence those shrouded visitors who came in the night,
who whispered things which, though half-understood, yet jolted them
back to a sense of their true identity? These "recognitions"—if they
may be so called—were the core of Afro-Americans' personal *and* national dilemma: they *were* African too; or, to paint the problem in bolder
colors, they were neither one nor the other—and they believed themselves to be both!

   The Bluesman both personified and solved this bewildering situation,
the epitome of the enigma, he was an American who believed in Hoodoo: he gave it free rein in his thoughts; it directed his seemingly direc-
tionless wanderings; it ensured his success in love and his luck in gambling. With its powers he could afford to be a rolling stone—sure to
overcome any impasse the world would throw in front of him.

Churchless, he praised God in his songs, and his listeners were reminded of the powers of the *loas*, of the forces the enemy could not understand, of their past glory and the history of their native land. These
powers were their birthright; they symbolized and brought into focus
those half-felt thoughts, those forms which unexpectedly dropped in
during the night.

Music is one of the principal aspects of African religion—a manifestation of the gods themselves. It participates in the "sacred" in the
African mind, which—excuse the analogy—conceives of it as an indivis-
ible trinity comprised of rhythm, dance, and sound; that it should lack
one of these is a concept alien to Africans' minds. To them music is *matter* and cannot exist without shape, form, and mass. An African definition of music might be expressed as "a movement born of sound." This
sound as traced by the human body is dance. Africans re-create the
sound with their bodies and mimic it with their voices, the greatest of
which is, for them, the drum. As the most consummate of manifestations, music is most worthy of being the vehicle of transport to the
gods—it is the supreme offering, a synthesis of devotion, the ritual of
power in motion. The body, the voice, become invocations to the Supreme. It is the means by which Africans overcome the opposition of the
rational and break through to make contact with the spiritual: through
music they come to the collective unconscious of the Ancestors. Freed
from their everyday selves, they find their true selves, the essence of their
beings, the Spirits of their blood. This magic called music is the key, the
open sesame to the treasure house of the stored images of the primeval
past. Having crossed the threshold they are in the presence of the gods,
of the eternal messages of, specifically, their race, and universally, of
Mankind.

Black Americans were divorced from all this—they had no natural organized Church of their own, no *houngan*, no rites, no prayers—in short,
no ceremonial by which to give interpretation to their spiritual needs.
The society they lived in had uprooted and destroyed all but the haziest
remnants of their religion, which was represented only by the rare Hoodoo Queen or Root Doctor. Besides, things were so contrived that they
had to give nearly all their time to worrying about existence in a land of
unrelenting hostility where their very color was tantamount to a crime
and relegated them to *official* poverty. Composed of violence and poverty,
their life was a recipe for hopelessness.

On this bleak, troubled landscape there appeared a man ... He was as
poor and harassed as the rest of his brethren; as wretched and unedu-

cated, as persecuted and disenfranchised as the rest. And yet, he was somehow different, possessing some kind of mysterious power, he posed an inexplicable threat to the order of things. He was a lone, restless, unstable figure; his shiftless, trouble-ridden life seemed the very synthesis of the black man's problem. As such he posed a challenge to what the country stood for, and, more importantly, to his own people: if nothing else he was *free*. After all, there was a hint of defiance in his holding up his blue mirror in front of these people, singing of brown-skinned gals, jook dancing, and hootchie-cootchie. "Look," he seemed to say, "and be proud of yourselves!" Of course he affected different people in different ways—some loved and others hated him. Some thought it best to forget the past; others to remember and cherish it. Those who saw "black" as a stigma berated him for his "nigger" ways, while others rejoiced that here was a man who had not lost his roots. The black Christian Churches, as we have seen, condemned him for playing "the Devil's music."

He was an unwelcome, incongruous figure, a would-be artist in a land which, having refused to acknowledge that blacks had ever had a culture, refused to credit him with the ability to participate in "art"—*that* was the preserve of white people; artists came from Boston or New York and preferably from Europe. And since black people had long ago been relegated to their "place," there was no need for them to have spokesmen.

Bluesman: the name itself sums up the black man's predicament. Maligned and misunderstood, he yet created the most important art form in American culture.

—1986

Mance Lipscomb

The blues was an original type a dance, see. You was out there in the woods dancin. An when I'm playin them, we called em breakdowns: hurry up an dance an hurry up an be in the moods, swingin—used ta have a dance called swing-out. But now that wadn no kind of blues dance.

Blues is something you should be payin tension to it. You set an listen ta the verses that you sangin the blues about. Some a them verses you put in there will reach somebody's feelin, what done hapm ta them. Some a their people that they know. Yo loved one, place you wanta go an caint go. Thangs you wanta do an caint do it. You got ta set an concentrate on the blues. It puts you ta thankin. Study slow. Thankin over thangs.

Blues is a slow step. Take it, an jest move around on the flow. An you caint dance it fast, cause blues not sposed ta be played fast. Jest be swingin around, an hold on ta yo podna, she holdin on ta you. An go around maybe two steps thisaway, an turn around, an dance back ta this forward step, an turn around an go back yonda a ways, to an for. Blues is a slow motion.

I dont like ta play blues until somewhere along about twelve or one o'clock. Because, I'm got a blues feelin along about that time a night. An I kin memorize all a those verses. I kin sang blues, an put maybe fifteen or twenty verses inta one song.

See, all my songs are what you call True Story Songs. Life Story Songs. That music was jest in my mind ta learn it, cause I like it. If you like a thang, it'll folla ya. If you jest pick up sumpn as a habit, you kin soon furgit about it. Thats how most music oughta be workt up: if you play sumpn the way you like it, somebody else gonna like it, cause its coming direckly from you. Then its gonna run through ya, see. It means sumpn to ya, an you kin hand it ta the individual.

But now a song if it dont have no feelin: well, you dont feel nothin from it when the fella hands it to ya. Its kind of dead. I been playin my songs maybe foedy years. An when I go, there wont be the blues that you hear me play on my issues. It wont sound like me. They'll be mostly writin. There's mighty few people gonna have the feelin—the worryin— because people dont take worry now. They git through what they gonna do right in a minute. They rush theyself. Its so fast movin now. They dont take time ta learn the feelin a what blues is.

Well, you might say blues wadn nothin but a cow huntin fur a calf. She lowed down in the field somewhere, jest bawlin ta brang her calf back around her. Well, she look fur her calf, she's worried about im. She had it inside a her she wanta find her calf. Thats a feelin she had. Thats what you call the calf blues. Not the people blues. When she find that calf, why then she satisfied. You got ta be unsatisfied to have the blues.

—1970s

Mance Lipscomb

Oh I got, lemme see, six records fur Ahhoolie. I got three fur Warner Brothers, but they didn put but the one out. Thats seven albums. Then I got some records combined wit other people. Like you sang one song, I sang anothun, an make a album outa it. I dont know miny them split records I aint got.

Frank Sinatra was tied up with them Brothers some kinda way. He lives someplace out in Califownya, heard me at one a my plays out there. I had jest stawted goin out ta places an playin. So, he came up ta me an say, "Mista Lipscomb, I got a little yacht settin out there in the ocean. Wonder could you come stay with me an my friends a couple a days, an play a little music?"

I say, "Well, I dont swim too good. An I done been babtized. Naw, I blieve I'd be better off on solid ground."

Say, "You dont hafta git in no water, man. Jest walk around on the decks an thangs to eat when you feel like it. Come on an go with us, Mista Lipscomb. Set out an enjoy the view."

So I got out there on that big waters. He had a little low girl wit im, she had shawt hair near about like a man. Called her Mia, I blieve. Purdy little old thang. An I sot out there an played fur them, two nights. She was holdin on ta him an he was holdin on ta her. Lookin at one anothuh. Say, "I show do like you music, Mista Lipscomb."

I dont know what they didn have on that boat, man. I et inythang I wanta, they got it an brung it ta me. So, he told them Warner Brothers ta make a record outa me.

—1970s

Houston A. Baker, Jr.

The task of adequately describing the blues is equivalent to the labor of describing a world class athlete's awesome gymnastics. Adequate appreciation demands comprehensive attention. An investigator has to *be* there, to follow a course recommended by one of the African writer Wole Soyinka's ironic narrators to a London landlord: "See for yourself."

The elaborations of the blues may begin in an austere self-accusation: "Now this trouble I'm having, I brought it all on myself." But the accusation seamlessly fades into humorous acknowledgement of duplicity's always duplicitous triumph: "You know the woman that I love, I stoled her from my best friend,/But you know that fool done got lucky and stole her back again." Simple provisos for the troubled mind are commonplace, and drear exactions of crushing manual labor are objects of wry, in situ commentary. Numinous invocations punctuate a guitar's resonant back beat with: "Lawd, Lawd, Lawd ... have mercy on me/ Please send me someone, to end this misery." Existential declarations of lack combine with lustily macabre prophecies of the subject's demise. If a "matchbox" will hold his clothes, surely the roadside of much-traveled highways will be his memorial plot: "You can bury my body down by the highway side/So my old devil spirit can catch a Greyhound bus and ride." Conative formulations of a brighter future (sun shining on the back door some day, wind rising to blow the blues away) join with a slow-moving askesis of present, amorous imprisonment: "You leavin' now, baby, but you hangin' crepe on my door," or "She got a mortgage on my body, and a lien on my soul." Self-deprecating confession and slack-strumming growls of violent solutions combine: "My lead mule's cripple, you know my off mule's blind/You know I can't drive nobody/Bring me a loaded .39 (I'm go'n pop him, pop that mule!)." The wish for a river of whiskey where if a man were a "divin' duck" he would submerge himself and never "come up" is a function of a world in which "when you lose yo' eyesight, yo' best friend's gone/Sometimes yo' own dear people don't want to fool with you long."

Like a streamlined athlete's awesomely dazzling explosions of prowess, the blues song erupts, creating a veritable playful festival of meaning. Rather than a rigidly personalized form, the blues offers a phylogenetic recapitulation—a nonlinear, freely associative, nonsequential meditation—of species experience. What emerges is not a filled subject, but an anonymous (nameless) voice issuing from the black (w)hole. The blues singer's signatory coda is always *atopic*, placeless: "If anybody asks you who sang this song/Tell X done been here and gone." The "signature" is a space already "X"(ed), a trace of the already "gone"—a fissure rejoined. Nevertheless, the "you" (audience) addressed is always free to invoked the X(ed) spot in the body's absence. For the signature comprises a scripted authentication of "your" feelings. Its mark is an invitation to energizing intersubjectivity. Its implied (in)junction reads: Here is my body meant for (a phylogenetically conceived) you.

The blues are a synthesis (albeit one always synthesizing rather than one already hypostatized). Combining work songs, group seculars, field hollers, sacred harmonies, proverbial wisdom, folk philosophy, political commentary, ribald humor, elegiac lament, and much more, they constitute an amalgam that seems always to have been in motion in America—always becoming, shaping, transforming, displacing the peculiar experiences of Africans in the New World.

—1984

Edward Kamau Brathwaite

BLUES

i woke up this mornin
sunshine int showin through my door
i woke up this mornin
sunshine int showin through my door
'cause the blues is got me
and i int got strength to go no more

i woke up this mornin
clothes still scattered cross the floor
i woke up this mornin
clothes still scattered cross the floor
las night the ride was lovely
but she int comin back for more

sea island sunshine
where are you hidin now
sea island sunshine
where are you hidin now
could a sware i left you in the cupboard
but is only empties mockin at me in there now

empty bottles knockin
laugh like a woman satisfied
empty bottles knockin
laugh like a woman satisfied
she full an left me empty
laughin when i should a cried

this place is empty bottles
this place is a woman satisfied
this place is empty bottles
this place is a woman satisfied
she drink muh sugar water
till muh sunshine died

i woke up this mornin

sunshine into showin underneath my door
i woke up this mornin
sunshine int showin underneath my door
she gone an left me empty
and i should a died ...

—1976

Leon Forrest

The eternal search for the Blues Singer is quite similar to that of the working novelist: to try to find true words to capture the ever-changing conditions of life upon the highly vulnerable heart. A life which is essentially tied to rupture, chaos, celebration, agony, humor, and always trouble. The migrating scenes often lived out by the wandering blues men and women can be heard of course in their music. Oftentimes these were men who supported themselves in a variety of odd jobs, as they looked for work continuously, on the farms or plantations of the South.

For the blues singer, personal, existential experience always outweighs handed-down wisdom. He is always after true feeling, which must be expressed rawly and sincerely; at its base the blues is always about how to deal with troubles. Blues people seem to accept the idea of trouble as the condition for initiation into the gospel of the good news of the blues. This angle of vision is perhaps comic at base, and is probably why there is so much wicked humor in the blues. We might say, then, that Trouble is always at your back door and, if you would but look, at your front door as well. Out of this you can recreate your life, by constantly crafting out new side doors in the menacing mansions and old houses of life. The lyrics of the blues are often highly evocative and filled with oracle-like secular street wisdom, culled from the essence of existence, at the very cutting edge of life (surely Big Bill Broonzy's image of the many uses of the knife come back to haunt us here). Indeed the worst thing that can happen to you, if you are a blues believer, is the loss of the blues. It is an eternal education. You lose the blues at the risk of losing your hold on existence. You lose your tragic sense of life ...

—1988

Samuel A. Floyd, Jr.

The blues is a solo manifestation of the values of the ring, possessing similar cathartic, affirming, and restorative powers. For African Americans, Esu's appearance as the Devil at the crossroads affirmed African custom and tradition, an affirmation so vital to their spiritual survival that they treasured the memory of this trickster and behaved as if the legend were true long after they had stopped believing it, as evidenced, as we have seen, by the music and the statements of bluesmen such as Robert Johnson, Tommy Johnson, and Peetie Attester. Armed with the elements of the ring and the interpretive gifts of Esu, early bluesmen brought new music into the twentieth century.

Musically, the blues probably took its most significant features from the calls, cries, and hollers of field slaves and street vendors and from the spirituals of brush harbors and church houses. It is a remarkable manifestation of some of the primary features of African and African-American song expression, making wide use of call-and-response figures, elisions, repeated short phrases, falling and pendular thirds, timbral distortions, ululations, vocables, hums, moans, and other devices typical of music derived from the ring.

Whatever their African source, early blues melodies were based on a pentatonic arrangement that included blue notes—or the potential for blue notes—on the third and fifth degrees of its scale. As the same neutral intervals are found in the music of some African societies, the blues intonation was not new to African Americans; it was new and strange only to those who were not in tune with the culture. Early blues was as free as the other African-American genres, only later becoming tamed and forced into the eight-, twelve-, and sixteen-bar frameworks that became somewhat common.

The lyrics of the blues were acquired from two primary sources: from life as the singer saw it, lived it, and survived it, and from the "traveling" lyrics of African-American culture. They represent a wide expressive spectrum, spanning "proverbial wisdom, folk philosophy, political commentary, ribald humor, elegiac lament, and much more" (Houston Baker. *Blues, Ideology, and Afro-American Literature: A Vernacular Theory,* 1984), including satire; they describe social phenomena and treat romantic relationships. Unlike the spiritual—a communal testimony oriented toward the next world—the blues song is a personal statement about an individual's view of his or her current circumstances. Blues singers composed their songs by combining fragments and verses from the hundreds or thousands of formulas that were floating around in black communities everywhere, spread by the traveling songsters. Black creativity combined

these fragments with African-American performance practices, transforming them into original works of musical poetry.

The blues, as they emerged during or after Reconstruction, were a way
of coping with the new trials and realizations brought by freedom. There
were blues songs about voodoo, estrangement, sex, protest, bad luck, de-
ceit, war, joblessness, sickness, love, health, evil, revenge, railroading, and
a variety of other life experiences, some sad, others not. These tropes express, in text and in tune, the variety of struggles and fulfillments of
African-American life in their new manifestations. African Americans
were no longer bemoaning their condition in the disguised lament and
protest of the spirituals, which sang of escape from the tribulations of
this life into the next, because following Emancipation, death was no
longer a release from slavery. As the blues poet sang:

> Oh-oh: death is awful
> Oh-oh: death is awful
> Oh-oh: death is awful
> Spare me over, another year.

In common with the spiritual, though, the blues was full of implica-
tion, albeit secular:

> Went to Church, put my hand on the seat
> Lady sat on it, said: "Daddy you sure is sweet,
> Mr. diddie wa diddie
> Mr. diddie wa diddie"
> I wish somebody would tell me what diddie wa diddie means

The blues recognized and represented independence, autonomy, a certain amount of liberation, and release from the oppression of slavery.
According to [Robert] Barlow [*Looking Up at Down: The Emergence of Blues
Culture*, 1989], bluesmen "acted as proselytizers of a gospel of seculariza-
tion in which belief in freedom became associated with personal mobil-
ity—freedom of movement in this world here and now, rather than salvation later on in the next." In black culture, this freedom of movement
was symbolized by songsters traveling rural roads with guitars on their
backs; it was epitomized by the railroad train. For fretting parents, the
passenger car was the primary means of relocating one's family to a less
hostile and oppressive environment; for songsters, their freight was the

means of getting from a turpentine camp to a jook miles away. They sang about these trains and imitated them with mouth harp and guitar—hence the trope of the train and train whistle in blues music. The words and the music of blues songs express both the profundities and the trivialities of the black experience in America.

In the moans, hollers, hums, falsetto, and elisions ... together with the timbre of the guitar and harp—distorted by bottleneck and hand-muffling, respectively—the heterogeneous sound ideal was realized in the blues, revealing the derivation of the music from the spirituals and the ring, even down to the use of "Oh, Lawdy" in a musical form that is, from the standpoint of Christianity, unabashedly profane. And the improvisatory potential ... prefigures jazz and confirms the presence of melodic extemporization in the African-American musical arsenal. [...]

Sadness [and] lamentation [are] traits that have been exaggerated—by well-meaning promoters of the black social cause and by not-so-well meaning record producers—to such a degree that it is commonly thought that the expressive range of the blues is limited to that one quality. Followers of the blues know that much of its repertoire is optimistic, some of it violent, some of it romantic, and some merely descriptive; and, while no blues recordings were made in the nineteenth century, it is logical to assume that this wide, expressive range was characteristic even then. [...]

As a communication system, the blues, as had the spirituals earlier, spoke in code—a semantic code that included euphemisms for sex such as Bessie Smith's "deep sea diver," "black snake," "ain't no more 'taters: the frost have killed the vine," and so one. But the blues also spoke a musical code in which, according to Baker, "the harmonica's whoop and the guitar's bass can recapitulate vast dimensions of experience" and in which the guitar's "growling vamp" signifies something other than what it speaks of. In short, instrumental blues spoke a musical code decipherable by knowers of the culture but inaccessible to those outside it. It is this code and its interpretation that links the blues to other black modes of expression. The code itself is interpretive, traditionally taught to blues people by Esu, the African god of interpretation and connector of the people to their African past.

The blues was a new expression, created by a people coming to grips with the changes wrought by the onset of Reconstruction and the dawning of a new century. As the genre developed, certain musical elements of the ring became so prominent that they emerged as primary tropes, and other genres began to borrow heavily from it. Since the blues appears to be basic to most forms of black music, and since it seems to be the most prominent factor in maintaining continuity between most of them, we might think of it as the Urtrope of the tradition.

—1995

Thomas A. Dorsey

Blues were really born shortly after slaves were free and they were sung the way singers felt inside. They were just let out of slavery or put out, or went out, but they hadn't gotten used to freedom. Their spirituals had a kind of feeling, you know, a depressed feeling. They poured out their souls in their songs. They still had the feeling for a number of years, but not the persecution and all that. But blues is a digging, picking, pricking at the very depth of your mental environment and the feelings of your heart. Blues is more than just *blues*. It's got to be that old low-down moan and the low-down feeling; you got to have feeling.

—1976–77

Robert Pete Williams

Music begin to follow me then. I been trying to stop playing, thinking 'bout preparing my soul for Jesus ... Just look to me like I can't put music down. Time I get hold of one guitar and I maybe sell it to somebody, well music just come back to me and worry me so, I just have to go back and buy me another guitar ... All the music I play I just hear in the air. You can hear the sound of it coming forth, sounding good.

Robert Wilkins

In blues it's what you call a felt-inward feeling—of your own self. It's not a spiritual feeling that you have; it's some kind of sorrowful feeling that you have of your own self. It's something that happened to you and cause you to become sorry or something, maybe grievous about it. Then you would compose the song to that feeling that you have. And then you would sing it and after you begin to sing it, then you become accustomed to it through psychology that 'most anybody could have that same feeling as you did. It's universal, but it don't bring joy in the spirit.

—1969

Lorenzo Thomas

BLUES CADET
after Sunnyboy Williamson

I'd rather take flying lessons.

I've worn out the pictures on the carpet
Just pacing my room

Ever since you went away
My life's portion of gloom
Increased a thousand fold

And in my four-walled room around me
The walls are closing like a door.

—1973

James H. Cone

Both the spirituals and the blues are the music of black people. They should not be pitted against each other, as if they are alien or radically different. One does not represent good and the other bad, one sacred and the other secular. Both partake of the *same* black experience in the United States.

Living under the harsh reality of slavery and segregation, the spirituals and the blues tell what black people did to keep together and endure. Blacks have always known that they were more than the little black sambos the whites imagined them to be. But it is one thing to know that you are a human being and quite another to create a world so that your humanity can be acknowledged. Through the power of human imagination, defined by their struggle against slavery and segregation, blacks created a separate world for themselves—a world defined by justice and peace, where women, men, and their children can freely love and be loved.

Music has been and continues to be the most significant creative art expression of African-Americans. Blacks sing and play music (in their churches and at juke-joint parties) as a way of coping with life's contradictions and of celebrating its triumphs. We sing when we are happy and when we are sad; when we get a job and when we lose one; when we protest for our rights and when the formal achievement of them makes no difference in the quality of our life. Singing is the medium through which we talk to each other and make known our perspectives on life to the world. It is our way of recording and reflecting on our experiences—the good and the bad, the personal and the political, the sacred and the secular.

Most blacks do not acknowledge these dualisms. They believe that reality is one. The spirituals and the blues record black people's feelings—their hopes and disappointments, their dreams and nightmares. We must view them as two artistic expressions of the same black experience. [...]

Gospel music replaced the spirituals as the most dominant music in the churches and jazz followed the blues—all communicating strong messages about love and hate, right and wrong, God and the world. Today a new form of musical discourse has emerged in the black community. It's called "rap" music. It is a musical-talk, extremely popular among young people who are searching for meaning in the world that has no place for them.

Whatever form black music takes, it is always an expression of black life in America and what the people must do to survive with a measure of dignity in a society which seems bent on destroying their right to be human beings. The fact that black people keep making music means that we as a people refuse to be destroyed. We refuse to allow the people who oppress us to have the last word about our humanity. The last word belongs to us and music is our way of saying it. Contrary to popular opinion, therefore, the spirituals and the blues are not songs of despair or of a defeated people. On the contrary, they are songs which represent one of the great triumphs of the human spirit.

—1972

William Barlow

The blues tradition fifty years after its birth on the cotton plantations of the South was a mature and familiar touchstone within urban black culture. Over the years, it had again and again made important contributions to the oral tradition, and had consequently remained on the cutting edge of African-American cultural resistance to white domination.

The components of that resistance were fourfold. At a primary level, there was the blues sound, or, perhaps more appropriately, the blues soundscape—all those "weird," "visceral," "suggestive," "dirty" sounds, "out of tune" and "off key" if judged by European musical standards. The use of blue notes was at the heart of the blues sound; they gave it its subversive character, a dissonance instantly recognizable in both vocal and instrumental renderings. In addition, the blues sound relied heavily on the use of tonic chord, which provided immediate release from musical tensions. They were, in effect, a wellspring of instant gratification. The release of pleasurable energy was also encouraged by the use of polyrhythms, which exploded tensions by stacking different rhythms on top of each other, thereby adding a dense, repetitive, and fluid locomotion to the overall blues sound. Finally, there were the wide variety of vocal techniques, like falsetto, melisma, slurring, and moaning, used to embellish the songs. These were based on affective pitch tones that masked the blues voice in order to evoke tonal memories. The "deep" blues sounds of pioneers such as Charley Patton, Blind Lemon Jefferson, Ma Rainey, and Bessie Smith were resurrected in the vocals of Muddy Waters, Howling Wolf, Billie Holiday, and Dinah Washington.

The blues texts were also bulwarks of cultural resistance, providing a composite view of American society from the bottom. They were not linear narratives, but were circular and indirect in their discourse, in keeping with African custom. They focused on the everyday lives of the black masses—their working conditions, living conditions, prison experiences, travels, and sexual relationships. The texts fall into two broad categories: cautionary folktales—lessons on how to survive in a hostile social environment—and prideful songs of self-assertion. While the former caution the listener through example to be ever vigilant against misfortune, the latter tend to urge an artist and audience alike to greater heights of emotion, endurance, pleasure, and even ecstasy. Blues texts, sung in the vernacular of the black masses, were the "true songs" or "reals" of hope, despair, humor, and struggle, which documented from within the epic African-American exodus out of the rural South and into the industrial centers of urban America during the first half of the twentieth century. In the words of St. Louis bluesman Henry Townsend:

> Although they call it the blues today, the original name given to this kind of music was "reals." And it was real because it made the truth available to the people in the songs—if you wanted to tell the truth. Most good blues is about telling the truth about things. Just as gospel music is songs about people in biblical times, the blues are songs about black folks today—and these songs are dedicated to the truth. I'm telling stories that were told to me or events that happened to me—just like all blues singers. The blues is one of the few things that was born here in America by black people. It's our music.

—1989

Thomas A. Dorsey

Some have asked what is the blues. It would be hard to explain to anyone who has never had a love craving, or had someone they loved dearly to forsake them for another, a wounded heart, a troubled mind, a longing for someone you do not have with you, and many other things I could mention ... Blues would sound better late at night when the lights were low, so low you couldn't recognize a person ten feet away, when the smoke was so thick you could put a hand full of it into your pocket. The joint might smell liked tired sweat, bootleg booze, Piedmont cigarettes, and Hoyttes Cologne ... The piano player is bending so low over the eighty-eight keys, you would look for him in time to swallow the whole instrument. He is king of the night and the ivories speak a language that everyone can understand.

—1976–77

Booker White

I just reach up and pull them out of the sky—call them sky songs.

I like to talk and have a nice time—like a fish—take him out of the water and lay him on the bank in the hot sun and he'll soon dry up and die—that's the way I am—if you don't put me someplace where I can have fun I won't live long ...

Like I said, though, things used to get rough in them days. Not that they don't these days, but back then they wouldn't think no more about killing a Negro than they would about killing a chicken. I became more acquainted with lynchings than I was with hanging up my socks ...

I had a first cousin to get lynched. His name was Robert Lee Hatchett. He was just about eighteen years old. A bunch of white boys was drinking one Saturday night and Robert Lee was coming home and they killed him and laid his body on the railroad tracks for the train to run over. But the engineer stopped. The white boys went home and went to bed and nothing was ever done to them. And that was one of the things that started me to being mean ...

I never wrote songs about nothing like that, though. I didn't do it then and I won't do it now. It just gets on my nerves. I can think of other things to sing about. It's so much of that kind of thing happening every day and I just don't want to make no songs out of it ...

I could lay down and die today. What am I gon' to worry about? All I want to do is make it in. On the earth, I have really gained a victory of a poor man having what he's supposed to have and I have no kick coming. When I die, I don't want to die with a frown on my face, 'cause I don't want nobody to think that I left something that I was supposed to get and didn't get it and I left with a frown ...

—1969

Son House

I bought an old piece of guitar from a fella named Frank Hopkins. I gave him a dollar and a half for it. It was nearly all to pieces, but I didn't know the difference.

... I kept on playing and got better and better, you know. I'd set up and concentrate on the songs, and then went to concentrating on my rhyming words, rhyming my own words. "I can make my own songs," I said. And that's the way I started.

... "Preachin' Blues," "Black Mama," "Mississippi Country Farm," and "Clarksdale Moan." Willie Brown and I played that last one together. I think that's about all. Close as I can get to it. It's been so long ... I got paid forty dollars for making those records ... forty dollars! ... It'd take me near about a year to make forty dollars in the cotton patch ...

This is on me. Just as well admit it. This is the truth. 'Course some of it is a little addition, but the biggest of it is the truth. I used to be a preacher. I was brought up in the church and started preaching before I started this junk ... And I began to wonder, now how can I stand up in the pulpit and preach to them, tell them how to live, and quick as I dismiss the congregation and I see ain't nobody looking and I'm doing the same thing ... I says, well, I got to do something, 'cause I can't hold God in one hand and the Devil in the other one ... I got to turn one of 'em loose. So I got out of the pulpit. So I said, the next time I make a record, I'm gon' to name it "Preachin' Blues." I'm preaching on this side and the blues on that side ...

—1969

Julio Finn

Did Robert Johnson seek out or meet a Hoodoo Doctor during his wanderings in the bayous who initiated him into the cult, thus providing him with the knowledge to invoke Legba, the master of the crossroads? Did he make a pact with this "Devil" in order to play "the Devil's music"? We'll never know. What is certain is that in the span of a couple of years he went from playing the guitar so badly that it hurt people's ears to being a performer in a class by himself. At the same time, from being a "boy" he became a man with extraordinary charisma, capable of moving a crowd to tears and attracting many men, destined to become famous in their own right, as his disciples. We also know that he was secretive to a fault about his technique. Most importantly, he himself told his friends that he had made a deal with the Devil, and that he would have it pay for it. His fellow musicians believed him, seeing nothing implausible in the undertaking. Not only his playing, but his "new" personality lent credence to the assertion. He had gone seeking strength and had come back a man of power—not just a bluesman, but a *Hoodoo* bluesman. The way the postulated thesis of his going to the crossroads fits into the Hoodoo tradition is almost uncanny. Compare, for instance, his story with that of the Dahomean tale "Man Against the Creator":

Awe reached the sky. Mawu (Legba's mother) said to him:

"What are you looking for?" Awe said to Mawu: "My knowledge is great. I now seek to measure my knowledge with you."

He made a statue of a man. But it could not breathe, nor talk, nor move.

Mawu said to him: "Your knowledge is not enough."

Mawu left Awe, and Awe went back to earth. But Mawu sent death to follow him.

However, Awe mastered Legba's knowledge and became a practitioner of magic. Awe and Death are the two friends of the world.

Legba (the seventh son of Mawu) led this man down the road to the market, and told him all that had to be done to make magic charms.

Moreover, music as a magic medium is an accepted idea in black culture. [...]

Johnny Shines voices the idea of music and magic in the comment he made about the first time he saw Howling Wolf perform: "I thought he was a magic man. They had an old saying about people who sold their soul to the Devil to be able to play better than anyone else. I thought Wolf was one these."

People think wrongly about magic: magic looks exactly like reality—only its effect is different.

In spite of the evidence, Johnson's biographers are either skeptical or deny outright his having made a pact. It is significant that none of them brings Hoodoo into the picture. But, then, how could they have, when none of them knew about Legba, or the *loa* stones, or of the African concept of the partnership between music and magic? This is pardonable, but their arrogance is not. They deal, not with what Johnson believed, but what *they* themselves believe. They don't believe in Hoodoo, so ... But, *whose* story is this? The only thing which matters is what Johnson believed. Possession? Why not? To hoodooists, the thing is not only possible, but desirable, a sign of high favor. Perhaps it was Johnson's misfortune not have been born in Brazil or Haiti—for, a few hundred miles from the clinical climes of the Great Union, possession takes place daily, and no one finds it "impossible." When I read the whitewashed accounts which have so far appeared of Robert Johnson, I experience a kind of vertigo, so similar in attitude are they to the earlier accounts by whites of African culture and music. The old taboos, rehashed and updated, lurk beneath the "objective" interest. While extolling Johnson's music—the Devil's music—they erase the obvious role Hoodoo played in it. The fact that Mister Bluesman Son House, Mister Bluesman Johnny Shines, and Mister Bluesman Robert Jr. Lockwood believed in his "pact" goes for nothing. So be it. But stop obscuring the history of the blues with your ideas, stop "interpreting" for the world how black people think—because you don't know! Robert either made or believed he made a deal with the Devil, and whichever way he did it—physically, symbolically, or imaginatively—he did it out of desperation. However it was, he certainly contracted a mystic obligation with the spiritual world. Those stones in his path, the midnight vigil at the crossroads, the flight from Satan's hounds—all became so inextricably bound up with his vision of the world that they became the signposts of his destiny. The ever-mounting consciousness that he himself was a "crossroad" all but unhinged him, and left him tottering in a nightmare world on the borders of which were insanity. [...]

By some kind of genial mysticism he transformed the chaos of his life into art, forging a new path for the blues to follow and giving a new interpretation to Hoodoo, breathing new life into the most awesome of the initiations, the Crossroads.

Revelations pass unseen to the uninitiated. Johnson was "called" to Hoodoo the same as he was "called" to the blues: to bear witness. With his "Hell Hound on My Trail" he gave utterance to the well-nigh hopeless condition of his people. In this sense, his art is the logical outcome of events, while life is the blues revealed, a towering monument to the music he played. His story encapsulates the whole of its history and his songs are the archetypal expression of its true meaning. There were stones in his pathway; he left gems in ours.

—1986

Jon Michael Spencer

What made the urban blues less priestly, ritualistic, and religious was, in part, capitalism. Capitalism naturally bred artists—artistic entrepreneurs—who *took* (money), rather than fashioning priests—preachers of blues—who *gave* (ministry). This commercializing of black sorrow was perfectly illustrated in a political cartoon in the *Defender* by Jay Jackson, a well-know artist and cartoonist of his day. The cartoon pictured a well-dressed black woman coming out of a "Music Publishing House." The woman was wearing a fur coat and, having just recorded a hit blues, had money overflowing from her pocketbook. The advertisement in the window of the publishing house read, "Divorced Woman Blues. Hear it, Greatest Blues since St. Louis Blues." And who did the newly famed blues singer run into on her way out of the store, begging for money in his tattered clothes; and what did he say? Waving a handful of bills beneath the nose of her ex-husband, the woman said, as the caption read, "Remember when you used to give me the blues? Well I made something out of them."

———

Another influence in the commercial reduction of the traditional cosmology of the blues was the trivializing (if not minstrelizing) of the music, first by white-owned vaudeville companies and then by white-owned recording companies. Paramount Records, for instance, advertised Trixie Smith's "Praying Blues" in an almost sacrilegious way, following an excerpt from the blues in which Smith begged the Lord to please hear her plea and send her a man "that wants nobody else but me." The advertisement then read, "It's a riot—a scream—a sensation—that Trixie Smith and Her Downhome Syncopators have made ... It's the best prayer we ever heard on record—'Mournful' won't describe it, it's that sad." It is evident in the innumerable advertisements like this one that the promotion of classic blues was plagued by the old "coon song" stereotypes of Tin Pan Alley. For instance, Okeh Race Records advertised Sippie Wallace's "Underworld Blues" with religious indifference: "The newest Okeh Record of Sippie's is some powerful wicked blues and no mistake. It's probably the sobbin'est, groanin'est, weepin'est, moanin'est blues you ever heard." [...]

These advertisements illustrate that white recording executives were significantly responsible for shaping Chicago's city blues. Their concern not for the traditional religious cosmology of many of the artists they recorded, but for money, power, and social relations (which were thought to be able to control good and evil), made blues into an increasingly rationalized "urban" art, one that eventually could be performed by white blues "artists." In this respect, the complaints Mississippian Jimmy Rogers had regarding his recording sessions with Chess in the early fifties are understandable: "Only time it'd be a rerun or somethin' Chess would want to change, and that would be the end of a good record. When he changed it, he'd take all the soul and everything from it. And that happened quite a few times." Just as the newspaper advertisements of the major record companies reduced the traditional cosmology of the blues to mere vaudeville, so did the record producers, for capitalistic reasons, play a significant part in this denaturement as city blues developed into its sophisticated urban offspring.

Capitalism also helped denude the blues of its mythologies, theologies, and theodicies in that it blurred moral polarities. This blurring of the moral distinction between good and evil, effected by capitalism, also caused African-American culture to shift increasingly from more absolutist judgments of good and evil to more relativist judgments. This is the significance of the front-page *Defender* article of 1950 that carried a large photograph of Billie Holiday and the caption "Billie Holiday Has Right to Sing Blues." Here the jazz-styled blues singer "has the *right* to sing blues," when three decades earlier blues and jazz were severely ridiculed, and blues worse than jazz.

—1993

Robert Hayden

HOMAGE TO THE EMPRESS OF THE BLUES: BESSIE SMITH

Because somewhere there was a man in a candystripe silk shirt,
gracile and dangerous as a jaguar and because some woman moaned
for him in sixty-watt gloom and mourned him Faithless Love
Twotiming Love Oh Love Oh Careless Aggravating Love,

She came out on the stage in yards of pearls, emerging like
a favorite scenic view, flashed her golden teeth, and sang.

Because grey lathes began somewhere to show from underneath
torn hurdygurdy lithographs of dollfaced heaven;
and because there were those who feared alarming fists of snow
on the door and those who feared the riot-squad of statistics,

She came out on the stage in ostrich feathers, beaded satin,
and shone that smile on us and sang.

—1962

Clyde E. B. Bernhardt

I ran a lot of errands for people. That's how I met the great black singer
Madame Gertrude Rainey, that everybody called Ma. It was June 1917
when her own all-colored minstrel show, "The Georgia Smart Set," came
to Badin for a few weeks. They set up their big canvas tent right behind
the cemetery, on Falls Road.

I was always hanging around her tent in case she got thirsty, then run
to the store for some Coca-Cola. She loved Coca-Cola. Cost five cents a
bottle, but I knew where to get three bottles for a dime. And she tip me
a dime. During the day the whole company be outside cooking or exer-
cising. Or just talking about show business. And I was running around
keeping busy, getting a nickel here and a dime there. Sometimes I made
almost a dollar a day that way. But I was so thrilled being around those
show folks I would of done it for nothing.

The people were all so nice, especially Ma Rainey. She was then
treated to be the greatest blues singer in the world. Ma was very dark,
had a wide nose, big lips, and a mouth full of gold-capped teeth. She

wasn't pretty—her natural complexion was black, but on the show she looked much lighter, almost high-yella.

"Honey," she say, "it's hard work to be light like me. Take a hour to put that makeup on and another to get the damn stuff off."

She spoke with a little lisp-tongue, but you couldn't hear it when she sang. I liked Ma Rainey. She was a happy-go-lucky person, a religious person. You could see it in her. Always helping the underdog.

Everybody talked about her famous gold necklace. I never seen such a necklace before—one-hundred-dollar gold coins all strung together with some fifty-dollar, twenty-dollar, and ten-dollar ones stuck in between. The smallest was five-dollar pieces. It was like a trademark for her. One day I found her scrubbing her necklace with Old Dutch Cleanser in her washbasin.

At night I was right down front in the colored section to watch the show. The tent was big and square, almost two-hundred-feet long. Men selling popcorn and roasted peanuts in the shell.

I remember she had a string band in front of the stage. A bass fiddle, violin, viola, piano, and drums, and it was the first time I seen the big bass played while straddled. Couldn't stop from laughing.

After the band overture, the curtain opened and out danced eight long-legged gals in short costumes. They weren't the prettiest I seen, in fact they were downright ugly. With light makeup they were passable, but they could sure dance up a streak. Then the chorus boys came out and danced in the same line. The audience just loved the old gals and boys.

As they danced off, the backdrop came down showing a large illustration of a cotton field. Two blackface rubes came out dressed in stovepipe pants that ended just below the knees to show white socks going down in their big, extra-long shoes. When they started telling those old, funny stories, everybody broke up.

Bertha Forbes was one of the ballad singers on the show, and John Miles was another that sang "Sweet Adeline" dressed in a long tailcoat with walking trousers and a top hat. They also had a terrific dancer doing buck and wing steps and some tap. Another comedy act was hip-bumping Roxy Caldwell and her lady partner. These were two funny women.

It was a straight two-hour show, no intermission. One time this funny juggler, the name was Joe Fraser, put two oil lamps on his head and both were lit. He turned his body up, down, around, back flipped, and never dropped a lamp. Didn't even blow out. Later, a man riding a bicycle came on dressed as a Japanese and holding an umbrella. Rode that thing every which way, sitting, standing, on his head, on his back, and finally one wheel fell off and he rode it as a unicycle. He was good.

Ma Rainey closed the show. When she was ready to go on, the great lady start singing in the wings and as the curtain opened, strutted out flashing those gold-plated teeth and her expensive gold necklace. She wore a long, gold silk gown that swept along the floor, gold slippers, and carried a rhinestone walking cane. Her hat was high and wide with large feathers stuck in it, had gold earrings dangling and diamond rings on all her fingers. When she got to center stage under those amber spotlights, the audience just went wild. She was all of what show business was suppose to be. She *was* show business.

Her first song was "St. Louis Blues" in a slow-drag tempo. Then maybe "Yellow Dog Blues" with a spoken introduction about her "easy rider" and other problems. She close with her own "See, See Rider Blues" and for the big finale go into "Walkin' the Dog," which was also called "Get Over Sal, Don't You Linger." Then the whole chorus line come stepping out behind her and she dance along, kicking up her heels. The song had dance instructions in the lyrics, and as she call a step, everybody would do it. Soon the whole cast was out on stage, jugglers, riders, singers, comedians, all dancing wild with Ma Rainey shouting and stomping. She call "WALK!" and everybody walked together before breaking out fast. She call "STOP!" and everybody froze. After many calls she finally holler "SQUAT!" and the whole group squatted down with a roar. Including Ma Rainey.

It was a exciting show and the audience kept cheering and whistling. The whites in the audience usually applauded the longest.

—1986

Thomas A. Dorsey

The room is filled with a haze of smoke, she walks into the spotlight, face decorated with Stein's Reddish Make-up Powder. She's not a young symmetrical stream-lined type; her face seems to have discarded no less than fifty some years. She stands out high in front with a glorious bust, squeezed tightly in the middle. Her torso, extending in the distance behind, goes on about its business from there on down. She opens her mouth and starts singing:

It's storming on the ocean, it's storming on the sea.
My man left me this morning, and it's storming down on me.

When she started singing, the gold in her teeth would sparkle. She was in the spotlight. She possessed her listeners; they swayed, they rocked, they moaned and groaned, as they felt the blues with her. A woman swooned who had lost her man. Men groaned who had given their week's pay to some woman who promised to be nice, but slipped away and couldn't be found at the appointed time. By this time she was just about at the end of her song. She was "in her sins" as she bellowed out. The bass drum rolled like thunder and the stage lights flickered like forked lightning:

> I see the lightning flashing, I see the waves a dashing
> I got to spread the news; I feel this boat a crashing
> I got to spread the news; my man is gone and left me
> Now I got the stormy sea blues.

As the song ends, she feels an understanding with her audience. Their applause is a rich reward. She is in her glory. The house is hot. Then she lets go again:

> Lawdy, Lawdy I hear somebody calling me,
> It ain't my regular, it must be my used-to-be.
> If I had wings and could fly like Noah's dove,
> I'd heist my wings and fly to the man I love.

By this time everybody is excited and enthusiastic. The applause thunders for one more number. Some woman screams out with a shrill cry of agony as the blues recalls sorrow because some man trifled on her and wounded her to the bone. [Ma Rainey] is ready now to take the encore as her closing song. Here she is tired, sweaty, swaying from side to side, fatigued but happy. Then she sings:

> Honey, Honey, Honey, look what you done,
> You done made me love you, and now your woman done come.
> If anybody ask you who wrote this lonesome song,
> Tell 'em you don't know the writer,
> But a lonesome woman put it on.

—1976–77

William "Big Bill" Broonzy

The first time I tried to play anything was in 1914. It was a home-made fiddle and I couldn't play it right away. That was in Arkansaw near where the Mississippi and Arkansaw Rivers came together. I had first heard a home-made fiddle played by a blues singer we knew as See Rider. Don't know his name—everybody called him just See See Rider, because he used to sing a blues by the name. Later on Ma Rainey made record of that tune, but I first heard it down around my home. I never saw anyone else play a home-made fiddle except See See Rider. He was born and raised in Redale, Arkansaw, and he played for everybody around there. Hearing him made me want to do something too.

Me and a boy named Louis made a fiddle and guitar from wooden boxes we got from the commissary. The neck was a broomstick and we'd get broken strings from See See Rider and patch them up. I made me a bow out of hickory wood by bending it and leaving it to dry. We'd cut a tree with an axe and go back the next day for rosin. I kept the fiddle hid because my old man and woman didn't want me to play it. Me and Louis would play every chance we got and one day a man heard us and took us to his house to play a piece. He liked it and said he'd get us a good fiddle and guitar. He sent to Sears-Roebuck in Chicago but it was a long time before I could play a regular fiddle. My home-made fiddle had only two strings and I played two strings on the new one fine, but it took a while to learn to use all four strings. After I could play it, I couldn't tune it. We used to go on picnics and barbecues and I'd play my fiddle, with Louis on guitar and a bass player named Jerry Sanders. But my brother-in-law would have to go along to tune the fiddle.

The first job I had playing music in a public place was in Little Rock. That was after I got out of the army in March 1919 and lasted until February 1920. Then I went to Chicago and got a job as a yard-man for the Pullman Company. I didn't play any for a few years until I met Charlie Jackson in 1924. He found out I could play a fiddle and had me come around. John Thomas, Theodore Edwards, and Charlie were all playing then on the West Side. Later I played guitar on a record for Teddy Edwards and the tunes were "Barbecue Blues" and "Louise Louise Blues."

Charlie first got me started on guitar at that time and showed me how to make chords, and I played around a little with John Thomas. Charlie was a well-known recording artist at that time and he got me to Mayo Williams, who was working for Paramount then. John Thomas and I auditioned two numbers for Williams—"Big Bill Blues" and "House Rent Stomp"—but he said we didn't play well enough. I guess it wasn't very good because I was just starting on guitar. I had my job for the Pullman Company and only played once in a while at house parties. We made those two numbers for Williams later on though. That was in 1926 and when we go to the studio, Aletha Dickerson, who was Williams's secretary, asked me my name. I told her, "William Lee Couley Broonzy," and she said, "For Christ's sake, we can't get all that on the label." She said she'd think of a name for me and later on when she wanted me for something she said, "Come here, Big Boy." That gave her the idea to call me Big Bill and that's the way I've been known ever since. I think I recorded six sides for the Paramount Company, but the first was "Big Bill Blues" and "House Rent Stomp."

There were a lot of good guitar players and blues singers around Chicago in those days and I knew all of them from playing around at different places. Shorty George recorded the first guitar blues of my knowing. Barbecue Bob was one of the first too—I met him around Chicago. I worked with Georgia Tom about that time—he was the leader of the Hokum Boys and wrote all their tunes, and when we made a record, we'd use a tune that they made, like "Somebody's Been Using That Thing." One day in 1930, we all piled into a Ford and drove to New York. There was Georgia Tom and I, a girl named Mozelle, Lester Melrose—he was the manager of the record company—and two members of the Hokum Boys, Arthur Pettis and Frank Brandswell. They sang but they didn't play and we made records like "Come On In," where Mozelle, Tom, and I sang and Tom played the piano and I played guitar. We also made records for the Starr Piano Company in Richmond, Indiana, with Georgia Tom on piano. Later on I made records there with Black Bob on piano. Georgia Tom's name was Thomas A. Dorsey and he was on a lot of records, including all of Tampa Red's, until he quit for the church about 1933.

All this time I was working during the day and they'd pay me to play all night. I was making records too and we'd all get together in the recording studio. I always went around to watch when Ma Rainey was recording. Maybe I'd be making records in one studio and Ma in another and others would be there, like Blind Blake, Charlie Jackson, Blind Lemon Jefferson, and Leroy Carr. I never worked with him but I think Leroy Carr was the greatest blues singer I heard in my life. I knew him from seeing him around and listening to him and he was the best guy you ever met. He played piano on all his records and usually worked with Scrapper Blackwell. He really could sing the blues and he couldn't have been more than thirty when he died.

—1945

Eileen Southern

Slave fiddlers had their own methods for producing "hot" music as the dancing became wilder and more abandoned....

The fiddler sang and stomped his feet as he played, the boy handling the needles all the while. An expert fiddler "could stomp the left heel and the right forefoot and alternate this with the right heel and the left forefoot, making four beats to the bar."

Holiday dances were generally all-night affairs. When the fiddler grew tired, the slaves provided a different kind of dance music by "pattin' juba." Basically, this procedure involved foot tapping, hand clapping, and thigh slapping, all in precise rhythm. There seem to have existed, however, a number of ways to accomplish this feat. [...] In Georgia the patter tapped his foot in regular time while he alternately clapped his hands lightly and slapped his thighs. On the plantation in Louisiana where Northrup was enslaved, the patting was performed by striking the hands on the knees, then striking the hands together, then striking the right shoulder with one hand, the left with the other—all the while keeping time with the feet, and singing, perhaps, this song:

> Harper's creek and roarin' ribber,
> Thar, my dear, we'll live forebber;
> Den we'll go to the Ingin Nation,
> All I want in dis creation,
> Is pretty little wife and big plantation.*

Northup tells us that the juba song typically was "one of those unmeaning songs, composed rather for its adaptation to a certain tune or measure than for the purpose of expressing any distinct idea." And patting juba made "a most curious noise, yet in such perfect order that the slaves had no difficulty in dancing to it."

There were as many ways to pat juba (or juber) as there were patters. On a Maryland plantation, a boy sang the "words of a jig in a monotonous tone of voice, beating time meanwhile with his hands alternately against each other and against his body [James Hungerford, *The Old Plantation, or What I Gathered There in an Autumn Month*, 1859]." The principal "juber rhymer" on that plantation was a girl named Clotilda who improvised the verses for the dancing and *recited* them in a "shrill sing-song voice, keeping time to the measure ... by beating her hands sometimes

---

*Solomn Northup, *Twelve Years a Slave*, 1853.

against her sides, and patting the ground with her feet." After each stanza, she paused a bit—perhaps to collect her thoughts for the next improvised stanza—but continued to beat her hands and pat her foot without ceasing.

Numerous variants of the juba song were current in the nineteenth century. Generally they had in common only the juba refrain and the idea of indicating in the verse the steps to be followed in the dancing. The following is an example of Clotilda's song:

JUBER'S DANCE

Laudy! how it make me laugh
Ter see de niggers all so saf';
See um dance de foolish jig,
Un neber min' de juber rig.
Juber!

(Negroes dancing every one after his or her own fashion, but keeping time to the beat.)

Juber lef' un Juber right;
Juber dance wid all yo' might;
Juber here un Juber dere,
Juber, Juber, ebery where.
Juber!

(The dancers get into confusion in their frantic efforts to follow the directions. *Clotilda* rebukingly,

"Git out, you silly breed!
Can't you dance de Juber reed?")

Once ole Uncle Will
Gwine ullong de side de hill,

Stump his toe uggin er weed,
Un spill all his punkin seed.
Juber!

(Ludicrous imitations of Uncle Will stumbling and trying to recover himself, and to prevent his pumpkin seed from falling at the same time. *Uncle Will,* with great disgust, "Imperdin piece!")

Dere's ole Uncle Jack
Hab er pain in his back;

Every time he try ter skip
Den he hab ter get er limp.
Juber!

(Active skips suddenly changed to a variety of awkward limps expressive
of great pain in the back. *Uncle Jack,* angrily, "De outrageous hussy!")

Guess I knows er nigger gal—
Dere she is, her name is Sal—
Un she hab to min' de baby,
Show us how she rock de cradle.
Juber!

(A variety of swaying motions, intended to represent cradle-rocking
in a ridiculous view. *Sall,* a daughter of Aunt Kate, and nurse of a baby
sister, indignantly, "I alwus said Clotildy was crazy!")

Ebery body knows Aunt Jinny,
Nothing ken be said uggin her;
When she fever nigger take,
My! how dat ole lady shake.
Juber! *etc*

In addition to instrumental dance music and pattin' juba, the dance-
music repertory of the slaves included "fiddle-sings," "jig-tunes," and
"devil songs." Regretfully, few of these were preserved. Most of the song
collecting took place on plantations where slaves, having been converted
to Christianity, came to regard dancing as sinful and no longer indulged
in it. As suggested above, there were collectors who realized that they
might be neglecting an important repertory in failing to record the non-
religious music, but apparently they were in the minority. There might
have been other reasons—one of them that the texts of dance songs
tended to be nonsensical. Who would bother to record such an absurdity
as the following except, perhaps, a slave:

Who's been here since I've been gone?
Pretty little gal wid a josey on.
Hog eye!
Old Hog eye!
And Hosey too!
Never see de like since I was born.

A number of dance songs have come down to us, however, from Catholic Louisiana, where dancing was not discouraged. Six such songs are included in the *Slave Songs of the United States* (William Allen, Charles Ware, and Lucy Garrison, 1867), all "obtained from a lady who heard them sung before the war on the Good Hope Plantation, St. Charles Parish, Louisiana," according to the editors of that 1867 collection. A song titled "Calinda" accompanied a kind of contradance in which the two lines of the dancers faced each other, advancing and retreating in time to the music. The *bamboula* was a lively couple-dance accompanied by the song "Musieu Bainjo;" its name probably points to the African bamboo-drum music originally associated with the dance. Four songs in the 1867 collection served as accompaniment songs for the group dance *coonjai* (counjaille); *Belle Layotte* (Pretty Layotte), *Remon, Aurora Braider,* and *Caroline.* The … collection includes a description of the music for the dancing:

> When the *Coonjai* is danced, the music is furnished by an orchestra of singers, the leader of whom—a man selected both for the quality of his voice and for his skill in improvising—sustains the solo part, while the others afford him an opportunity, as they shout in chorus, for inventing some neat verse to compliment some lovely *danseuse,* or celebrate the deeds of some plantation hero. The dancers themselves never sing, as in the case of the religious "shout" of the Port Royal negroes; and the usual musical accompaniment, besides that of the singers, is furnished by a skillful performer on the barrel-head drum, the jawbone and key, or some other rude instrument.

The most common plantation instruments were the fiddle and the banjo. Some slaves purchased their instruments with money earned from working in their free time, and others received instruments as gifts from their masters or other whites, but most had to content themselves with home-made instruments.

Depending upon the place and custom, various kinds of materials were used for the fiddles and banjos. Given a good pocketknife, some pine boards, and gut from a slaughtered cow that had been carefully cut into strips, dried, and treated, a skilled craftsman could produce a fairly good fiddle. In some places, fiddles were made of gourds and the strings and bows were made of horsehair. A banjo might be made from half of a fruit with a very hard rind, such as a calabash or gourd, by stretching a thick skin or piece of bladder over the opening, adding two or three strings made from gut, and raising the strings on a bridge. Banjos were also constructed by stretching the tanned hide of a ground hog or woodchuck over a piece of timber fashioned like a cheesebox. Sometimes the bowl of the gourd was not cut away, and the instruments had the appearance of a mandolin. While there seem to be no references to slaves playing "store-bought" mandolins, we know that after the emancipation the instrument became popular among black folk musicians.

For other than string instruments, the slaves used any and every kind of material that could be forced to produce a musical sound—old pieces of iron, ribs of a sheep, jawbones of a cow or horse, pieces of wood and sticks, even a jawbone and key in Louisiana, the key being rubbed against the bone. Slaves made flutes of all kinds from natural materials and made panpipes of "canes, having different lengths for different notes, and blowed like mouth organs."

In the deep South there were laws that expressly prohibited the slaves "using and keeping drums, horns, or other loud instruments which call together or give sign or notice to one another." Slaveholders were well aware of the African tradition for "talking instruments," and made every effort to eliminate that source of secret communication among the slaves. On the other hand, in the Upper South horns were often used for practical purposes: the conch horn, for example, to call slaves to work at daybreak, or a long-trumpet type at tobacco auctions in Virginia.

The most frequent combination of instruments for dancing coupled the fiddle and the banjo, to which might be added various kinds of small percussions, such as triangles, tambourines, castanets, and sticks. As mentioned above, homemade percussions of unlikely origin also were used. One account mentions music played on a "banjor (a large, hollow instrument with three strings)" and a "quaqua (somewhat resembling a drum)." In the mid-nineteenth century, a Virginian recalled that dancing on Sundays "resounded with the sounds of jollity—the merry strains of the fiddle [and] the measured beats of the quaw sticks ..."

—1971

Arthur Brown

CALLIN BUDDY
                    BOLDEN

callin buddy   bolden callin
sweet
calls to and fo plumblack
shimmy
hipted congo loves
callin

CALLIN
(tongueless tunes)
big leg woman
why u be so mean
got plenty
hamfat woman
but u cut so lean
big leg woman
why u
cut yo meat so lean

CALLIN
cutta cuttin bolden
dap black buddy bolden
who play new orleans
louisianna blues f real
who say

SHAKE YO ASS
TO THE BRASS
BUDDY BOLDEN WHO TALK BAD
who play f pimps n them
who say

i'm buddy bolden
n i'm king
in lincoln park
its me that come to see

play f happy
play f sad
birth death day
n boogie
in the dark

CALLIN BUDDY BOLDEN
HORN RISING LIKE
A SPECIAL RISING SUN
BUDDY WHOSE NOTES DANCE N
    WRING WITH THE YOUNG FINE ONES
LIKE WIND IN THE CANE
man say play clean
laweyers doctors
teachers things
inside

i play f them
dont wonta hide
play f hannah
play f rain

CALLIN BUDDY BOLDEN
CALLIN BUDDY BOLDEN
CALLIN BUDDY BOLDEN
WHO'S GONE INSANE

—1985

Early Jazz and the Jazz Age

Daphne Duval Harrison

Blacks were heard on records as early as 1895 when George W. Johnson recorded "Laughing Song" on an Edison phono-cylinder. There were also a 1901 Victor recording by the brilliant young comedian, Bert Williams; a 1902 recording by the Dinwiddle Colonel Quartet; recordings by Carroll Clark, a vocalist who sang so-called plantation melodies; the Fisk Jubilee Singers singing their "sorrow songs"; and coon songs by a few black minstrel men (some of whom would express their regret a few years later).

These early recordings featured comic monologues and black college choral versions of religious music, but no blues, except for one blues title among forty-nine music rolls issued in a 1906 series, *Music for the Aeolian Grand.* Perhaps this was an anomaly, but it was the precursor of blues rolls issued ten years later. With typical irony, it was the active search for and use of blues songs by major white entertainers that thrust the blues into the center of the entertainment industry. According to Ronald Foreman, a scholar on the history of jazz and race records, it was Sophie Tucker's interest in the blues and their subsequent adoption by Blossom Seely, Al Bernard, Nora Bayes, and other white headliners that "invested the word [blues] with musical meaning for many vaudeville and theater patrons."

For persons who could not attend live performances, there were occasional issues of blues on music rolls prior to World War I; and between March 1917 and April 1918, G.R.S., Connorized, Standard Music, Universal Music, and Vocalstyle released lists of new blues titles.

The profitable sales of jazz and blues piano rolls was the impetus for the phonograph companies' search for black or white talent to feature on jazz and blues recordings. The rise in race consciousness among blacks after the war facilitated the search. In 1919, James Reese Europe and his Army band were instrumental in pointing out the value and beauty of black music to blacks. This raised consciousness led black musicians and entertainers to seek involvement in the entertainment industry beyond stage performances. The phonograph companies initially made only modest attempts to respond to blacks' aspirations for acceptance as both buyers and producers of recordings. The popularity of black artists was not attributed to their talent by white promoters but rather to the type of music they played. Many hours were spent by Perry Bradford and

W.C. Handy trying to convince the record companies that black women blues singers had a ready market of black consumers who wanted to buy their recordings. They repeatedly approached the companies from 1919 on and were rebuffed by managers who claimed that the black women's voices were unsuitable, or that their diction was different from that of white women, or that they could not fill the requirements.

But Bradford was a hustler. His persistence may have been considered a nuisance by some but that did not deter him. As he pounded the New York pavements, he hit upon what he thought was a surefire plan—convince a recording company to sign up a singer for his songs and win a big audience. He had been writing, playing, publishing, and hawking his compositions for quite a few seasons when he decided that Mamie Smith, the star of *Maid of Harlem*, a musical review, would be an attractive offering on the recording market. To his credit, Bradford had produced some tuneful, danceable melodies which were already on piano rolls and sheet music, and this helped him get an appointment with RCA Victor Records on 10 January 1920 for a trial session featuring Mamie Smith singing "That Thing Called Love," a vaudeville-type ballad. Although Victor did not release it, Bradford and Smith did not give in to one failure. They continued up and down Tin Pan Alley, knocking on the doors of recording studio managers, seeking a fair shake in the expanding record market. Bradford hit pay dirt on 14 February at General Phonograph's Okeh studios, with Smith singing "That Thing Called Love" coupled with "You Can't Keep a Good Man Down." A stellar group of musicians led by Johnny Dunn, trumpet, and including Willie "The Lion" Smith, piano, backed the vocals. The recording lay dormant until summer when General Phonograph released it in its regular entries of popular titles without any special attention or fanfare.

In March 1920, the black press hailed the upcoming release as an event:

> Now we have the pleasure of being able to say that they [the record company] have recognized the fact that we are here for their service; the Okeh Phonograph Company has initiated the idea by engaging the handsome, popular, and capable vocalist, Mamie Gardener Smith of 409 W. 135th Street, N.Y.C., and she has made her first record ... apparently designed to be one of that great company's big hits. ["Making Records," *Chicago Defender*, 13 March 1920.]

Although General Phonograph did no special promotion, the recording was an overwhelming success. Blacks purchased every copy that could be found. Some estimates were in the 100,000 range, stupendous for the times, especially because these were sold exclusively to blacks.

Okeh rushed to capitalize on its new find by recording "Crazy Blues" on 10 August of the same year. At that session the studio orchestra was dubbed Mamie Smith's Jazz Hounds and was expanded to include Johnny Dunn on cornet, Dope Andrews on trombone, and Leroy Parker on violin. The cover for the sheet music of "Crazy Blues" featured a photograph of Smith and the band and the Okeh record catalog number. This time, much advertising fanfare accompanied its release.

"Crazy Blues" set off a recording boom that was previously unheard of. The target of the publicity campaigns soon became known as the "race market," a term supposedly coined by Ralph Peer, the Okeh recording manager. In less than a year, the race market was jumping with "discovery after discovery" of blues singers touted as the "best yet" by their record companies. Meanwhile, Mamie Smith was propelled into the limelight by the rave reviews appearing into the black press. She was pointed to with pride as the first artist of the race to record popular songs. Her entry into the market was a boon to music publishing companies as well as to music stores in every town and city. The *Chicago Defender* ran an ad by the Pace and Handy Music Company for their latest sheet music release, which included Bradford's "You Can't Keep a Good Man Down." The interesting feature of this ad was its exploitation of Smith's name: "Sung by Mamie Smith on Okeh record. The first Colored girl to make a record of a popular song, and it's great." W.C. Handy acknowledged in an article appearing a few weeks later that the increase in profits for publishers and writers, and in the number of contracts for other singers, was "following up the good works of Mamie Smith with the Okeh record people ...

—1988

David N. Baker

Various social factors provided the cultural climate needed for the birth of jazz in New Orleans. This city was the largest in the South at the time, and it was relatively "liberal." The French and Spanish residents winked at what their WASP neighbors would have found immoral. In this easy-going city, the Black man had more freedom than anywhere else in the South, at least by 1900, and the higher wages attracted many Southern Negroes. An additional stimulus was the fact that New Orleans used music for practically all occasions, and that fitted right in with the African thing.

The instruments the early players got were generally second-hand, from a Confederate band. In addition to these conventional instruments, you had a body of ad hoc instruments like fly swatters, jugs, washboards, combs, buckets, plungers—any thing that could make sound (and we've always been a resourceful people). Any book on jazz will describe the marching bands of 1870 and 1890 which played for parades and funerals. Fraternal and labor organizations had their own bands, just as they do today in Indianapolis. You go in now to the YMCA band and find usually older duds with awful instruments, but these cats still want to play and do their thing. Most of the Indianapolis musicians who made names for themselves came through something like this, like the Prince Hall Elks Band, where J.J. Johnson got his start. He still gives credit to a little old man with one leg too short who started him off. Freddie Hubbard came through one of those bands. I came through more than one because I didn't play so well and had to do a lot of traveling.

The dance music used before hot bands got going was sweet stuff, using strings and piano. Salon music. The hot brass band, from around 1890, marked a revolution in popular music. Ensemble playing was heterophonic, rather than polyphonic, and blues was the common denominator. Instrumental jazz developed from the mergings of the New Orleans band tradition and urban blues. The art of group improvisation, like the blues, was associated with the uptown section of New Orleans. As in folk music, two creative forces were involved: the group and a gifted individual. The tension between the collective harmonic rhythm and individual rhythms is what later came to be described as swing.

Despite the brass and marching band precedents, jazz was different from march music. The early jazzmen depended on their imagination and preferred (in many instances from necessity) to improvise rather than read music. It was not all improvisation, of course. From the very beginning, jazz musicians used what we call band "arrangements," but they weren't written down. They simply came to be because they were played that way several times and got crystallized.

The music came from a million sources. Many of the pieces were stolen from old marches. Band leaders stole tunes and, because they couldn't read, played the tune with many variations. After the leader showed the trumpet player the way he thought the tune went, the trumpeter would play it for the band and then the players made their arrangement. It was every man for himself, with the trumpeter taking the lead. True to the oral tradition and that of personalizing the music, the early jazzmen infused their music with speech and vocal qualities: growls, pitch variations, slurs, smears, and the cadence of conversation. The idea of ensemble playing was on the surface an imitation of brass bands, but it was more than that when one considers the music from social and psychological viewpoints.

The classic form of the New Orleans band crystallized with Joe "King" Oliver, the first master of referential improvisation (i.e., using a melody for the point of departure). We're going to see some dichotomies set up here in a minute, but his whole philosophy was based on the perfect rendition of a completely predictable result. Ensemble music, Black or White, jazz or not, always has this goal. The music produced excitement from its effective realization. The excitement of the performance came from the perfected rendition of certain traditional devices and patterns, the unanimity of conception. The greatness was within prescribed limits. Gunther Schuller, in Early Jazz, calls this "a circus psychology where each succeeding performance had to top the original." We know that's a dead-end street. The only tolerated surprises were the breaks (and these, by the way, were direct links to spirituals, work songs, blues, and—when they were expanded—they became the first solos in jazz).

Once a single player could hold the listener's attention, the collective ensemble was no longer as important, and that brings us to Louis Armstrong. When the soloist began to predominate, we have one-voice music over a two-beat metrical bass. The next stage would be four-beat harmonic bass for collective improvisation, as we had with King Oliver. The third stage, which is the gateway to today, is the emergence of a soloist coming from the ensemble's homophony. Satchmo was able to break free because he had a technical prowess unmatched by any other player of his time, and he had a fertile imagination, and unbridled sense of solo construction and influences from King Oliver and Bunk Johnson. His innovations were in rhythmic treatment primarily. He relaxed the time and effected the departure from what has been described as a ricky-tick rhythm section. He introduced rhythm to the straight tone (what Gunther Schuller calls "terminal vibrato"), and you could recognize this in his playing all of his life: that vibrato widens and almost breaks at the end of a tone.

—1973

Ishmael Reed

THE OLD MUSIC

The great migration of Afro-Americans which took place in the 1940s changed their culture and politics.

North became the immigrant's "streets paved with gold," while the South became their "Old Country." Somebody from that neck of the woods became your "homeboy." "Country" became a word of disparagement meaning a backward, innocent way of life. Relatives wrote relatives "down home," about how wonderful it was in Detroit, Chicago, and New York. They were often lying and writing these letters in a furnished room with only the blues to keep them warm. The best novel about the results of this migration is Richard Wright's *Native Son*.

The intellectuals came in contact with nihilistic philosophies and heard utopian ideas from immigrant "radicals." The artists became "avant-garde," not the true "avant-garde" which, as in VooDoo, treats "tradition as a contemporary function," but an "avant-garde" which viewed the past as "reactionary."

Jelly Roll Morton got a cold reception when he went to New York, which he referred to as "bitter"; he returned to Los Angeles to die. The Northeastern "avant-garde" dismissed Louis Armstrong as a "Tom."

This school of thought has dominated Afro-American culture until recently.

One who realizes his tradition recognizes Jelly Roll Morton, a HooDoo believer, as the guardian of spirit rhythms and Louis Armstrong as the King Zulu, the New Orleans Houngan, worthy of the respect due to his office: "Strong-armed bodyguards and shiny black limousines, rented from the Geddes and Moss Undertakers, always accompany him to the Royal Barge at the New Basin Canal and South Carollton Avenue. Cannons are fired, automobile horns blast, throats grow hoarse acclaiming him."

A riot nearly developed when Louis Armstrong was not accorded the King Zulu's funeral. He was buried in Queens and not in New Orleans.

By rejecting their traditional music, this "avant-garde" rejected the one medium next to dance which acted as the preserver of their ancient art forms, for there are parallels between the coherent confusion one finds in New Orleans music (what Ortiz Walton terms "Classical Afro-American" music, what Creole Tom Dent of New Orleans, a HooDoo worker, ethnographer, archivist, refers to as "Old Music," and what is commonly called "Dixieland") and VooDoo rites, the art form with origins in Africa whose simplified American version is called HooDoo.

The instruments in the old music substitute for the spirits who possess the human hosts in a ceremony; in old music the instruments sound like "voices." Early New Orleans music even bore HooDoo titles such as "Up Jumped LaBas," most likely Creoles trying to say Legba, protector of the Holy Gates and Guardian of the Crossroads; Stackalee's real love was a HooDoo Queen in New Orleans.

It can be argued that the majordomo who precedes the mourners in the funeral parade where the "second line" occurs is a symbol of Baron Samedi, lord of the cemetery. The majordomo wears the costume of Baron Samedi, and uses his whistle to summon the *loas* (spirits) and his baton is the symbol of Ghede, a New World *loa* of satire with no European and African antecedents according to Zora Neale Hurston. A *loa* which came about through an ancient process—a process which probably gave rise to forms like "Rags" and "Blues"; the "Blues" is often treated as a *loa:* "Good Morning, blues/blues how do you do," from "Jailhouse Blues," the Houngan greeting a *loa.*

The performers of the old music weren't interested in knowing esoteric scales or rhythms or even "reading" music though their inventions often startled professors. Being a virtuoso at the instrument didn't become an end in itself, which you could prove by playing real fast. They weren't ashamed of the banjo, an Afro-American invention, and played the tuba like a bass. They had a sense of humor and wit and didn't turn their backs on the audience, what Kropotkin called showing your behind to the bourgeoisie. In fact, they encouraged audience participation and played for HooDoo holidays, parades, marriages, and funerals.

The "avant-garde" played professor music—music you couldn't dance to. Music played to impress a new breed of critics who had developed a whole industry of pedantic newspeak criticism; loaded down with bibliographies; dwelling upon minutiae about who played with so-and-so on what date at which studio in what town and what-not. The new Monks. For years they ruled and often misappropriated Afro-American music in order to further their political ends. Their reign is coming to an end.

The kids of Martin Luther King Junior High School who are now listening to Ohio Players, Little Beaver, Rufus, Earth Wind and Fire, and the Miracles will soon be asking their parents to buy them Jelly Roll Morton, King Oliver, Bunk Johnson, Kid Ory, The Preservation Hall Band, The Eureka Marching Band, and the King HooDoo Zulu Louis Armstrong as well.

—1975

Robert Hayden

Of death. Of loving too:
Oh sweet sweet jellyroll:
so the sinful hymned it while
the churchfolk loured.

I scrounged for crumbs:
I yearned to touch the choirlady's hair,
I wanted Uncle Crip

to kiss me, but he danced
with me instead;
we Balled-the-Jack
to Jellyroll

Morton's brimstone
piano on the phonograph,
laughing, shaking the gasolier
a later stillness dimmed.

—1978

Lorenzo Thomas

Between 1910 and 1920, the black population of Los Angeles increased 105%; Chicago, 148%; Cleveland, 307%; Detroit, 611%; and Gary, Indiana, 1,283%. New York City's 66% increase effectively made Harlem the "Negro metropolis of the United States."

What African-American artists—painters, blues singers, poets—recorded of the era was not statistical data but the social, psychological, and spiritual impact of the period. "The migrant masses," wrote Alain Locke [in *The New Negro*] in 1925, "shifting from countryside to city, hurdle several generations of experience at a leap, but more important, the same thing happens spiritually in the life-attitudes and self-expression of the young Negro in his poetry, his art, his education, and his new outlook, with the additional advantage, of course, of the poise and greatest certainty of knowing what it is all about."

If he didn't know, the New Negro certainly found out very quickly. [Robert B.] Grant writes:

The reaction of northern whites to the arrival of southern black was heavily dependent on racist preconceptions. These preconceptions … were amply supported by the behavior of the undereducated, unhealthy black masses flocking to the cities, for the migrants generally lacked both industrial skills and preparation for urban life. Whereas these deficiencies were often characteristic of white immigrant groups and of city immigrants generally, Negroes felt the disapproval of Caucasians with special force.

At its worst, race prejudice led to violence and even murder. [*The Black Man Comes to the City: A Documentary Account from the Great Migration to the Great Depression, 1915–1930*, 10–11.]

While the cruel reception many migrants received is well documented and sometimes discussed in the poetry of the Harlem Renaissance, that was *not* the subject of the blues.

The blues, after all, remained essentially a dramatic conversation confined to, and carefully encoded for, those who intimately shared the same experience. While sophisticated white people in the 1920s were avid for African-American music, the blues and jazz were not primarily designed for their amusement. The songs were more likely intended as a crash course in urban survival—cautionary tales designed to get the new arrival "hep" as quickly as possible.

The truth of the matter is, perhaps, hidden and revealed in that word "hep" and its current version "hip." The word is certainly *not* derived, as sociolinguist Thomas Kochman once suggested, from a "kinetic cryptosememe for the role the hip plays in dancing, where it can be viewed as a synedoche for the body and the locus of movement." Our word *hip* is, rather, a rendering of southern black refugees' dialect pronunciation of the word "help." Nineteenth-century writers recording black or white southern speech might have spelled it *he'p*. The true significance of the expression can be guessed by reconstructing the circumstances of its usage in the early part of this century. The first thing the migrant to the big city needs is help. His homefolks will help him find a room, tell him where they're hiring workers, tell him what's what and what's happening. Of course, the city also harbors those who would help the newcomer to hand over his traveling cash, the belongings in his bag, and anything else they might get away with. As Louis Armstrong wrote of his experiences in the years before the First World War: "As the days rolled on, I commenced get hep to the jive. I learned a great deal about life and people."

—1990

Ethel Waters

I was learning a lot in Harlem about music and the men up there who played it best. All the licks you hear, now as then, originated with musicians like James P. Johnson. And I mean all of the hot licks that ever came out of Fats Waller and the rest of the hot piano boys. They are just faithful followers and proteges of that great man, Jimmy Johnson.

Men like him, Willie "The Lion" Smith, and Charlie Johnson could make you sing until your tonsils fell out. Because you wanted to sing. They stirred you into joy and wild ecstasy. They could make you cry. And you'd do anything and work until you dropped for such musicians.

The master of them all, though, was Lucky Roberts. Everybody called him Pop, but reverently. He now runs a restaurant up on the hill in Harlem. I don't call it Sugar Hill. I don't use that kind of language. Any night you can go up to Pop Roberts's place and hear operatic arias sung magnificently by the great singers who are waiters and waitresses there.

Fine singers! People I know, people I admire, people I've worked with! But they are Negroes and have to wait on tables because they can't get any work in show business. They are colored. Period.

—1950

Sidney Bechet

I did a lot of things in my life that I wanted to do and I am quite sure that there is nothing that I would be ashamed of. If I had to live my life over again, I would do the same that I have done again because some things that people probably say was bad, probably seem bad to them, but in a time when something happens and you know that you have done wrong, you sort of take your own judgment and try to get out of it the best way you can. Anyway, I am very happy now and I am living a life pretty easy. And I'll always play music as long as I possibly can. All them crotchets, I'll put them down with my clarinet or saxophone and I'll play as long as I have breath. I think I did the best I could with my life. I made everybody happy close to me. I had a lot of worries, but now I have decided I have figured that out because I figured the day would come when I'd have to leave here, which everybody does. Nobody lives for a lifetime. I'm not worried about the body. If I didn't do with it what they want, I have used it and it is finished and I am satisfied.

I am an old man now; I can't keep hanging on. I'm even wanting to go; I'm waiting, longing to hear my peace. And all I've been waiting for is the music. All the beauty that there's ever been, it's moving inside the music. Omar's voice, that's there, and the girl's voice, and the voice the wind had in Africa, and the cries from Congo Square, and the fine shouting that came up from Free Day. The blues, and the spirituals, and the remembering, and the waiting, and the suffering, and the looking at the sky watching the dark come down—that's all inside the music.

—1960

Louis Armstrong

All the big, well known Social Aid and Pleasure Clubs turned out for the last big parade I saw in New Orleans. They all tried to outdo each other and they certainly looked swell. Among the clubs represented were The Bulls, The Hobgoblins, The Tamanays, The Young Men Twenties (Zutty Singleton's club), The Merry-Go-Rounds, The Deweys, The Tulane Club, The Young Men Vidalias, The Money Wasters, The Jolly Boys, The Turtles, The Original Swells, The San Jacintos, The Autocrats, The Frans Sa Mee Club, The Cooperatives, The Economys, The Odd Fellows, The Masons, The Knights of Pythias (my lodge), and The Diamond Swells from out in the Irish Channel. The second liners were afraid to go into the Irish Channel which was that part of the city located uptown by the river front. It was a dangerous neighborhood. The Irish who lived out there were bad men, and the colored boys were tough too. If you followed a parade out there you might come home with your head in your hand.

To watch those club parades was an irresistible and absolutely unique experience. All the members wore full dress uniforms and with those beautiful silk ribbons streaming from their shoulders they were a magnificent sight. At the head of the parade rode the aides, in full dress suits and mounted on fine horses with ribbons around their heads. The brass band followed, shouting a hot swing march as everyone jumped for joy. The members of the club marched behind the band wearing white felt hats, white silk shirts (the very best silk), and mohair trousers. I had spent my life in New Orleans, but every time one of those clubs paraded I would second-line them all day long. By carrying the cornet for Joe Oliver or Bunk Johnson I would get enough to eat to hold me until the parade was over.

When a club paraded it would make several stops called "punches" during the day at houses of the members, where there were sandwiches, cold beer and, of course, lots of whiskey. The whiskey did not interest me at that time. All I wanted was to be allowed to hang around with the fellows.

When all the clubs paraded it took nearly all day to see them pass, but one never got tired watching. Black Benny was always the star attraction. He was the only man, musician or not, who dared to go anywhere, whether it was the Irish Channel, Back o' Town, the Creole section in the Seventh Ward, or any other tough place. Nobody would have the nerve to bother him. He was just that tough and he was not afraid of a living soul. Wherever he went outside of our ward to beat the drums or to dance he was always treated with the greatest respect.

By the year 1922 I had become so popular from playing in Kid Ory's band and the Tuxedo Brass Band that I too could go into any part of New Orleans without being bothered. Everybody loved me and just wanted to hear me blow, even the tough characters were no exception. The tougher they were the more they would fall in love with my horn, just like those good old hustlers during the honky-tonk days.

Joe Oliver had left New Orleans in 1918, and was now up in Chicago doing real swell. He kept sending me letters and telegrams telling me to come up to Chicago and play second cornet for him. That, I knew, would be real heaven for me.

I had made up my mind that I would not leave New Orleans unless the King sent for me. I would not risk leaving for anyone else. I had seen too many of my little pals leave home and come back in bad shape. Often their parents had to send them the money to come back with. I had had such a wonderful three years on the excursion boats on the Mississippi that I did not dare cut out for some unknown character who might leave me stranded or get me into other trouble. Fate Marable and the Streckfus brothers had made it impossible for me to risk spoiling everything by running off on a wild goose chase.

After I had made all my arrangements I definitely accepted Joe's offer. The day I was leaving for Chicago I played at a funeral over in Algiers, on August 8, 1922. The funeral was for the father of Eddie Vincent, a very good trombone player. When the body was brought out of the house to go to the cemetery the hymn we played was "Free as a Bird," and we played it so beautifully that we brought tears to everybody's eyes.

The boys in the Tuxedo Brass Band and Celestin's band did their best to talk me out of going up to Chicago. They said that Joe Oliver was scabbing and that he was on the musicians' union unfair list. I told them how fond I was of Joe and what confidence I had in him. I did not care what he and his band were doing. He had sent for me, and that was all that mattered. At that time I did not know very much about union tactics because we did not have a union in New Orleans, so the stuff about the unfair list was all Greek to me.

When the funeral was over I rushed home, threw my few glad rags together and hurried over to the Illinois Central Station to catch the 7 PM train for the Windy City. The whole band came to the station to see me off and wish me luck. In a way they were all glad to see me get a chance to go out in the world and make good, but they did not care so much about having me play second cornet to Joe Oliver. They thought I was good enough to go on my own, but I felt it was a great break for me even to sit beside a man like Joe Oliver with all his prestige.

It seemed like all of New Orleans had gathered at the train to give me a little luck. Even the old sisters of my neighborhood who had practically raised me when I was a youngster there. When they kissed me good-bye they had handkerchiefs at their eyes to wipe away the tears.

When the train pulled in all the pullman porters and waiters recognized me because they had seen me playing on the tailgate wagons to advertise dances, or "balls" as we used to call them. They all hollered at me saying, "Where are you goin', Dipper?"

"You're a lucky black sommitch," one guy said, "to be going up North to play with ol' Cocky."

This was a reference to the cataract on one of Joe's eyes. The mean guys used to kid him about his bad eye, and he would get fighting mad. But what was the use? If he had messed around fighting with those guys he would have ended up by losing his good eye.

When the conductor hollered all aboard I told those waiters: "Yeah man, I'm going up to Chicago to play with my idol, Papa Joe!"

—1954

Alain Leroy Locke

In New York between 1905 and 1912 or 1915, four Negro conductors and arrangers of real genius raised Negro music out of a broken, musically illiterate dialect and made it a national and international music with its own peculiar idioms of harmony, instrumentation, and playing. These men saw the future of Negro music; they had the courage to be original. These men were Ford Dabney, James Reese Europe, Will Marion Cook, and W.C. Handy. Dabney revolutionized the Negro dance orchestra and started the musical fortunes of Florenz Ziegfeld when he was experimenting with roof-garden productions. Jim Europe, a member of the "Memphis Students," alternated with Cook as musical director of the Cole and Johnson shows, and organized the famous Clef Club Orchestra. Europe was later to make Negro music the preferred rhythm in the new dance vogue started by Vernon and Irene Castle. As will be noted later, Irene Castle gave Europe full credit for the fox trot, which she labeled the most popular dance of the day. Cook not only gave Negro music its first serious orchestral works, but with his "Syncopated Orchestra" surprised and converted audiences in London, Paris, and Berlin in 1919–20. Handy, as is well known, championed the despised Mississippi folk music between 1909 and 1912 and created the "blues."

In May 1912, three Negro conductors led a syncopated orchestra (today we would say jazz orchestra) of one hundred and twenty-five Negro musicians in a "Concert of Negro Music." The concert was at Carnegie Hall; the audience included some of New York's most sophisticated music-lovers; the atmosphere resmbled that of any concert of "classical music." The compositions were conducted by their own composers or arrangers. Perhaps the transformation was too sudden; many did not recognize this folk music in "full dress." Some thought it was incongruous (some of it was), but those who recall only the epoch-making conert of "Classical Jazz" by Paul Whiteman in 1924 or a similar concert by Vincent Lopez the same year should be reminded of the historically more significant concert by The Clef Club in May 1912. At that time ragtime matured fully and the age of jazz really began. [...]

In spite of the obvious development of ragtime and jazz from Negro sources and the pioneer artistry of Negro dancers and musicians, the question frequently comes up: "How Negro is Jazz after all?" No one will deny that the elements of ragtime and jazz can be found elsewhere in the world, not only in other folk music, but as a device of syncopation in some of the most classical music, that of Beethoven, for example. But jazz and ragtime are nonetheless distinctively Negro. Original jazz is more than syncopation and close eccentric harmony: it has a distinctive intensity of mood and a peculiar style of technical performance. These can be imitated, but their original pattern was Negro. Inborn with the folk Negro, this is a quality detected in a stevedore's swing, a preacher's cadenced sermon, a bootblack's flick, or the "amen" from a corner of a church.

But this can be said only of the early jazz, which was not only the most racial, but musically the most powerful. To sense the difference instantly one has only to contrast, for example, one of the early blues, like Bessie Smith's old version of the "Gulf Coast Blues," with any contemporary blues. Another classic case in point is W.C. Handy's "The Memphis Blues," the first jazz classic. Handy began experimenting with the blues form in 1909 after having watched the earliest jazz-makers, the itinerant piano-players who moved through the Mississippi area improvising music which, as J.A. Rogers puts it, reproduced the sentiments and moods of the dock laborers, railroad gangs, and simple folk. Until 1897 his concern was exclusively with classical music, but when, during that year, he discovered the appeal of real "down home" music, he initiated a serious search for folk music. "The Joe Turner Blues," an early lesson in the folk idiom, led to his adopting it as the novelty feature of the Pythian Band that he organized in Memphis. In 1909, still in Memphis, Handy composed his third blues, "Mr. Cromp," which helped elect the city official of that name. No one of the three was accepted for publication, and eventually Handy sold the rights to the composition to a white promoter for one hundred dollars. In a garbled version, in which the rhythm was simplified and words were added, it was republished in New Youk and earned a fortune for the copyright owners. Handy, refused permission by the owner to use "The Memphis Blues" in his own *Blues Anthology* thirteen years later, was thus "Father of the Blues," though disinherited from his rightful recognition and rewards. [...]

Another cradle element of jazz was in Handy's blues. It was the habanera or tango rhythm, first used by that composer in the original "Memphis Blues." The justification for the use of the tango rhythm as characteristically Negro and its popularity among Negroes became very plausible when we recall that this is originally an African rhythm (the native word for it is *tangana*) and that it probably became Spanish through the Moors. This is corroborated by the fact that this same tango rhythm is basic in the purest and oldest strains of Afro-Cuban music, the folk music of Mexico, in Brazil, where the Negro influence has been dominant, and in Negro dances of even the Bahamas and Barbados.

In addition to jazz rhythm and harmony, jazz improvisation emerged from the blues. It grew out of the improvised musical "filling in" of the gap between the short measure of the blues and the longer eight-bar line, the break interval in the original folk form of the three-line blues. Such filling in and compounding of the basic rhythm are characteristic of Negro music from Africa to South Carolina, from the unaccompanied hand-clapping of the streetcorner "hoe-down," to the interpolations and shouts in Negro church revivals. Handy's own theory of jazz is that it is, in essence, "spontaneous deviation from the musical score," in other words, an impromptu musical embroidery woven around and into the musical tune and the regular harmony. This means short, daring, and in-spired music. When this style was incorporated into orchestral music, a new sort of instrumental music was born out of the folk jazz. Thus jazz is a towering and elaborate superstructure built upon the basic founda-tion of the blues. The controversy as to whether jazz is a new type of music or another method of playing music can be resolved by this fact, because it shows the difference between superficial jazz and the really solid type. The one is merely a series of musical tricks by which any tune can be ragged or jazzed. The other is an organic combination of jazz rhythm, harmony, and creative improvisation. [...]

What is deeper and more important is the mood out of which [jazz] is generated and the instinctive gift for doing it spontaneously. No really Negro musical group worries about what the other musicans are going to do; they are just as likely to vary and embroider at will and whimsy as to follow a score. No one approaching the issue from the side of experi-ence rather than that of academic debate could be in doubt about the racial color and feeling of jazz. [...] Louis Armstrong, in his *Swing That Music*, says that "to become a front rank 'swing player' a musician must learn to read expertly and be just as able to play to score as any 'regular' musician. Then he must never forget for one minute of his life that the true spirit of swing lies in free playing and that he must always keep his own musical feeling free. He must try to originate and not just imitate. And if he is a well-trained musician in the first place, he will be able to express his own musical ideas as they come to him with more versatility, more richness, and more body.... To be a real swing artist, he must be a composer as well as a player."

For the process of composing group improvisation, the jazz musician must have a whole chain of musical expertness, a sure musical ear, an in-stinctive feeling for harmony, the courage and gift to improvise and interpolate, and a canny sense of the total effect. This free style, which Negro musicians introduced into playing, really has generations of expe-rience behind it. It is derived from the voice tricks and vocal habits of

Negro choral singing. Out of the voice slur and quaver between the flat and the natural come a whole jazz cadenza and all the jazz tone devices. Out of the use of a single sustained voice tone as a suspension note for chorus changes of harmony came the now elaborate jazz harmonic style. It is interesting to note that the African has this same fluid, shifting musical scale, even more subtle than the scale-shifts of the American Negro folk music. In fact, it seems that many American Negro musical traits are the original African ones modified by the more regular pattern of European music. These basic racial idioms are more apparent in the simpler, earliest forms of jazz, and more in the vocal than in the instrumental pieces. As Sterling Brown has rightly said: "There is rich material on hand for the reevaluation of the Negro folk. Out of penitentiaries, in the deep South, John and Alan Lomax have brought the musical memories of singers with names such as Iron Head, Clear Rock, and Lightning. From what is more truly folk culture these men and others like John Hammond, Willis James, and John Work have brought hidden singers and songs." Whenever Negro folk music is evaluated or reevaluated, the old cheap Okeh and Columbia records of The Memphis Students, the McKinney Cotton Pickers, The Chicago Rhythm Kings, The Dixieland Orchestra, and the early blues singers—Bessie, Clara, and Mamie Smith, and Ma Rainey—will prove to be priceless materials, not only, as Sterling Brown implies, to round out the true picture of Negro folk music, but also to show how jazz was created.

—1956

LeRoi Jones / Amiri Baraka

When jazz first began to appear during the twenties on the American scene, in one form or another, it was introduced in a great many instances into that scene by white Americans. Jazz as it was originally conceived and in most instances of its most vital development was the result of certain attitudes, or empirical ideas, attributable to the Afro-American culture. Jazz as played by white musicians was not the same as that played by black musicians, nor was there any reason for it to be. The music of the white jazz musician did not issue from the same cultural circumstance; it was, at its most profound instance, a learned art. The blues, for example, which I take to be an autonomous black music, had very little weight at all in pre-jazz white American culture. But blues is an extremely important part of jazz. However, the way in which jazz utilizes the blues "attitude" provided a musical analogy the white musician could understand and thus utilize in his music to arrive at a style of jazz music. The white musician understands the blues first as music, but seldom as an attitude, since the attitude, or world-view, the white musician was responsible to was necessarily a quite different one. And in many case, this attitude, or world-view, was one that was not consistent with the making of jazz.

There should be no cause for wonder that the trumpets of Bix Beiderbecke and Louis Armstrong were so dissimilar. The white middle-class boy from Iowa was the product of a culture which could *place* Louis Armstrong, but could never understand him. Beiderbecke was also the product of a subculture that most nearly emulates the "official" or formal culture of North America. He was an instinctive intellectual who had a musical taste that included Stravinsky, Schoenberg, and Debussy, and had an emotional life that, as it turned out, was based on his conscious or unconscious disapproval of most of the sacraments of his culture. On the other hand, Armstrong was, in terms of emotional archetypes, an honored priest of his culture, one of the most impressive products of his society. Armstrong was not *rebelling* against anything with his music. In fact, his music was one of the most beautiful refinements of Afro-American musical tradition, and it was immediately recognized as such by those Negroes who were not busy trying to pretend that they had issued from Beiderbecke's culture. The incredible irony of the situation was that both stood in similar places in the superstructure of American society: Beiderbecke, because of the isolation any deviation from mass culture imposed upon its bearer; and Armstrong because of the socio-historical estrangement of the Negro from the rest of America. Nevertheless, the music the two made was as dissimilar as possible within jazz. Beiderbecke's slight, reflective tone and impressionistic lyricism was the most impressive example of "the artifact given expression" in jazz. He played "white jazz" in the sense I am trying to convey, that is, as a music that is the product of attitudes expressive of a peculiar culture. Armstrong, of course, played jazz that was securely within the traditions of Afro-American music. His tone was brassy, broad, and aggressively dramatic. He also relied heavily on the vocal blues tradition in his playing to amplify the expressiveness of his instrumental technique.

I am using these two men as examples because they were two early masters of a developing American music, though they expressed almost antithetical versions of it. The point is that Afro-American music did not become a completely American expression until the white man could play it! Bix Beiderbecke, more than any other of the early white jazzmen, signified this development because he was the first white jazz musician, the first white musician who brought to the jazz he created any of the *ultimate concern* Negro musicians brought to it as a casual attitude of their culture. This development signified also that jazz would someday have to confront the idea of its being an art (since that was the white man's only way into it). The emergence of the white player meant that Afro-American culture had already become the expression of a particular kind of American experience, and what is most important, that this experience was available intellectually, that it could be learned.

—1963

Henry Crowder

So the devil and I continued riding together. Often during the four following years I would ask myself if I was going to continue like that forever. Each time the question arose I would tell myself no but still I stayed with my mistress and worked in the brothel.

Entering the place where I worked often reminded me of the great change that had taken place in my life in such a short period. It was a strange experience for me. With all of my religious training, beliefs, and thoughts, the work there furnished a marked contrast to all of the things I had been taught to respect and desire.

How well I remember my first introduction to the district and how very timid I was about ringing the bell of the pretentious-looking house to which the little colored man had sent me. I remember just as well the events that followed.

What a surprise it was to me when a gorgeously gowned and jeweled woman came to the door. Under the soft white and red lights she looked like a white woman but I was too amazed at her striking appearance to be sure.

I told her why I was there and she politely asked me to enter. The floor of the house was covered with a thick, soft carpet. From there I was shown into a magnificently furnished room and told to wait.

It was the first time I have ever been in a house of ill-fame and I was none too comfortable. I took in my surroundings with the greatest surprise and interest. Rich curtains, half concealed by heavy drapes, hung at the windows. The furniture seemed of the best quality and was beautifully upholstered. Two large oil paintings of nude women hung on the wall.

In the midst of my bewildered thoughts a stout mulatto woman, clad only in a yellow silk robe, entered and told me she was the "Madam." We immediately started talking business. I was to report to work at nine o'clock in the evening and play piano and sing until the house closed in the morning. The pay was two dollars a night and tips. I accepted and was told to come to work the following night.

My mind was in a whirl as I left the house. I had never imagined places of that sort could be so grand.

The following evening I presented myself at the door promptly at nine o'clock. I was startled upon entering, however, by being told that since I was the first man to enter the house that night I would have to hand over a piece of silver money for luck. If I did not have the money I would have to wait until some other man proceeded me and gave a present. Being anxious to get in and get my bearings I surrendered my last dime.

I was shown into the ballroom where I was to play and sing. It was furnished with a lovely piano and a number of chairs. The floor was highly polished and the windows draped in thick red plush. The usual nude pictures hung on the walls.

A number of beautiful mulatto women sitting in the room eyed me curiously as I entered. They were all dressed in magnificent evening gowns, and their faces powdered and painted as though an expert had applied their make-up.

I was terribly ill at ease. I very shyly took a chair that was near the piano and began to wonder what the start would be like.

This house was the famous Mahogany Hall of Washington, D.C. A lot of southern cities have houses called by the same name but I dare say they are not as magnificent as the original was in those days.

All of the women who worked there were light colored and catered to white men only. As the pianist I was the only black man permitted in the place. I was immediately dubbed "The Professor" and was never called by any other name as long as I was there.

I did not exactly know what to do on my first night there and was beginning to softly play a few tunes when my little colored maid friend who steered me into the job appeared and put me at my ease.

She told me that I need not play except when "company" was there and that it was strictly against the rules of the house to bring whiskey or gin into the house or to flirt with any of the girls. Violation of any of these cardinal rules meant immediate dismissal I was told.

It was not difficult for me to strictly observe these two rules at first but after working there for a while I would smuggle whiskey in for the girls. On those occasions I always received handsome tips.

As time passed I became accustomed to the life the place and earned good money. The "Madam" and all the girls liked me so I got on very well. The girls had no interest for me personally. I soon discovered that on the whole they were a pretty ignorant, low type. They used filthy language and were generally disgusting when no white men were there.

During the entire two years I worked there I only saw two women who I thought were of a better grade mentally. They both confided to me that they were there only for the purpose of getting some quick money for a special reason. Neither of them stayed long.

The girls were allowed to go out but they had to swear not to associate with colored men. Needless to say that oath was freely violated. In fact I think the only pleasure those girls had was when they were with men of their own race.

The method employed by the Madam to hold her girls was rather crude but it worked. When they entered the house they were bought new gowns for the parlors. The price charged a newcomer was always double what the dress cost. The Madam always paid in cash and the girl would repay for her clothes out of her earnings. Madam always insisted on three dresses to start with and a new one whenever she deemed necessary. The girls received half of the fee charged in the house and out of their pay they had to pay half to Madam for their clothes. The women could never get out of debt.

The police of the district, who were in the pay of the Madam, would uphold her in preventing any girl from leaving if she owed anything. This of course was only terrorism but the girls fell for it although a few did run away in despair and desperation. At best it was a terrible life for them and I felt very sorry for some of them.

The white clients were as a rule very orderly though there were a few brawls and fights started by drunks on Saturday night.

As I worked there almost two years I came to know all of the other colored men and women of the district. A short time before I started working in the "Division," as the district was called, the police had made the life of the Negro men who worked in the house miserable. They were continually arresting the boys and charging them with vagrancy.

The practice was stopped, however, by a ruling from the police court which said that the playing of a piano in a house of ill-fame did not constitute a violation of the vagrancy law. Thereafter, the piano players were safe.

When I quit my job in the Mahogany Hall I went to work in the most select house in the district. That house catered only to white men of the highest social and wealthy circles. The girls were all white and wore the most extravagant evening dresses. Needless to say, it was a most expensive house. The only drink sold was champagne and in the event a client desired beer or whiskey it was given free of charge.

Only three men worked in the house. There was a porter and I was assisted by a banjo player. We were all colored. The Madam there would not hire white musicians or maids under any circumstances.

I made more money there than ever before in my life. Sometimes I took home as much as $80 or $90 for a night's work and I never received less than $7.

—1935–36

Thomas L. Morgan and William Barlow

In spite of the groundswell of interest in black popular music after World War I, ASCAP's growing membership roll remained predominantly white. By 1920, there were only ten African Americans in the organization, but many more were knocking on the door as Tin Pan Alley attracted increasing numbers of black songwriters hoping to benefit from the boom in jazz and blues.

Some of the best-known African American tunesmiths based in New York City during the 1920s were W.C. Handy, Bessie Smith, Clarence Williams, Perry Bradford, Eubie Blake, Alberta Hunter, J. Rosamond Johnson, Henry Creamer, James P. Johnson, Porter Grainger, Cecil Mack, Shelton Brooks, and Spencer Williams. Many of the men in this group, like Handy and Clarence Williams, also established their own publishing firms to collect all the royalties on the songs they wrote.

Black songwriters tended to be more respectful of their musical heritage than their white counterparts and drew many of their themes, lyrics, melodies, and song structures from the black oral tradition. This was especially the case when the composer was from the South and was personally familiar with the African American folklore and folk music there. As Clarence Williams stated in an interview ... "Why, I'd never have written the blues if I had been white. You don't study to write blues, you feel them."

After World War I, the record labels continued to favor recording white entertainers' "cover" versions of black popular songs over producing

African American renditions of the same material. Covering was a frequently used technique designed to introduce the popular music of a smaller subculture to the audience of a larger cultural group. In this instance, its purpose was both to entice a curious white public to purchase recordings of the new black music and to "upgrade" it.

Upgrading was synonymous with commercializing; it attempted to bring African American music more in line with European musical conventions, while superimposing upon it a veneer of bourgeois Anglo-American respectability. The net result was that a significant percentage of the blues and jazz recorded in the teens and twenties was drained of its African American characteristics and working-class content. This diluting process and the technical constraints inherent in the early recording process, like fidelity and the length of a disc, converged to stifle somewhat both authenticity and innovation in black popular music.

The Victor label's first jazz and blues releases by white entertainers, issued in 1917, included two discs destined to be among the biggest commercial hits of the era. The hit record in the blues category was Sophie Tucker's version of W.C. Handy's classic "St. Louis Blues," which sold over a million copies. In the jazz category, the Original Dixieland Jazz Band's (ODJB) first release, "Livery Stable Blues," also sold over a million copies.

The ODJB was a group of five young white musicians from New Orleans who had been inspired by the burgeoning "hot" ensemble style of jazz in vogue among that city's black working class while they were growing up. The group's first national booking was in Chicago in 1916. Several months later, the band moved on to New York, and within a matter of weeks their popularity soared. The new hot music they played became the rage of the city, and they were immediately signed to record for the Victor label. "Livery Stable Blues" was a jazz novelty tune featuring cornet and trombone barnyard imitations of cows and horses, and the minstrel mentality it suggests may have accounted for the band's stylized, self-conscious approach to this new genre. The spectacular success of the ODJB was one of the catalysts that launched the Jazz Age for a youthful "lost generation" of white artists, musicians, writers, and radical intellectuals. The music came to symbolize the rebellious spirit of the fabled Roaring Twenties.

A handful of black-owned record companies were also launched in the

1920s, only to meet a fate similar to that of the small white-owned labels. W.C. Handy and his partner Harry Pace founded the Black Swan Record Company in 1921. The label reported more than $100,000 in sales during its first year of operation, but three years later it was in serious debt, and the owners were forced to sell the company to Paramount Records. Other black-owned labels included the Sunshine label, based in Los Angeles; Merritt records, based in Kansas City; and Mayo "Ink" Williams's Black Patti label in Chicago. All folded after a year or two.

Even the two dominant companies, Columbia and Victor, which jumped on the blues and jazz bandwagon when it became apparent that a new African American market for discs did in fact exist, were experiencing financial trouble due to the advent of commercial radio. Columbia's sales plummeted from $7 million in profits to a loss of $4.5 million, forcing the company to file for bankruptcy in 1923. Victor's sales declined from $51 million to $25 million between 1923 and 1925.

Okeh, Columbia, and Paramount emerged as the leaders in the recording of black music. The pacesetter was Okeh, and by 1923, the label had released forty discs by black artists; six jazz instrumentals, eleven religious records, and twenty-three blues recordings.

At first, Okeh advertised this material as "Colored" records and grouped them together in a "Colored Catalogue." In 1922, however, the label placed advertisements in the *Chicago Defender* for "Race phonograph stars" and Okeh "race records." Within a year, the company had dropped the word "colored" from its advertising. Ralph Peer, the man who supervised the label's black releases, would later take credit for coining the term "race record." However, it is more likely that he adopted it from the *Chicago Defender*, which frequently used "race" as a progressive designation for African Americans. "Race" was symbolic of black pride and solidarity in the 1920s, and it was usually favored over "colored" or "Negro" by African Americans in the urban North. Peer did not want to offend black consumers, which is probably why he made the switch in the first place. In any event, soon thereafter the term "race records" was being used by all of the other record labels that sold discs by black artists.

—1992

Sterling Brown

CABARET
> (*1927, Black & Tan Chicago*)

Rich, flashy, puffy-faced,
Hebrew and Anglo-Saxon,
The overlords sprawl here with their glittering darlings.
The smoke curls thick, in the dimmed light
Surreptitiously, deaf-mute waiters
Flatter the grandees,
Going easily over the rich carpets,
Wary lest they kick over the bottles
Under the tables.

The jazzband unleashes its frenzy.

> *Now, now,*
> *To it, Roger; that's a nice doggie,*
> *Show your tricks to the gentlemen.*

The trombone belches, and the saxophone
Wails curdlingly, the cymbals clash,
The drummer twitches in an epileptic fit

> Muddy water
> Round my feet
> Muddy water

The chorus sways in.
The "Creole Beauties from New Orleans"
(By way of Atlanta, Louisville, Washington, Yonkers,
With stop-overs they've used nearly all their lives)
Their creamy skin flushing rose warm,
O, le bal des belles quarteronnes!
Their shapely bodies naked save
For tattered pink silk bodices, short velvet tights,
And shining silver-buckled boots;
Red bandannas on their sleek and close-clipped hair;
To bring to mind (aided by the bottles under the tables)
Life upon the river—

> Muddy water, river sweet

(Lafitte the pirate, instead
And his doughty diggers of gold)

> There's peace and happiness there
> I declare

(*In Arkansas,*
Poor half-naked fools, tagged with identification numbers,
Worn out upon the levees,
Are carted back to the serfdom
They had never left before
And may never leave again)

> Bee-dap-ee-DOOP, dee-ba-dee-BOOP

The girls wiggle and twist

> *Oh you too,*
> *Proud high-stepping beauties,*
> *Show your paces to the gentlemen.*
> *A prime filly, seh.*
> *What am I offered, gentlemen, gentlemen . . .*

> > I've been away a year today
> > To wander and roam
> > I don't care if it's muddy there

(*Now that the floods recede,*
What is there left the miserable folk?
Oh time in abundance count their losses,
There is so little else to count.)

> Still it's my home, sweet home

From the lovely throats
Moans and deep cries for home;
Nashville, Toledo, Spout Springs, Boston,
Creoles from Germantown;—
The bodies twist and rock;
The glasses are filled up again . . .

(*In Mississippi*
The black folk huddle, mute, uncomprehending,
Wondering "how come the good Lord
Could treat them this a way")

shelter
Down in the Delta

(Along the Yazoo
The buzzards fly over, over, low,
Glutted, but with their scrawny necks stretching,
Peering still.)

I've got my toes turned Dixie ways
Round that Delta let me laze

The band goes mad, the drummer throws his sticks
At the moon, a *papier-mache* moon,
The chorus leaps into weird posturings,
The firm-fleshed arms plucking at grapes to stain
Their corralled mouths; seductive bodies weaving
Bending, writing, turning

My heart cries out for
M U D D Y W A T E R

(Down in the valleys
The stench of the drying mud
Is a bitter reminder of death.)

Dee da dee D A A A AH

—1932

W. E. B. DuBois

[This piece is from a book review of Nigger Heaven *by Carl Van Vechten.]*

The author [Carl Van Vechten] counts among his friends numbers of
Negroes in all classes. He is an authority on dives and cabarets. But he
masses this knowledge without rule or reason and seeks to express all of
Harlem life in its cabarets. To him the black cabaret is Harlem; around it
all his characters gravitate. Here is their stage of action. Such a theory of
Harlem is nonsense. The overwhelming majority of black folk there
never go to cabarets. The average colored man in Harlem in an everyday
laborer, attending church, lodge, and movie and as conservative and as
conventional as ordinary working folk everywhere.

Something they have which is racial, something distinctively Negroid
can be found; but it is expressed by subtle, almost delicate nuance, and
not by the wildly, barbaric drunken orgy in whose details Van Vechten

revels. There is laughter, color, and spontaneity at Harlem's core, but in the current cabaret, financed and supported largely by white New York, this core is so overlaid and enwrapped with cheaper stuff that none but a fool could mistake it for the genuine exhibition of the spirit of the people. [...]

In *Nigger Heaven* there is not a single lovable character. There is scarcely a generous impulse or a beautiful ideal. The characters are singularly wooden and inhuman. Van Vechten is not the great artist who with remorseless scalpel probes the awful depths of life. To him there are no depths. It is the surface mud he slops about in. His women's bodies have no souls; no children palpitate upon his hands; he has never looked upon his dead with bitter tears. Life to him is just one damned orgy after another, with hate, hurt, gin, and sadism.

Both Langston Hughes and Carl Van Vechten know Harlem cabarets; but it is Hughes who whispers

> One said he heard the jazz band sob
> When the little dawn was grey.

Van Vechten never heard a sob in a cabaret. All he hears is noise and brawling. Again and again with singular lack of invention he reverts to the same climax of two creatures tearing and scratching over "mah man"; lost souls who once had women's bodies; and to Van Vechten this spells comedy, not tragedy.

—1926

Harold Cruse

But the superficial Negro creative intelligentsia, who have become so removed from their meaningful traditions, cannot see things this way, so blindly obsessed are they with the modern mania for instant integration. They do not understand the cultural history of America and where they fit in that historical scheme. They understand next to nothing about the 1920s and how the rather fluid, contending cultural trends among blacks and whites were frozen in that decade, once white control of cultural and creative power patterns was established to the supreme detriment of blacks. They are not aware that the white critics of that time were saying that Negro creative artists were, for the most part, primitives; and that Gilbert Seldes, for example, asserted that Negro musicians and composers were creatively and artistically backward. They are not aware that for critics likes Seldes, the Negroes were the anti-intellectual, uninhibited, unsophisticated, intuitive children of jazz music who functioned with aesthetic "emotions" rather than with the disciplined "mind" of white jazzmen. For such critics, the real artists of Negro folk expression were the George Gershwins, the Paul Whitemans, and the Cole Porters. Seldes asserted in 1924:

> Nowhere is the failure of the Negro to exploit his gifts more obvious than in the use he has made of the jazz orchestra; for although nearly every Negro jazz band is better than nearly every white band, no Negro band has yet come up to the level of the best white ones, and the leader of the best of all, by a little joke, is called [Paul] Whiteman. (*The Seven Lively Arts,* 1924.)

This was a personal opinion, but whether true or false, it typified the white cultural attitude toward all forms and practices of Negro art: Compared to the Western intellectual standards of art and culture, the Negro does not measure up. Thus every Negro artist, writer, dramatist, poet, composer, musician, et al, comes under the guillotine of this cultural judgment. What this judgment really means is that the Negro is artistically, creatively, and culturally inferior; and therefore, all the established social power wielded by the white cultural elite will be used to keep the Negro creative artist in his place. But the historical catch in all this is that the white Protestant Anglo-Saxon in America has nothing in his native American tradition that is aesthetically and culturally original, except that which derives from the Negro presence.

Seldes's mixed feelings and critical ambivalence concerning Negro music stemmed from his awareness that jazz would have to become America's national music, or at least form its basic ingredients. This grievously worried many white critics then, and it explains why they still maintain the artistic superiority of the European symphonic music tradition. From these attitudes on the cultural arts, based on racial values, whites have cultivated their own literary and cultural critique. But it has been a critique predicated on the cultural ideals of a group whose English-North European antecedents have been too culturally ego-ridden, unoriginal, ultra-conservative, and desiccated to generate a flourishing national culture. Hence historically, there has been on the cultural front in America a tense ideological war for ethnic identity and ascendancy. This competition has taken on strange and unique patterns. Often it is between WASPs and Jews, but more often than not, it is a collaboration between WASPs and Jews, on high levels, against the Negro. Since it is less possible for the Negro to "pass" for a WASP than for a member of any other ethnic group, it is the Negro minority who is the most vulnerable and defenseless on the cultural front. In this war of identity over cultural art standards, the Negro functions under a double or triple jeopardy: Without a literary and cultural critique of its own, the Negro cannot fight for and maintain a position in the cultural world.

—1967

Patricia A. Turner

When I was a child, one of my favorite grown-ups was a friend of my parents who had been a Cotton Club dancer in the mid-1920s. When I knew her, Lillian was a domestic worker in the employ of a wealthy white widow. She dressed in crisp uniforms with elaborate costume jewelry or intricately folded floral handkerchiefs pinned to the bodice. Although she never looked tawdry, she wore lots of makeup and perfume. She entertained me for hours with stories about the beautiful women and handsome men she had known in the Harlem of her youth. She talked of parties and vacations. She taught me the steps to some of the dances she remembered. She created G-rated stories of her love affairs. She still bore a grudge against a good-looking beau who left her in pursuit of Nina Mae McKinney, star of several all-black films of the 1930s. She said she had known Lena Horne and Duke Ellington. None of these names meant a whole lot to me at the time, but the adults were impressed so I was too.

In all of Lillian's stories of her Harlem adventures, never once did she mention organized crime or anything to do with the white patrons/owners of the nightspot. If she was still alive, I would have a ton of questions for her. How well did Duke Ellington and Cab Calloway get along? Was Ellington jealous when Calloway was so successful when he filled in while Ellington and his Washingtonians took a leave to appear in a Hollywood film? Was Ellington as much of a ladies' man as they say? What kind of relationships developed among the women, such as Josephine Baker, Lena Horne, and Ethel Waters, backstage? How did it feel to perform on a stage in a club where your own parents couldn't get in to see you?

It is unlikely that any of these stories will reach the big screen. Since a movie entitled *The Cotton Club* has already been made, producers will be hesitant to underwrite another film on this cultural landmark. I suppose this is my biggest problem with all of these films. The stories of Delta bluesmen, the Cotton Club performers, and the early ragtime pianists will not get told, at least by filmmakers. These films, which sandwich the accomplishments of black musicians into stories about the very people who exploited them, will prevent the real stories from being presented to a mass audience.

Since the centuries during which slavers forced their west African captives to sing and dance during the Middle Passage—the interval on board slave ships en route from Africa to the New World—in order to maintain their physical fitness aboard slave ships, the dominant culture has exploited and commodified the music of Americans of African descent for purposes lucrative and beneficial to itself. During slavery, traders forced their chattel to sing on the auction block so as to raise their selling price. In the aftermath of slavery, African Americans were forced to "blacken up" to compete with white minstrels. Groups such as the Fisk Jubilee singers kept their college running on the money they made by selling polished versions of spirituals. At every juncture in our history it has seemed as if the dominant culture appreciates us mainly for our music. Wouldn't it be nice if fledgling adolescent white musicians could redeem the souls of elderly black men, all the while enhancing their rock careers, as is the case in [the movie] *Crossroads*? Wouldn't it be nice if, as is the case in *The Big Chill*, whites could just dance to the music without ever encountering real African Americans? The people who make these films probably don't perceive themselves as belonging to the same category as those who cracked the whip on the slave ships. Our responses may not be as visceral as those of our ancestors. Yet when film after film, commercial after commercial, episode after episode hinges on the music and lyrics of our hearts and souls, we feel a decided kinship with our ancestors. It's the same old song, but with a different meaning to those of us compelled to sing it.

—1994

Rudolph Fisher

"Ladies and gentlemen!" sang Curry to the tense crowd that gorged the Arcadia. "Tonight is the night of the only contest of its kind in recorded history! On my left, Mr. Bus Williams, chief of the Blue Devils. On my right, Mr. Fessenden Baxter, leader of the Firemen. On this stand, the solid gold loving-cup. The winner will claim the jazz championship of the world!"

"And the sweet mama too, how 'bout it?" called a wag.

"Each outfit will play three numbers: a one-step, a fox-trot, and a blues number. With this stop watch which you see in my hand, I will time your applause after each number. The leader receiving the longest total applause wins the loving-cup!"

"Yea—and some lovin'-up wid it!"

"I will now toss a coin to see who plays the first number!"

"Toss it out here!"

"Bus Williams's Blue Devils, ladies and gentlemen, will play the first number!"

Bus's philosophy of jazz held tone to be merely a vehicle of rhythm. He spent much time devising new rhythmic patterns with which to vary his presentations. Accordingly he depended largely on Tappen, his master percussionist, who knew every rhythmic monkey-shine with which to delight a gaping throng.

Bus had conceived the present piece as a chase, in which an agile clarinet eluded impetuous and turbulent traps. The other instruments were to be observers, chorusing their excitement while they urged the principals on.

From he moment the piece started something was obviously wrong. The clarinet was elusive enough, but its agility was without purpose. Nothing pursued it. People stopped dancing in the middle of the number and turned puzzled faces toward the platform. The tap-drummer was going through the motions faithfully but to no avail. His traps were voiceless, emitted mere shadows of sound. He was a deaf mute making a speech.

Brief, perfunctory, disappointed applause rose and fell at the number's end. Curry announced its duration:

"Fifteen seconds flat!"

Fess Baxter, with great gusto, leaped to his post.

"The Firemen will play their first number!"

Bus was consulting Tappen.

"For the love o' Pete, Tap—?"

"Love o' hell. Look a' here."

Bus looked—first at the trapdrum, then at the bass; snapped them with a finger, thumped them with his knuckles. There was almost no sound; each drum-sheet was dead, lax instead of taut, and the cause was immediately clear; each bore a short curved knife-cut following its edge a brief distance, a wound unnoticeable at a glance, but fatal to the instrument.

Bus looked at Tappen, Tappen looked at Bus.

"The cream-colored son of a buzzard!"

Fess Baxter, gleeful and oblivious, was directing a whirlwind number, sweeping the crowd about the floor at an exciting, exhausting pace, distorting, expanding, etherealizing their emotions with swift-changing dissonaces. Contrary to Bus Williams's philosophy, Baxter considered rhythm a mere rack upon which to hand his tonal tricks. The present piece was dizzy with disharmonies, unexpected twists of phrase, successive false resolutions. Incidentally, there was nothing wrong with Baxter's drums.

Boiling over, Bus would have started for him, but Tappen grabbed his coat.

"Hold it, papa. That's a sure way to lose. Maybe we can choke him yet."

"Yea—?"

"I'll play the wood. And I still got cymbals and sandpaper."

"Yea—and a triangle. Hell of a lot o' good they are."

"Can't quit," said Tappen.

"Well," said Bus.

Baxter's number ended in a furor.

"Three minutes and twenty seconds!" bellowed Curry as the applause eventually died out.

Bus began his second number, a fox-trot. In the midst of it he saw Jean dancing, beseeching him with bewildered dismay in her eyes, a look that at once crushed and crazed him. Tappen rapped on the rim of his trap drum, tapped his triangle, stamped the pedal that clapped the cymbals, but the result was a toneless and hollow clatter, a weightless noise that bounced back from the multitude instead of penetrating into it. The players also, distracted by the loss, were operating far below par, and not all their leader's frantic false enthusiasm could compensate for the gaping absence of bass. The very spine had been ripped out of their music, and Tappen's desperate efforts were but the hopeless flutterings of a stricken, limp, pulseless heart.

"Forty-five seconds!" Curry announced. "Making a total so far of one minute flat for the Blue Devils! The Firemen will now play their second number!"

The Firemen's fox-trot was Baxter's re-arrangement of Burleigh's "Jean, My Jean," and Baxter, riding his present advantage hard, stressed all that he had put into it of tonal ingenuity. The thing was delirious with strange harmonies, iridescent with odd color-changes, and its very flamboyance, its music fine-writing and conceits, delighted the dancers.

But it failed to delight Jean Ambrose, whom by its title it was intended to flatter. She rushed to Bus.

"What is it?" She was a-quiver.

"Drums gone. Somebody cut the pigskin the last minute."

"What? Somebody? Who?"

"Cut 'em with a knife close to the rim."

"Cut? He cut—? Oh, Bus!"

She flashed Baxter a look that would have crumpled his assurance had he seen it. "Can't you—Listen." She was at once wild and calm. "It's the bass. You got to have—I know! Make 'em stamp their feet! Your boys, I mean. That'll do it. All of 'em. Turn the blues into a shout."

"Yea? Gee. Maybe—"

"Try it! You've got to win this thing."

An uproar that seemed endless greeted Baxter's version of "Jean." The girl, back out on the dance floor, managed a smile as Baxter acknowledged the acclaim by gesturing toward her.

"The present score, ladies and gentlemen, is—for the Blue Devils, one minute even; for the Firemen, six minutes and thirty seconds! The Devils will now play their last number!" Curry's intonation of "last" moved the mob to laughter.

Into that laughter Bus grimly led his men like a captain leading his command into fire. He had chosen the parent of blues songs, the old St. Louis Blues, and he adduced every device that had ever adorned that classic. Clarinets wailed, saxophones moaned, trumpets wept wretchedly, trombones laughed bitterly, even the great bass horn sobbed dismally from the depths. And so perfectly did the misery in the music express the actual despair of the situation that the crowd was caught from the start. Soon dancers closed their eyes, forgot their jostling neighbors, lost themselves bodily in the easy sway of that slow fateful measure, vaguely aware that some quality hitherto lost had at last been found. They were too wholly absorbed to note just how that quality had been found: that every player softly dropped his heel where each bass-drum beat would have come, giving each major impulse a body and breadth that no drum could have achieved. Zoom-zoom-zoom-zoom. It was not a mere sound; it was a vibrant throb that took hold of the crowd and rocked it.

They had been rocked thus before, this multitude. Two hundred years ago they had swayed to that same slow fateful measure, lifting their lamentation to heaven, pounding the earth with their feet, seeking the mercy of a new God through the medium of an old rhythm, zoom-zoom. They had rocked so a thousand years ago in a city whose walls were jungle, forefending the wrath of a terrible black God who spoke in storm and pestilence, had swayed and wailed to the same slow period, beaten on a wild boar's skin stretched over the end of a hollow tree-trunk. Zoom-zoom-zoom-zoom. Not a sound but an emotion that laid hold on their bodies and swung them into the past. Blues—low-down blues indeed—blues that reached their souls' depths.

But slowly the color changed. Each player allowed his heel to drop less and less softly. Solo parts faded out, and the orchestra began to gather power as a whole. The rhythm persisted, the unfaltering common meter of blues, but the blueness itself, the sorrow, the despair, began to give way to hope. Ere long hope came to the verge of realization—mounted it—rose above it. The deep and regular impulses now vibrated like nearing thunder, a mighty, inescapable, all-embracing dominance, stressed by the contrast of wind-tone; an all-pervading atmosphere through which soared wild-winged birds. Rapturously, rhapsodically, the number rose to madness and at the height of its madness, burst into sudden silence.

Illusion broke. Dancers awoke, dropped to reality with a jolt. Suddenly the crowd appreciated that Bus Williams had returned to form, had put on a comeback, had struck off a masterpiece. And the crowd showed its appreciation. It applauded its palms sore.

Curry's suspense-ridden announcement ended:

"Total—for the Blue Devils, seven minutes and forty seconds! For the Firemen, six minutes and thirty seconds! Maybe that was the Devils' last number after all! The Firemen will play their last number!"

It was needless for Baxter to attempt the depths and heights just attained by Bus Williams's Blue Devils. His speed, his subordination of rhythm to tone, his exotic coloring, all were useless in a low-down blues song. The crowd, moreover, had nestled upon the broad, sustaining bosom of a shout. Nothing else warmed them. The end of Baxter's last piece left them chilled and unsatisfied.

But if Baxter realized that he was beaten, his attitude failed to reveal it. Even when the major volume of applause died out in a few seconds, he maintained his self-assured grin. The reason was soon apparent: although the audience as a whole had stopped applauding, two small groups of assiduous handclappers, one at either extreme of the dancing-area, kept up a diminutive, violent clatter.

Again Bus and Tappen exchanged sardonic stares.

"Damn' if he ain't paid somebody to clap!"

Only the threatening hisses and boos of the majority terminated this clatter, whereupon Curry summed up.

"For Bus Williams's Blue Devils—seven minutes and forty seconds! For Fess Baxter's Firemen—eight minutes flat!"

He presented Baxter the loving-cup and a hubbub of murmurs, handclaps, shouts, and hisses that drowned whatever he said. Then the hubbub hushed. Baxter was assisting Jean Ambrose to the platform. With a bow and a flourish he handed the girl the cup.

She held it for a moment in both arms, uncertain, hesitant. But there was nothing uncertain or hesitant in the mob's reaction. Feeble applause was overwhelmed in a deluge of disapprobation. Cries of "Crooked!" "Don't take it!" "Crown the cheat!" "He stole it!" stood out. Tappen put his finger in the slit of his trap-drum, ripped it to a gash, held up the mutilated instrument, and cried, "Look what he done to my traps!" A few hardboiled ruffians close to the platform moved menacingly toward the victor. "Grab 'im! Knock his can off!"

Jean's uncertainty abruptly vanished. She wheeled with the trophy in close embrace and sailed across the platform toward the defeated Bus Williams. She smiled into his astonished face and thrust the cup into his arms.

"Hot damn, mama! That's the time!" cried a jubilant voice from the floor, and instantly the gathering storm of menace broke into a cloudburst of delight. The romance-hungry multitude saw Bus Williams throw his baton into the air and gather the girl and the loving-cup into his arms. And they went utterly wild—laughed, shouted, yelled, and whistled till the walls of the Arcadia bulged.

Jazz emerged as the mad noise subsided: Bus Williams's Blue Devils playing "She's Still My Baby."

—1930

Mary Lou Williams

Mr. Jelly Lord was a more frightening proposition. He was considered a big deal then, and he had me scared. When the guys dragged me into his office downtown we were surprised to see him playing duets with an ofay piccolo player. At a convenient break, they introduced me and told Jelly they would like for him to hear me. Indicating that I should park my hips on the stool, Jelly gave over the piano and I got started on my favorite Morton piece, "The Pearls."

Almost immediately I was stopped and reprimanded, told the right way to phrase it. I played it the way Jelly told me, and when I had it to his satisfaction, I slipped in one of my own tunes. This made no difference. I was soon stopped and told: "Now that passage should be phrased like this."

Jelly Roll had a mouthful of diamond and spoke with a stammer when he got excited. He was what we call a "big mouth," and the sound of his voice had me shaking in my boots. Any minute I was expecting to get up off the floor because I had played his "Pearls" wrong. That's how they trained you in these days (half the chorus girls had black eyes!), and Morton had the reputation of being a demanding taskmaster. Musicians—they really have it easy now!

—1954

Melvin B. Tolson

IVORY FRYSINGER

Though he drank nothing stronger than black coffee
And avoided love affairs with easy women
And never gambled,
Ivory was a welcome guest in shady resorts.
Proprietors were glad to see his moony grin
Because he attracted wandering customers.

Okay Katie said
That liquor and gambling and a double-dealing woman
Had made him what he was:
An itinerant piano player
Who sang in a plaintive baritone
And wrung from the ivory keys
Astonishing rhythms.

Sometimes a hollow-eyed black Ulysses would say:
"I'm homesick, Ivory, homesick,
Strike up Papa Handy's "St. Louis Blues."

Since playing and singing for the benefit of others
Was Ivory's religion,
No one had ever heard him refuse to grant a request.

When Ivory played
His mind became a tapestry of color-tones.
With his head sidewise

As if taking a cue
From someone hidden in the sanctum of the piano,
His sensitive fingers caressed the ivories,
His full-bodied baritone swam into the verse,
His ebony face glowed with wonder.
When Ivory sang
Folk forgot to talk.

Sometimes his winging fingers
Dipped lightly over the keys
Like the shadow of gulls
Skimming the surface of mirroring waters.
Sometimes his rigid fingers fell
Like pneumatic hammers
Upon the quaking keyboard.

Ivory's mad genius
Could change the shape and mood of music
By fashioning an anthem into a waltz,
Or a spiritual into blues,
Or a classic into jazz.

—1935

Claude McKay

The "Song of Harlem" was the latest hit. It was written by a Harlem
Negro about the time when the popular taste began craving hot jazz or
swing music. But the composer could find no publisher willing to take it.
There is no Harlem like that in words and music, they said. People don't
want that kind of Harlem stuff. The public wants Harlem hot. The composer kept his song. At last a white sympathizer introduced him to the
leader of a Negro orchestra. The Negro musician added it to his repertoire and put it over the radio.

The "Song of Harlem" became an immediate success. It came the
tempo of the country had reached a turning point and the public was
ready for a different version of Harlem.

So Pucksar played the "Song of Harlem."

In Harlem you may find what joy you seek,
But forget not that sorrow lingers there,
Where in the shadows dwell the weak and meek,

Of broken lives whose homes are cold and bare,
Like broken lives of outcasts everywhere,

The dusk benignantly enfolds the street,
And gathers Harlem's children to her breast,
And brown madonnas kiss their babies' feet
And tenderly they cradle them to rest:
Oh golden hearts of Harlem in the night,
Oh souls of Harlem searching for the light.

In Harlem there is laughter, music, wine,
And beauty bold in strangely haunting eyes,
And also wholesome lives like yours and mine,
And quiet homes wherein the sacred ties
Of love and faith bind humble families.

The music was an indolent onestep, a kind of pain-in-the-spine shuffle, and out-of-work Pucksar in Paris played it with heart-rending feeling
for Harlem. He built up a picture of Harlem there in the room: Lenox
Avenue and its fried fish and coffee pots, Eighth Avenue and its vegeta-
bles and fish market, Seventh Avenue and its saloons and brown faces
against the window panes.

All the guests—Africans, Aframericans, Europeans—swayed to the
melody like a cradle rocking to a lullaby. But while the others danced
from left to right, the Senegalese dancer moved her head up and down in
a kind of subdued interpretation of the primitive Senegalese dance.
Achine, captivated and calmed by the music to which she had objected,
was rocking in Buster's arms.

But Princess Fanti had sat down in a corner and Millinda had insisted
on sitting with her. "I love that song," said the princess, caressing the
heavy purple window drapery against her.

"It's pretty," said Millinda, "perhaps you like it because it has a little
tango in it."

"No, it's the Negro I like in it more than the hot jazz. It was that kind
of Negro I knew. And I found Negro life like that when my husband
took me to Africa to present me to the chiefs of his tribe. Everywhere
there was that strange undertone of melancholy." She wiped her eyes
furtively and said: "Excuse me. I told you I wanted to go home."

"Oh, it's alright," said Millinda, "I understand you. But I didn't know
you had been to Africa."

"Oh yes, Prince Fanti took me there two years before his death, so his people could salute me. And he was never right after he returned. I think something happened to him there."

"Did you like Africa?"

"I liked the visit and the people they were so lovely to me. But I wouldn't want to live there."

"Perhaps I should have visited Africa too," said Millinda. "Now it's too late."

"Why too late? Are you going back to New York?"

"I don't know where I'm going—perhaps to hell. Let's drink and forget," said Millinda, getting up.

—1943

Sidney Bechet

You know there's people, they got the wrong idea of Jazz. They think it's all that red-light business. But that's not so. And the real story I've got to tell, it's right there. It's Jazz.

What it is—how it come to be what it is.

People come up to me and they ask me, "Are you going to play 'Tin Roof Blues'?" They ask me, "What's be-bop?" or what do I think of some record Louis Armstrong put out. But if I was to answer that, I'd have to go back a long way. That's why I have to tell a lot more than people would expect.

They come to tell me they like this record or that, and they ask me what I'm trying to do by my music. They ask me, what's going to happen to Jazz? Where's it going? One night a man came to see me when I was playing in Paris; I'd known his son in New York. He came in with this party, and after the band had finished playing I got to talking with him. He started to tell me it meant a lot to him to hear me play; he'd had an experience he'd never had before. I told him I played like I always played. That's really all I can say.

But he was in a kind of feeling he wanted to talk. He was coming to me because there was something he wanted to know. So he told me he wanted to tell me a story, how he hadn't planned on coming to this place, this Vieux Colombier. He'd been off somewhere, very happy; his people, they had been enjoying themselves. And then someone suggested they come to hear me, that's what he said. And this man, he'd heard me and I was still playing the old music, I was still playing New Orleans. That's when he told me. "This music is your music," he said.

But, you know, no music is my music. It's everybody's who can feel it. You're here ... well, if there's music, you feel it—then it's yours too. You got to be in the sun to feel the sun. It's that way with music too.

But what that man said started me thinking. I began to think there's a whole lot of people, all they've been hearing is how ragtime got started in New Orleans, and as far as they know it just stopped there. They get to think in a memory kind of way all about this Jazz; but these people don't seem to know it's more than a memory thing. They don't seem to know it's happening right there where they're listening to it, just as much as it ever did in memory.

This man that come to see me in the Vieux Colombier went on to tell me about the band, about the French kids. "You gave them the spark," he said. "They didn't have it until you played." And then he wanted to know what was going to happen to Jazz when people like me weren't around any more.

But you know, Jazz isn't just me. It isn't just any one person who plays it. There'll always be Jazz. It doesn't stop with me, it doesn't stop anywhere. You take a melody ... people can feel a melody ... as long as there's melody there's Jazz, there's rhythm. But this man didn't stop there; he went on to say it was me who made the music—me and the old bunch: Buddy Bolden, Kid Ory, La Rocca, and all the others. That's where I tell him no. People's got an idea, I tell him, but it isn't like that; they think it started with one person—Bolden, Oliver, someone—but it wasn't like that. I'm trying to explain it to this man, how it got started way back. I told him how my family beat time with their hands on drums ... how that's Jazz too, how you can just beat on the table and it can be Jazz.

But what that man was saying ... he was worried that if people like him don't hear about it, stumble on to it, just like he did that night when he was persuaded to come, it wasn't going to be around. "Jazz comes out of an environment," this man said. "Something makes it. We can't have today what we should have to make it and keep it going. All we have to go on is a lot of legends. We'll remember river boats and never know how they were. We'll read about all those early days, and all we'll have is some bigger mystery except for maybe getting together with some friends from time to time and playing over all the records. We won't have anything of our own to add to it. The kids who take it up now, where are they going to go when they're looking for their background in Jazz? When they can't just walk down the street and hear it anywhere?"

"Maybe it stopped in New Orleans," he said. "Maybe there's no more of it except for a few of the old ones. Maybe it's gone except for those who can remember it."

Well, that's what this man had in his mind. But let me tell you one thing: Jazz, that's a name the white people have given to the music. What does Jazz mean to you when I come up behind you: "Jazz," I say, "what does that do to you?" That doesn't explain the music.

There's two kinds of music. There's classic and there's ragtime. When I tell you ragtime, you can feel it, there's a spirit right in the word. It comes out of the Negro spirituals, out of Omar's way of singing, out of his rhythm. But Jazz—Jazz could mean any 'damn thing: high times, screwing, ballroom. It used to be spelled *Jass*, which *was* screwing. But when you say ragtime, you're saying the music.

But here's what I really mean. All God's children got a crown. My race, their music ... it's their way of giving you something, of showing you how to be happy. It's what they've got to make *them* happy. The spiritual, that's sad; but there's a way in it that's happy too. We can be told: "Maybe you don't belong in Heaven, and you haven't got a place on this earth; you're not in our class, our race." But somewhere, all God's children wear a crown, and someday we're going to wear ours too.

You know, the Negro doesn't want to cling to music. But he needs it; it means something; and *he* can mean something. He's always got to be honest, and people are always putting him to music. "That's your place," they say. How can you be honest to something when people are trying to make it unnatural for you?

But if you have a feeling for the music, you can understand him, and that's why he keeps it so important to himself. And he's always been trying. The black man, he's been learning his way from the beginning. A way of saying something from inside himself, as far back as time, as far back as Africa, in the jungle, and the way the drums talked across the jungle, the way they filled the whole air with a sound like the blood beating inside himself.

My story goes a long way back. It goes further back than I had anything to do with. My music is like that ... I got it from something inherited, just like the stories my father gave down to me. And those stories are all I know about some of the things bringing me to where I am. And all my life I've been trying to explain about something, something I understand—the part of me that was there before I was. It was there waiting to be me. It was there waiting to be the music. It's that part I've been trying to explain to myself all my life.

—1960

Duke Ellington

The City of Jazz is a place in which certain people live. Some are on their way out, while many others are on their way in. Some are rushing to get there, but others appear reluctant and are cautious in their approach. Still others claim they are afraid, and hesitate to expose themselves in this place where they feel so strange, this strange place where the most solid citizens are so hip, or slick, or cool. These hesitant ones fear they will feel like country folk in the metropolis, or like people on the Chinatown bus tour. They wonder if they will be taken for suckers or squares.

My experience on my many visits to and from the city (I do one-nighters, you know) has convinced me that its people are all very nice human beings. There are those who work for the city (the players), those who work at the city (the analysts), and those who just enjoy it (*these* are my people). The citizens of all three groups are more concerned with what they like than what they dislike. All of them, too, assume that they know one another. For instance, when they meet for the first time they embrace warmly like old college chums.

In the city's public square, you find statues of heroes. Some are of those who built the walls, like Buddy Bolden and King Oliver. They appear to have been sculpted in bars, after-hours joints, and houses of ill-repute. Some are of those who fought to save the city, like Fletcher Henderson and Paul Whiteman, and they are identified with the world of ballroom palaces. Some are of those who went down swinging, like Bix Beiderbecke and Chick Webb, and who were decorated posthumously for heroic performances above and beyond the call of duty. Last, in the same concert halls where they play the masterworks, are statues of some of the great ones who long defended the walls, like Bechet, Armstrong, and Hawk.

This City of Jazz does not have any specific geographical location. It is anywhere and everywhere, wherever you can hear the sound, and it makes you do like this—you know! Europe, Asia, North and South Americas, the world digs this burg—Digsville, Gonesville, Swingersville, and Wailingstown. There are no city limits, no city ordinances, no policemen, no fire department, but come rain or come shine, drought or flood, I think I'll stay here in this scene, with these cats, because almost everybody seems to dig what they're talking about, or putting down. They communicate, Dad. Do you get the message?

Villesville is *the* place—*trelos anthropos!*

—1973

Frank Marshall Davis

JAZZ BAND

Play that thing, you jazz mad fools!
Boil a skyscraper with a jungle
Dish it to 'em sweet and hot—
Ahhhhhhhhh
Rip it open then sew it up, jazz band!

Thick bass notes from a moon faced drum
Saxophones moan, banjo strings hum
High thin notes from the cornet's throat
Trombone snorting, bass horn snorting
Short tan notes from the piano
And the short tan notes from the piano

Plink plank plunk a plunk
Plink plank plunk a plunk
Chopin gone screwy, Wagner with the blues
Plink plank plunk a plunk
Got a date with Satan—ain't no time to lose
Plink plank plunk a plink
Strut it in Harlem, let Fifth Avenue shake it slow
Plink plank plunk a plunk
Ain't goin' to heaven nohow—
     crowd up there's too slow . . .
Plink plank plunk a plunk
Plink plank plunk a plunk
Plunk

Do that thing, jazz band!

Whip it to a jelly

Sock it, rock it; heat it, beat it; then fling it at 'em

Let the jazz stuff fall like hail on king and truck driver, queen
     and laundress, lord and laborer, banker and bum

Let it fall in London, Moscow, Paris, Hongkong, Cairo,
    Buenos Aires, Chicago, Sidney

Let it rub hard thighs, let it be molten fire in the veins of dancers

Make 'em shout a crazy jargon of hot hosannas to a fiddle-faced
jazz god

Send Dios, Jehovah, Gott, Allah, Buddha past in a high
    stepping cake walk
Do that thing, jazz band!

Your music's been drinking hard liquor
Got shanghaied and it's fightin' mad
Stripped to the waist feedin' ocean liner bellies
Big burly bibulous brute
Poet hands and bone crusher shoulders—
Black sheep or white?

Hey, Hey!
Pick it, papa!
Twee twa twee twa twa
Step on it, black boy
Do re me fa sol la ti do
Boomp boomp
Play that thing, you jazz mad fools!

—1935

The Thirties and Forties

Clyde E.B. Bernhardt

King Joe Oliver was a heavy man, about two hundred fifty pounds and kind of chubby, but not flabby looking, slouchy, or anything like that. He was neat and clean as a pin. Stood about just under six feet. He was fifty-four years old in 1931, and I remember I gave him a pack of Chesterfield cigarettes on his birthday and he told me how old he was. Was born in New Orleans, he said that too.

His hair was crew-cut style, kept real close. His feet was not as large as the average man his size—looked like he wore a ten at the most. Had no scars that I saw, only this one bad left eye that stuck out like a frog's and was bigger then the other. It was not noticeable unless he had his glasses off, and he made sure to keep them on almost all the time. Never heard him say he was blind in that eye, so I think he could see something out of it. Probably the reason he was not a good sight reader.

"I'm the slowest goddamned reader in my band," he would mumble in his low voice. "You guys might read faster but damn it, you better wait for me."

Oliver was a very dark man and always seemed conscious of that. "There three kinds of blacks," he once told me. "A *black*, a *lamb* black, and a *damn* black." He laughed at his joke and then added, "I'm black and I only seen two other damn people in the world blacker'n me," and then he laughed some more.

Oliver often said things like that. When he see somebody real dark he strike a match and whisper: "Who dat out dare? What dat movin'?" All that kind of stuff.

Everybody laugh and he laugh the loudest. Some New Orleanians have peculiar ways. You just have to understand them—they critical of others and very critical of themselves.

He just loved to play the dirty dozens—a kind of insulting game. The more insults tossed back and forth, the better he liked it. Herman Elkins and Walter Dennis always try to dozens him back but they didn't stand a chance. He tell them something bad about their mother or sister, about sleeping with them and what they did and how they did it and what they said about it and things like that. Everybody would die laughing, but the guys always let him go. He was no contest. His dozens won every time.

And man, could he *eat*. The only person that gave him competition eating was Fats Waller. Yesss Lord. Oliver eat a dozen fried eggs for breakfast and then say how he could eat more. He take about a pound of bacon, fried real crisp, and chew it piece by piece, then drink down maybe ten cups of coffee.

And he loved his grits and rice. Yes he did. And sweets—jam, preserves, and jelly piled high on bread and butter. Then sop everything up.

Once I saw him drink a half gallon of lemonade and twelve bottles of Coca-Cola.

"I know I'm not the smallest eater in town," he growl, "but damn it, I enjoy what little I do eat."

And the guys all laugh. "Well," they say, "we hate to see you when you hungry." Then everybody went into the dozens again.

Oliver never allowed any of us to drink on the job. He didn't either, although he smoked heavy. Sometimes we slip outside where there was a pint or quart jar of corn whiskey hidden. He was watching and sneak around back of the bus and peep in the window. "Alright," he shout, "if I catch any of you mothers drinkin' on your rest period, I'm gonna fine each of you two bucks."

He always watched us but never did catch us.

A couple of boys once bought some reefers in Dallas, a whole paper bag for a quarter. That was the first time I ever seen that stuff. Never saw it out east. The guys all talking about getting a Target Cigarette wrapping machine to roll their own, but didn't know where to buy it.

"That's one thing I like about this band," Oliver said, "ain't got no goddamn big reefer smokers in it."

Told me he tried it once. "Some ol' Mexican boy sold me some for a dime. I inhaled, did every damn thing, and that shit didn't bother me no kind of way. How in hell they get their damn kicks from that?"

He always used a gold-plated horn, a Conn I think—they cost more than a brass- or silver-plated one. Back then, really big-name bands wouldn't hire unless the musician had a gold-plated instrument. Man, it sure looked class.

Oliver used three mutes: a wah-wah—he was very good on a wah-wah—a cup mute, and a straight mute. I never heard any trumpet player take a wah-wah plunger and play "Sugar Blues" like he did. Sounded like he was crying and moaning—it was magnetic. The horn really talked.

I asked him once what it was saying. "Goddamn it, I was cussin' you mothers out."

He had all his teeth extracted in 1927 because of pyorrhea. Sometimes his denture plates hurt his gums after playing about a hour, and he have to stop, get off the stand, and stay alongside for a while. They had no paste in those days to hold the plates tight like they do now, but as long as they didn't bother him, his playing was not affected. He could hit a high D—never did play those high F's and G's like Louis Armstrong—the highest he go was around C and D. But he scream, on a D.

I say King Oliver still played more and was more exciting then a lot of younger men in their twenties and thirties. Of course he didn't sound the same every night. He did have his off days, but so did all of us.

Sometimes he was feeling terrific. "Goddamn it, I feel *good* tonight!" And he came up on the bandstand. "I'm gonna play you all a 1923 solo." And knocked everybody out. Every time.

—1986

C. L. R. James

I want to say a few words about jazz music. I have listened to it for several decades now. At the same time, as an amateur, I have paid a great deal of attention to the great composers. The most startling experience of my musical and artistic life is the level of musicianship of the great popular bands of the United States. Mozart and Beethoven would be at home in our modern concert halls. But I believe popular music in the United States would astonish them. It is difficult for me to conceive that at any time in history there has ever been a music of such quality, shared in so spontaneously and easily by the great mass of the population, as the bands and records of Louis Armstrong, Benny Goodman, Lionel Hampton, and heaps of others. Their musicianship, I have been told by musicians, has reached a high pitch. And it depends entirely upon popular support and popular interest.

I have noticed in the United States a great number of people, and especially young people, untrained in formal music, whose ear and sense of musicianship, sense of timing, combinations of tone, color, etc. have been developed to an extraordinary pitch by the interest that most of the younger generation seems to have in the popular musicians. Here is an extraordinary development of popular culture as never has existed before.

Furthermore, there is in the development of jazz from decade to decade, or even from year to year, a clear response to changes in the moods and attitudes of the American people, which in turn reflect economic and social development. Again the Depression marks the dividing line. They do not compose the songs as they did before 1929 (or a few years after). They do not even play in the same way. To me *this* is what

matters in the world of art today. Owing to the increasingly social organization of life and the corresponding technological changes and oppor-
tunities, the popular artists working for the mass are expressing powerful
currents of thought and feeling as never before in a way that is quite new.

—1953

Mary Lou Williams

I found Kansas City to be a heavenly city—music everywhere in the
Negro section of town, and fifty or more cabarets rocking on Twelfth
and Eighteenth Streets. Kirk's band was drawing them into the handsome Pla-mor Ballroom when my husband, John Williams, had me return to him in Kaycee. This was my first visit to Missouri's jazz metropolis, a city that was to have a big influence on my career.

With two sisters, Lucille and Louise, who knew every speak-easy in
town, I began to make the rounds from "Hell's Kitchen" on Fifth Avenue to a club on Eighteenth where I met Sam Price. Sammy was playing
an unusual type of blues piano which I thought could hardly be improved on. I had the luck to hear him again when we were both in New
York during 1934.

One night, we ran into a place where Ben Pollack had a combo which
included Jack Teagarden and, I think, Benny Goodman. The girls introduced me to the Texas trombonist, and right away we felt like friends.
After work, he and a couple of musicians asked us to go out, and we visited most of the speaks downtown. One I remember particularly, because it was decorated to resemble the inside of a penitentiary, with bars
on the windows and waiters in striped uniforms like down-South con-
victs. In these weird surroundings, I played for the boys and Jack got up
and sang some blues. I thought he was more than wonderful. While they
stayed in Kaycee, Jack and some of Pollack's men came round every
night, and I was very happy to see them.

Now at this time, which was still Prohibition, Kansas City was under
Tom Pendergast's control. Most of the night spots were run by politicians and hoodlums, and the town was wide open for drinking, gambling,
and pretty much every form of vice. Naturally, work was plentiful for
musicians, though some of the employers were tough people. For instance, when [Andy] Kirk moved from Pla-mor, the orchestra went to
work for a nationally feared gangster. He was real bad: people used to run
when you mentioned his name. At that time, Andy was playing tuba, and

the band was conducted by our singer, Billy Massey. Billy was a man not easily scared, and one day at the new job he ran off his mouth to the boss. The hood concluded he was crazy (which was not far wrong), and told the band to pack and leave—but fast. The rest of the guys were too nice, he said, for him to think about killing Billy.

I heard that Count Basie later worked for the same dracula, and also had a slight misunderstanding. As result, Basie had to work two weeks without pay.

Kaycee was really jumping—so many great bands having sprung up there or moved in from over the river. I should explain that Kansas City, Missouri, wasn't too prejudiced for a Midwestern town. It was a ballin' town, and it attracted musicians from all over the South and Southwest, and especially from Kansas.

Kansas City, Kansas, was right across the viaduct, just about five or six miles distant. But on the Kansas side they were much snootier. A lot of their musicians were from good families who frowned on jazz, so the musicians and kids would come across to Kaycee to blast. In Kaycee, nothing mattered.

I've known musicians so enthused about playing that they would walk all the way from the Kansas side to attend a jam session. Even bass players, caught without streetcar fare, would hump their bass on their back and come running. That was how music stood in Kansas City in those years around 1930.

Yes, Kaycee was a place to be enjoyed, even if you were without funds. People would make you a loan without asking for it, would look at you and tell if you were hungry and put things right. There was the best food to be had: the finest barbecue, crawdads, and other seafood. There were the races, and swimming, and the beautiful Swope Park and zoo to amuse you. There were jam sessions all the time, and big dances such as the union dance given every year by our local. As many as ten or twelve bands participated in this event, and you were sure to hear at least eight original styles there, as well as one or two outfits trying to imitate Duke.

For private entertainment we had our hot corn club every Monday, at which the musicians and wives would drink and play bridge, "tonk," or "hearts." At these meetings the boys drank corn whiskey and home brew—in fact, most anything with a high alcohol content—and they got laughs out of giving me rough liquor so strong it would almost blow the top of one's head off.

One of the regulars was Herman Walder, brilliant tenor player with Moten and brother saxophonist Woodie Walder. Herman asked me if I'd like a cool drink one night, and not knowing the taste of corn I gulped down a large glassful. The next thing I remember was people putting cold towels on my head. Being stubborn, I thought: if they can take it, so can I. So each Monday I tried to drink, with much the same result. The boys took to betting that I'd be high within ten minutes of entering— and they always won.

A wild Twelfth Street spot we fell in regularly was the Sunset, owned by Piney Brown, who loved jazz and was very liberal with musicians. Pianist Pete Johnson worked there with bass and drums, sometimes with Baby Lovett, a New Orleans drummer who became one of Kansas City's best. Now the Sunset had a bartender named Joe Turner, and while Joe was serving drinks he would suddenly pick up a cue for a blues and sing right where he stood, with Pete playing piano for him. I don't think I'll ever forget the thrill of listening to big Joe Turner shouting and sending everybody night after night while mixing drinks.

Pete Johnson was great on boogie, but he was by no means solely a boogie player. It was only when someone like Ben Webster, the Kaycee-born tenor man, yelled, "Roll for me ... come on, roll 'em Pete, make 'em jump," that he would play boogie for us.

Of course, we didn't have any closing hours in these spots. We could play all morning and half through the day if we wished to, and in fact we often did. The music was so good that I seldom got to bed before midday. It was just such a late morning occasion that once had Coleman Hawkins hung up. Fletcher Henderson came to town with Hawkins on tenor, and after the dance the band cruised round until they fell into the Cherry Blossom where Count Basie worked. The date must have been early 1934, because Prohibition had been lifted and whiskey was freely on sale. The Cherry Blossom was a new nightclub, richly decorated in Japanese style even to the beautiful little brown-skinned waitress.

The word went round that Hawkins was in the Cherry Blossom, and within about half an hour there were Lester Young, Ben Webster, Herschel Evans, Herman Walder, and one or two unknown tenors piling in the club to blow. Ben didn't know the Kaycee tenormen were so terrific, and he couldn't get himself together though he played all morning. I happened to be nodding that night, and around 4 AM. I awoke to hear someone pecking on my screen. I opened the window on Ben Webster. He was saying: "Get up, pussycat, we're jammin' and all the pianists are tired out now. Hawkins has got his shirt off and is still blowing. You got to come down." Sure enough, when we got there Hawkins was in his singlet taking turns with the Kaycee men. It seems he had run into something he didn't expect.

Lester's style was light and, as I said, it took him maybe five choruses to warm up. But then he would really blow; then you couldn't handle him on a cutting session. That was how Hawkins got hung up. The Henderson band was playing in St. Louis that evening, and Ben knew he ought to be on the way. But he kept trying to blow something to beat Hawkins and Herschel and Lester. When at last he gave up, he got straight in his car and drove to St. Louis. I heard he'd just bought a new Cadillac and that he burnt it out trying to make the job on time. Yes, Hawkins was king until he met those crazy Kansas City tenormen.

—1954

Pops Foster

Willie "the Lion" Smith used to live in the same apartment house I did in Harlem. Willie is what you call a born musician. He was a very slow reader and couldn't play in the big bands but was very good with the small ones. Willie could play in more keys than anyone except James P. (Johnson).

Willie and I used to play with Leadbelly. I think we were the only two guys who could play with him. Leadbelly didn't know which key he was going to play in. He'd play in all naturals and sharps. We'd have to listen to him then search around to find the keys. Then when we found it, we'd take off. Josh White and most of them guitar players aren't good musicians. They just play the blues. When Willie and I would play with them kinda guys, he'd come around to say, "We've got a hard date today, Pops." A lot of those guys can't even tune their instruments.

Leadbelly didn't know when to start or stop. The recording companies always had to go and splice his endings on. Leadbelly's wife's name was Irene and the tune of his "Irene" got to be a big hit. As soon as it did he died. Leadbelly was a mean and evil guy. He was in the penitentiary three times for killing guys and every time he played his way out. I was at his house one day when one of the partners of Asch Records talking about making some records, when he nearly killed a guy. Leadbelly's son-in-law insulted this guy's wife and he chased the son-in-law up to Leadbelly's door. They were fighting in the doorway when Leadbelly picked up an iron poker and started hitting the guy on the head with it. Me and the guy from Asch got out of the place and took off. When Leadbelly went before the judge for beating the guy we had to go to court with him. The judge knew about Leadbelly's singing and that he was on parole, and he didn't want to send him back to jail. So he told the guy he nearly killed that he had no business in Leadbelly's house and fined him, and withdrew the charges against Leadbelly.

When Leadbelly would get mad he'd just sit and grit his teeth. One time I told him he'd have to play a chord up on his guitar or we couldn't make no record. He just sat and started gritting his teeth. I told him he could grit his teeth all day, but if he didn't play the chord we couldn't play with him. He finally played it. Another time the government told him he had to pay taxes, and he was mad because he'd never paid before. He just sat and gritted his teeth; I told him to have the man take it out before he got paid. Leadbelly was just a mean and evil man. I just made records with him and never hung around with him at all.

—1971

Willie "The Lion" Smith

Our best customer was a prosperous Jewish family named Rothschild out on South Orange Avenue. They were in the wallpaper-hanging business. On Saturdays when I made deliveries there, a rabbi was at Mrs. Rothschild's home to teach her children their Hebrew lessons.

The chanting sounds coming out of the parlor during the lessons fascinated me from the beginning, and Mrs. Rothschild soon noticed. She permitted me to go into the study and sit and listen. It didn't take much time before I began to learn the meanings of the Hebraic words. When the rabbi saw how well I was doing, he took special pains to teach me, and it wasn't long before I was talking Hebrew as well as the Rothschild kids. It certainly did impress Mrs. Rothschild, who is still living, over ninety years of age, and when I go over to Newark I stop in to say hello to her.

As it turned out, I favored the Jewish religion all my life and at one time served as a Hebrew cantor in a Harlem synagogue. You could say I am Jewish partly by origin and partly by association. When I was thirteen years old, I had my bar mitzvah in a Newark synagogue. A lot of people are unable to understand my wanting to be Jewish. One said, "Lion, you stepped up to the plate with one strike against you—and now you take a second one right down the middle." They can't seem to realize I have a Jewish soul and belong in that faith.

—1964

Richard Wright

When off duty after a hard day of fighting, we are like spent troops, ready to plunge into pleasure to obliterate the memory of this slow death on city pavements. Just as in the South, in spite of the Lords of the Land, we managed to keep alive deep down in us the hope of what life could be, so now, with death ever hard at our heels, we pour forth in song and dance, without stint or shame, a sense of what our bodies want, a hint of our hope of a full life lived without fear, a whisper of the natural dignity we feel life can have, a cry of hunger for something new to fill our souls, to reconcile the ecstasy of living with the terror of dying ...

It is when we seek to express ourselves that the paradoxical cleavage in our lives shows most. Day after day we labor in the gigantic factories and mills of Western civilization, but we have never been allowed to become an organic part of this civilization; we have yet to share its ultimate hopes and expectations. Its incentives and perspectives, which form the core of meaning for so many millions, have yet to lift our personalities to levels of purpose. Instead, after working all day in one civilization, we go home to our Black Belts and live, within the orbit of the surviving remnants of the culture of the South, our naive, casual, verbal, fluid folk life.

Alone together with our black folk in the towering tenements, we play our guitars, trumpets, and pianos, beating out rough and infectious rhythms that create an instant appeal among all classes of people. Why is our music so contagious? Why is it that those who deny us are willing to sing our songs? Perhaps it is just because so many of those who live in cities feel deep down just as we feel. Our big brass horns, our huge noisy drums and whirring violins make a flood of melodies whose poignancy is heightened by our latent fear and uneasiness, by our love of the sensual, and by our feverish hunger for life. On the plantations our songs carried a strain of other-worldly yearning which people called "spiri-

tual"; but now our blues, jazz, swing, and boogie-woogie are our "spirituals" of the city pavements, our longing for freedom and opportunity,
an expression of our bewilderment and despair in a world whose meaning eludes us. The ridiculousness and sublimity of love are captured in
our blues, those sad-happy songs that laugh and weep all in one breath,
those mockingly tender utterances of a folk imprisoned in steel and
stone. Our thirst for the sensual is poured out in jazz; the tension of our
brittle lives is given forth in swing; and our nervousness and exhaustion
are pounded out in the swift tempo of boogie-woogie.

We lose ourselves in violent forms of dances in our ballrooms. The
faces of the white world, looking on in wonder and curiosity, declare:
"*Only* the Negro can play!" But they are wrong. They misread us. We are
able to play in this fashion because we have been excluded, left behind;
we play in this manner because all excluded folk play. The English say of
the Irish, just as America says of us, that only the Irish can play, that they
laugh through their tears. But every powerful nation says this of the folk
whom it oppresses in justification of that oppression. And, ironically,
they are angered by the exhibition of any evidence to the contrary, for it
disturbs their conscience with vague and guilty doubts. They smile with
cold disdain when we black folk say that our thirst can be slaked in art,
that our tensions can be translated into industry, that our energies can be
applied to finance, that our delight in the world can be converted into
education, that our love of adventure can find fulfillment in aviation. But
in one way or another, the white folk deny us these pursuits, and our
hunger for expression finds its form in our wild, raw music, in our invention of slang that winds its way all over America. Our adoration of color
goes not into murals, but into dress, into green, red, yellow, and blue
clothes. When we have some money in our pockets on payday, our laughter and songs make the principal streets of our Black Belts—Lenox Avenue, Beale Street, State Street, South Street, Second Street, Auburn Avenue—famous the earth over.

The Bosses of the buildings would have the world believe that we
black folk, after these three hundred years, have locked in our veins blood
of a queer kind that makes us act in this "special pattern." In their class-
rooms and laboratories they attempt to harness science in defense of
their attitudes and practices, and never do they so vigorously assail us as
"trouble-makers" as when we say that we are "this way" because we are
made to live "this way." They say we speak treasonably when we declare
that human life is plastic, that human nature is malleable, that men pos-

sess the dignity and meaning of the environmental and institutional forms through which they are lucky or unlucky enough to express themselves. They solemnly assert that we seek to overthrow the government by violence when we say that we live in this manner because the Black Belt which cradles our lives is created by the hands and brains of men who have decreed that we must live differently. They brand us as revolutionists when we say that we are not allowed to react to life with an honest and frontal vision.

We live on, and our music makes the feet of the whole world dance, even the feet of the children of the poor white workers who live beyond the line that marks the boundary of our lives. Where we cannot go, our tunes, songs, slang, and jokes go. Some of the white boys and girls, starved prisoner of urban homes, even forget the hatred of their parents when they hear our sensual, wailing blues melodies. The common people of the nation grow to love our songs so much that a few of us make our living by creating a haven of song for those who are weary of the barren world of steel and stone reared by the Bosses of the Buildings. But only a few of those who dance and sing with us suspect the rawness of life out of which our laughing-crying tunes and quick dance-steps come; they do not know that our songs and dances are our banner of hope flung desperately up in the face of a world that has pushed us to the wall.

—1941

Nelson Peery

The one dim street light hanging over the crossroad casts eerie shadows on the dance hall. The barnlike structure was set back, half hidden by the giant, moss-covered eucalyptus tree. A line of dim lights was strung across the front of the building. The door was open and the rough tables were lined up close to the walls to provide the maximum room for the dancers.

Brad and Bunk were waiting for us in the shadows before the dance hall. Introductions were made and the jug was passed around. Nearly strangling on the undiluted corn whiskey and gasping for air, I hid the jug in the underbrush. Regaining some composure, we went in. The organizers of the dance asked everyone to leave any liquor outside, because the sheriff might come by.

The dimly lit hall began to fill up. Little groups gathered around the tables, loading them up with 3.2 beer and red pop. The lanterns shone on hair slicked and plastered down with Murrays or "conked" into limp waves. The soft light reflected on gold-capped teeth, some of which held the engraved sword and star of the Prince Hall Order. These were dandies from De Ritter, Natchitoches, or Shreveport. They followed the dance band circuit into the smaller towns, selling whiskey, running card and dice games, or attempting to recruit fresh flesh for the whorehouses springing up around the training camps.

The combo arrived and set up their equipment. They tuned the instruments to the piano and the dance began. The snare drum, the sax, the trombone, the guitar, and the piano began a fast boogie-woogie introduction.

Sarah looked at me.

"I'm too out of practice for this one."

My head was swimming from the raw liquor. She seemed a bit hurt not to dance the first dance. Southern courtesy meant that she would have to dance the first and last dances with me. I hoped that something slow would be next.

———

Couples began the fast dancing. With snapping fingers and tapping feet they felt the common cadence. Twisting, bobbing individuals merged into a dancing mass. They caught the complex half steps and the steady eight full beats to the bar. This was dancing that I had never seen before—Black Belt dancing. He struts and pecks and spins. Contentiously thrusting first chest then groin forward, transported to a cosmos of boogie-woogie—a world of black fingers flying over the keys, pounding out the intoxication, sweat dripping from a tossing head, the free foot stomping out the beat. Strong fingers jerking up and down the neck of the guitar, chords mingling between and crowning the heavy rhythm of the piano. The trombone and sax court each other, filling with and contrasting to the wire snare dragged across and slapping the taut skin of the drum. Eyes half closed, rocking in rhythm, he dances, excited by, yet oblivious to, his fascinated oscillating partner. She responds, pulling the tight dress upward, unfettering muscular thighs, torquing gyrating hips to the east and breast to the west, strong white teeth glistening between full, excited, parted lips, head thrown back as rhythm captivates consciousness. Arcane Africa smiled and embraced her passionate children.

The music ended abruptly and the crowd left the dance floor sweating, embracing, applauding.

With reed instruments laid aside, the guitar player moved between the drums and the piano. Soft, mournful music of the Delta spread out from the combo. It penetrated the sultry air of the dance hall and brought the entire crowd to its feet, swaying to a familiar tempo. A young woman stood next to the piano, eyes closed, waiting for the proper chord. It was the song I had hoped for. I held out my hand and led Sarah to the floor. She leaned against me, right arm around my waist, left hand against my shoulder blade. Swaying against and moving across my pelvis, she pulled me into the sexuality of the music, the dance, the undulating, closely packed crowd. The woman began to sing the popular traditional blues:

> Oh, my easy rider
> See what you done done.
> Lawd, Lawd, Lawd,
> Easy rider,
> See what you done done.
> You made me love you
> An' now your gal has come.

Eyes closed, the world consists of the lamenting, whining soprano, the sweating cheek, the braless youthful breast, the oscillating thighs partially astraddle my leg. Music more felt than heard drifted out of earshot. The crowd, hypnotized by their motions, continued to dance a few moments without the music. There was no applause. Still entwined, the couples made it to the tables and the cool drinks. A few more numbers and the combo took their break. The dancing and partying intensified with the sweltering heat of the hall.

The minute hand moved to ten o'clock.

"Ten o'clock, sweetheart."

"We can stay a little."

"I promised your ma."

She rose, presented a sweaty cheek to Brad and Bunk, and we started the short walk home.

"When will I see you again?"

"I don't know. We have to finish the maneuvers, then I guess we'll go overseas."

"Guess you'd never want to come back to a place like Many."

"I'd like to see you again. We'll still be somewhere around here for another month."

"I'm not hard to find. I'm at home or at the school."

"When do you graduate?"

She laughed the laugh of an adult when a child says something silly.

"I been through school. I teach the little ones."

I was taken aback. Sixteen, through school, and teaching! Jesus Christ, I knew the South was different and poor; I didn't know it was this poor.

Her mother opened the door a crack, acknowledging that we were back in time. We sat on the porch talking about the South until her mother politely offered to make me a pallet on the floor. I declined and, pulling Sarah to the side of the house, kissed her and, pulling her tight against me, told her I'd be back soon.

I got back to the truck stop just in time to catch the 11:00 PM convoy to the bivouac. Excited, wanting her terribly, afraid of leaving her with a baby in this god-awful poverty, I lay awake a long time under the mosquito netting, listening to the buzzing of insects.

I tried to understand this grinding poverty and the inability of the South to combat it. I had seen enough evidence that the Southern white farmers and workers were not any different from people anywhere else. Somehow so many of them had bought the idea that the road out of their poverty lay in pushing the blacks farther down into it. Worst yet, those who didn't believe that seemed helpless to change it. I knew one thing for certain: the blacks had to defend themselves until the whites learned better. Each attack and each defense drove these natural allies further and further apart, so they would never be able to learn.

Bunk and Brad stumbled in and flopped fully clothed on their blankets. Their drunk snores overwhelmed the sounds of crickets and mosquitoes. I rolled over into a fitful sleep.

—1994

Duke Ellington

Americans have always listened to music, when they aren't busy making it. This is part of our culture. For some, hearing "live" music is a luxury. For others it's part of the daily diet. Everything depends on how the budget stacks up against the price of admission to Carnegie Hall or the cover charge at nightclubs giving out with the "hot" brand of music.

Well, when the war came along, a few years back, people wondered whether music was going to be one of the casualties. Would it have to take a back seat for a while? Would we have to sacrifice it at a time when bombs and bullets had an A-1 priority over Boogie-Woogie and Bach? I think these last few years have proved that music doesn't kick up its heels and call it quits under crisis. Music is staying by popular request of the fighting men and the folks they left behind. And that goes for all music.

Ours is a country of two major types of music—the concert hall variety and what goes under the general heading of "jazz." It wouldn't be right to draw too thick a line between them because nowadays we are beginning to see "jazz" moving into the Concert Hall—in the scores played by symphony orchestras, and the other way around. My own Carnegie Hall concert, recently, is an example of what I mean.

Swing is my beat. Not jazz in the popular sense of the word, which usually means a chatty combination of instruments knocking out a tune. Swing, as I like to make it and play it, is an expression of sentiment and ideas—modern ideas. It's the kind of music that catches the rhythm of the way people feel and live today. It's American music because it grew out of our folk music, picking up a little from every section of the country as it traveled from New Orleans to Chicago to Kansas City to New York.

Swing came along as a new brand of jazz. It wasn't the "hot" type, the "sweet" style and the so-called popular music that the boy friend was singing to his girl on the park bench. At the start, people said it was a fad and scheduled for a short life—if a happy one. But it fooled them, as any real style will. It didn't date but instead has become a brand of music in which people are creating as hardily as pioneers in any new field.

What swings? Rhythm. A few notes, a chord combination, a simple musical phrase is developed into a series of rhythm patterns which creates a form that is listened to as seriously as a concert hall piece. Part of the reason is that this rhythm hits home to the people who hear it. It speaks their language and tells their story. It's the musician and his audience talking things over.

When I get an idea, I write the melody and often work out the arrangement, too. But sometimes the band and I collaborate on the arrangement. I write the melody down and play it at rehearsal. Then the boys will start making suggestions in a "free-for-all." One of them might get up and demonstrate his idea of what a measure should be like. Then another one of the boys will pick it up and maybe fix it a little. Sometimes we'll argue back and forth with our instruments, each one playing a couple of bars his own way.

Still other times I might just sit down at the piano and start composing a little melody, telling a story about it at the same time to give the
mood of the piece. I'll play eight bars, talk a bit, then play another eight
and soon the melody is finished. Then the boys go to work on it, improvising, adding a phrase here and there. We don't write like this very often
and when we do it's usually three o'clock in the morning when we've
finished a date.

But this is a little off the point. What I am trying to get across is that
music for me is a language. It expresses more than just sound. I often
think of tones as colors or memories, and all that helps in composing.

I said that swing is my beat. But because of all the confusion about
what swing is and isn't, I prefer to say that I am carrying on the tradition
of American folk music, particularly the folk music of my people. In my
tone poem "Black, Brown, and Beige" I tried to parallel the history of
the Negro in my music. My opera, "Boola," which is still unproduced,
tells the story of the Negro in America.

What's the future of swing?

It has been said that it has no future because it's too narrow in its
forms. I don't think that's right. Swing at its best is "free" within the form
itself. Take, for example, the lyrical "Stardust" and then take the more recent "Your Socks Don't Match." The two are completely opposite in sentiment, mood, and character, but they are both a product of swing.

A number of composers have been experimenting with these new musical ideas on a large scale. I spoke of my own tone poem and opera.
Then there's the work of Gershwin, which is not the same but moves in
the same general direction. There are others, too, and I am convinced
that still others will come along and their music will stick. For swing is a
product of its time. Whether it's a jam session brand which is its purest
state, or music written down on paper for a market, it's alive, creative,
and that's what gives it its future.

—1944

Charles "Cow Cow" Davenport

The word *Boogie* was derived from our old grandmothers' use of the word
meaning the devil. When the kids broke the rules in any way such as
fighting, running away, or disobeying ... we were told that the "Boogie
man" was going to get us. The blues was considered bad music as it usually alluded to love affairs. In those days, only the lowest class of people

in the towns, or people who were known to be without self-respect, would dare to be heard singing the blues.

So whenever I'd get a chance I would slip away from my home to practice on some neighbor's piano and tried to play a blue tune, at the same time thinking of what my parents would think if they could hear me, and what they would say to me. I called my music "Boogie" music.

In 1917, before the First World War, there were several dances in vogue, namely: "walkin' the dog," "jazz dance," and "ballin' the jack," that were used in dance halls; other dances resembling the rhumba or "scraunch," etc., which were done in the honkey-tonks, joints where nice people did not go. I gave the name of "Boogie-Woogie."

When I began playing the "Cow Cow Blues," I was trying to imitate a train, and originally called them the "Railroad Blues." I was trying to get in a part where the switchman (with many of whom I had a personal acquaintance) boarded the train from the cow-catcher or the front of the train. The word *cow* somehow stuck with me and subconsciously, in a theater. I once ended my song with "Nobody here can do what Papa Cow Cow can do." The audience immediately picked up the song and those who liked the number were anxious to get acquainted with me. After the show they would walk up addressing me as "Papa Cow Cow" and from then on I have been called by such a moniker.

—1940s

Milt Hinton

Cab [Calloway] had a big following among both black and white people. He made some records, of course, but his real reputation came from the coast-to-coast radio broadcasts we'd do a couple of nights a week from the Cotton Club. Later, we had another radio show called "Cab Calloway's Quizzicale." I was a regular member of the cast, but I didn't have a name. I had a number—"62 Jones." Tyree [Glenn] and Eddie Morton, the dancer, were also on the show. It was basically a musical quiz program where listeners called in and tried to win prizes. We'd do jokes and other kinds of dialogue, so there was a regular script and lines to read, the same as other radio shows in those days. With all that exposure, wherever we played, any place in the country, people would come out just to see what Cab looked like.

I don't think we ever played for an all-black audience. We'd work plenty of segregated theaters where blacks had to sit up in the balcony. We'd also play a lot of all-white dances, but I can remember others where they'd allow whites and blacks in, then divide the room in half. There'd be a rope from the center of the bandstand down the middle of the dance floor. Whites danced on one side, blacks on the other. Many times the band would end up on the white side of the room. It was as dumb as that.

I remember once at a dance in Jacksonville, they roped off an aisle so we could go to the bathroom at intermission. When the break came, we started walking towards the colored men's room and some of the white guys in the audience stood on each side of the aisle and leaned across the ropes trying to hit us. It was like a nightmare parade and we were the star attraction.

We also played some strange places in Texas. I can recall a one-nighter in a Longview roadhouse which was beyond belief.

Apparently, for generations the people in this town had been small-time farmers—working the land and raising a few cows. They'd always had a lot of land, but it was barren and worthless. In fact, it was so bad that for years cattle had gotten sick grazing on some of the ranges.

Everything suddenly changed when it was discovered that the town was sitting in the middle of a very large oil field. In some places, oil was even found oozing out at ground level, which is the reason cattle got sick so often.

Soon these people had leased their land to a few big oil companies. The money started flowing in and the town went wild. Northern sharpies found out about the place quickly and came in selling Palm Beach suits for five hundred dollars and gold watches for much more. These people would buy whatever they were told rich people had in Houston or Dallas or up north.

That's how we came to play there. Some of the town people had been told about the great black bands from New York and they decided they had to have one play for them. Unfortunately we got the job.

Our train pulled into town late one afternoon. Before we left the Pullman we put on fresh uniforms. Then a dozen private cars picked us up and drove us about thirty miles out of town to a big wooden roadhouse. I remember by the time we arrived it was pitch black, except for the lights in the place. It really was the middle of nowhere.

Inside, the roadhouse was rustic. The stage was shaky and much too small—maybe about the right size for four or five guys. Somehow our valets managed to set up our equipment and we squeezed onto the bandstand.

We began playing and soon the place was filled with local people. Booze was everywhere and it didn't take long before most people were drunk. The more they drank, the louder they got and the more they seemed to want to fight.

Benny Payne was playing piano and I was standing right next to him. At some point during the evening, while we were in the middle of a number, a couple looking very loaded walked over to the piano. They watched Benny for a while and then the girl started talking to him. He ignored her, knowing what could happen if he let a conversation begin. But she wouldn't give up and she offered Benny a drink. He pretended not to hear but after she asked two or three times he told her, "No, thank you," in a very polite way.

Hearing that, she yelled, "You mean you ain't gonna take a drink that's offered you, boy?"

Benny knew immediately he had to take the drink, regardless of the risks. He took the glass from her and finished it in one gulp. But just as soon as he put it down on the piano, the guy with her leaned over close to Benny and told him, "Nigger, you can't be takin' whiskey from my girl."

I was so terrified I could barely move my fingers and I quickly looked around the room for an escape route. But it wasn't necessary—at least at that moment. Seconds later, a fight broke out between a few local guys on the other side of the room and it caught this guy's attention. He backed away from Benny, grabbed his girl's hand, and rushed over to check it out.

We kept playing. I felt relieved, but it didn't last long. A couple of minutes later I heard a commotion on the side of the stage and when I was able to get a clear view, I couldn't believe my eyes. Our road manager, Mr. Wright, a white man from Texas, was standing next to Cab shooing off five or six local guys. They were pushing and pulling, trying to hit Cab, and I could hear them shouting things like, "I'll give two hundred to hit the nigger." I didn't understand it then, but later I learned they had a town law about a fine you'd pay for assaulting blacks. That's what the two hundred dollars was about.

We tried to keep playing, but suddenly all hell broke loose. I couldn't believe the brawling. The place looked like one of those barroom scenes in an old Western movie—guys hitting each other with bottles, chairs, anything they could get hold of and swing.

We grabbed our instruments and rushed off the little stage, but there was no place to go. The windows were too small to climb through and with all the fighting, we couldn't make it across the room to the door. So we huddled together against the wall next to the stage.

A few seconds later, the manager of the place came over and shouted, "I'll try and save you niggers, but this is gettin' outta hand." He pulled up a trap door a few feet away from us and we went down a ladder, one by one, carrying our instruments into a dirt cellar.

We must've spent a couple of hours down there listening to the stomping and the glass breaking and feeling the vibrations from the room above us. It felt like an eternity. Everyone was scared to death.

Then it all got quiet and about a half hour later the manager opened the trap door and told us it was all over.

Cars were waiting for us outside. We drove back to the station, got back on our Pullman, and just as it started to get light, we pulled out of Longview.

—1988

Duke Ellington

I have already said that it is my firm belief that what is still known as "jazz" is going to play a considerable part in the serious music of the future. I am proud of that part my race is playing in the artistic life of the world. Paul Robeson, Roland Hayes, your own [Samuel] Coleridge-Taylor, are names already high in the lists of serious music; that from the welter of negro dance musicians now before the public will come something lasting and noble I am convinced.

The music of my race is something more than the "American idiom." It is the result of our transplantation to American soil, and was our reaction in the plantation days to the tyranny we endured. What we could not say openly we expressed in music, and what we know as "jazz" is something more than just dance music. When we dance it is not a mere diversion or social accomplishment. It expresses our personality, and, right down in us, our souls react to the elemental but eternal rhythm, and the dance is timeless ...

The characteristic melancholy music of my race has been forged from the very white heat of our sorrows and from our gropings after something tangible in the primitiveness of our lives in the early days of our American occupation.

—1931

Larry Neal

"Fate's being kind to me ... Fate doesn't want me to be too famous too young."

These were the words of Duke Ellington when he learned that the Pulitzer Prize advisory board had turned down the music jury's citation of Ellington for his achievements in modern music over a long period. The jury had in mind the sum total of Duke Ellington's work. We will return to this point.

The question is: How should we feel about this? Should we rather feel the Duke was cheated out of a well-deserved award; what the Pulitzer is—which has been long overdue? The manner in which this question is answered is ultimately related to how we see ourselves vis-à-vis the dominant society—white America. Should we really be concerned about recognition from a society that oppresses us, exploits us; and which will even use its "acceptance" of us as another instrument of enslavement? This time the enslavement is more psychological than physical.

This kind of enslavement furthers the idea of a liberal America, abundantly aware of the creative gifts of the black man; it further reinforces our dependency on white America.

All of this is not to say that Duke or anybody else receiving these awards should refuse them. (That wouldn't be a bad idea, though.) I am proposing that what we understand is the necessity of establishing our own norms, our own values; and if there must be standards, let them be our own. Recognition of Duke Ellington's genius lies not with the white society that has exploited him and his fellow musicians. It lies with us, the black public, black musicians and artists. Essentially, recognition of that sort, from a society that hates us and has no real way of evaluating our artistic accomplishments, is the meanest kind of intrusion upon the territory of black people.

We dig you, Duke. We play your music, sing your songs, and feel their relationship to our everyday life and needs. These are the words that must flow out of an organized body of black musicians or some black institutions. They are the words of brothers, and they act to reaffirm group consciousness and group obligation. They act to establish, once and for all, that we are collectively aware of our own artistic talents and that recognition from white America is simply incidental to recognition from black America.

Recognition from the dominant white society should not be the primary aim of the black artist. He must decide that his art belongs primarily to his own people. This is not to deny that there are some "universal" factors at work; but we are living in a specific place, at a specific time, and are a specific set of people with a specific historical development. In the confusion of today's struggle for human survival, the black artist cannot afford vagueness about himself and his people who need him.

Duke's approach to music has always been rooted in the materials found naturally among black people. His work stands as a monumental achievement in precision and form. Duke has never ceased to be an innovator. And we must feel that the sum total of his work belongs to us; it is we who must say what it is; it is we who must give the awards.

—1969

Duke Ellington

The Pulitzer Prize music committee recommend me for a special award in 1965. When the full Pulitzer committee turned down their recommendation, Winthrop Sargeant and Ronald Eyer resigned.

Since I am not too chronically masochistic, I found no pleasure in all the suffering that was being endured. I realized that it could have been most distressing and distracting as I tried to qualify my first reaction: "Fate is being very kind to me; Fate doesn't want me to be too famous too young."

Let's say it had happened. I would have been famous, then rich, then fat and stagnant. And then? What do you do with your beautiful, young, freckled mind? How, when, and where do you get your music supplement, the deadline that drives you to complete the composition, the necessity to hear the music instead of sitting around publishing your laurels, counting your money, and waiting for the brainwashers to decide what rinse or tint is the thing this season in your tonal climate?

—1973

From The Book of Negro Folklore

The simplest words in Jive are those relating to things—inanimate objects, the furniture in a room, objects which can be moved, sold, bought, exchanged, all concrete and tangible objects.

Alarm Clock—Chimer
Body—Frame
Corner—Three pointer
Door—Slammer
Elderly Man—Poppa Stoppa
Feet—Groundpads
Gun—Bow-wow
Hands—Grabbers
Jail—House of Many Slammers
Liquor—Lush, juice
Moon—Pumpkin
Nose—Sniffer
Overcoat—Benny or Bear

Verbal Names

These are words that move and "jump," the Jive verbs that give the language its appeal and spontaneity, that make Jive flexible.

Here we are dealing with the words which describe bodily motion, the movement of arms, legs, hands, and feet. They also denote intangible action having to do with thought, comprehension, a very important phase of Jive.

We start off by naming simple acts. [Previously] we discussed the name of things, we had you going home: and, instead of saying, "I am going home," you said, "I'm going to my pile of stone." "Am going" is a perfectly legitimate expression in English denoting an intention and describing an act already taking place. In Jive you would substitute the words *cop* and *trill* in place of "am going," and your statement would be: "I'm copping my trill for my pile of stone." Simple, isn't it? Even your great-aunt Hannah could understand that, couldn't she?

There are relatively few Jive verbs, since Jive is primarily a language consisting of descriptive adjectives rather than being replete with verbs denoting action. However, the few Jive verbs to balance the enormous number of nouns, or names of things, are thrillingly competent, graphic, and commanding. Two in particular are worthy of our attention. The verbs *knock* and *lay* are the basis of Jive. *Knock* in particular is found all through the process of a Jive conversation. It is one of the key words.

"Knock a nod," says the Jiver. He means going to sleep. "Knock a scoff," he says. He means, eat a meal. "Knock a broom" is found to mean a quick walk or brisk trot away from something. "Knock me down to

her" means to introduce me to a young lady; "knock me a riff" in musical parlance means for a musician to play a musical break in a certain
manner. "Knock a jug" means to buy a drink.

The verb *lay* is another vitally important verb in the Jiver's vocabulary.
It also denotes action. For example: "Lay some of that cash on me," says
a Jiver. His statement means literally what it says. But if he says, "He was
really laying it," he means someone was doing something out of the ordinary, as in a stage performance or musical program, or a well-dressed
person entering a room and suddenly becoming the object of all eyes.

Here are some other important verbs:

Blow—To leave, move, run away
Cop—To take, receive, understand, do
Dig—To understand, take, see, conceive, perceive, think, hand over
Drag—Humiliate, upset, disillusion
Stash—To lay away, hide, put down, stand, a place
Take a powder—Leave, disappear

Jive Adjectives, or Words Signifying Quality
Before the names of things, or objects, as in standard English we need to
know a special state or condition regarding them in order to get a clear
mental picture in our minds. For example, a *blue* sky, a *soft* chair, the *hot*
sun, etc. The language of Jive has plenty of such adjectives, more of
which are constantly being added every day. The following list may prove
helpful:

Anxious—Wonderful, excellent
Fine—All right, okay, excellent
Frantic—Great, wonderful
Groovy—To one's liking, sensational, outstanding, splendid
Mad—Fine, capable, able, talented
Mellow—State of delight, beautiful, great, wonderful
Righteous—Pleasing to the senses, glorious, pretty, beautiful, mighty
Solid—Very fine, okay, great, terrific

Jive Phrases, Simile and Hyperbole
As in standard English, Jive is flexible and infinitely capable of expressing
phrases or rare harmonic beauty and rhythmical force. The language of
the hepsters is constantly acquiring new descriptive phrases, narrative and

explanatory in content, which constitute an integral and necessary part of one's equipment for gaining proficiency in talking and writing Jive. Here are a few, some of which are self-explanatory, and others which are translated into English in italics:

Fine as wine
Mellow as a cello
Like the bear, nowhere
Playing the dozens with uncle's cousins—*doing things wrong*
I'm like the chicken, I ain't stickin'—*broke*
Dig what I'm laying down?—*understand what I'm saying?*
I'm chipper as the China Clipper and in the mood to play—
flying high and personally feeling fine
Swimps and wice—*shrimps and rice*
Snap a snapper—*light a match*
Like the farmer and the 'tater, plant you now and dig you later—
I must go, but I'll remember you.

Jive Rhyming and Meter
The language of Jive presents an unusual opportunity for experimentation in rhymes; in fact, a lot of it is built on rhymes, which at first hearing might be considered trite and beneath notice. However, Jive rhymes and couplets are fascinating and comparatively easy to fashion. As to meter, it is desirable that the syllables form a correct measure, but this is not essential. All that is necessary is that the end words rhyme; they do not necessarily need to make sense. Here are some examples:

Collars a broom with a solid zoom—*left in a hurry*
No lie, frog eye
What's your duty, Tutti-Frutti?
Joe the Jiver, the Stranded Pearl-Diver
Had some whiskey, feel kind o' frisky
Swing and sweat with Charley Barnet—*to dance to Barnet's music*
Are you going to the function at Tuxedo Junction?—*Tuxedo Junctions are places, dancehalls, candy-stores, etc., where hepsters gather.*
My name is Billie, have you seen Willie?—*used as a greeting or salutation among accomplished hepcats*
Ain't it a pity, you're from Atlantic City?—*salutation*
I can't frolic, I got the colic—*I drank too much.*

—1958

Malcolm X

From Small's I taxied over to the Apollo Theater. (I remember so well that Jay McShann's band was playing, because his vocalist was later my close friend, Walter Brown, the one who used to sing "Hooty Hooty Blues.") From there, on the other side of 125th Street, at Seventh Avenue, I saw the big, tall, gray Theresa Hotel. It was the finest in New York City where Negroes could then stay. (The Theresa is now best known as the place where Fidel Castro went during his U.N. visit, and achieved a psychological coup over the U.S. State Department when it confined him to Manhattan, never dreaming that he'd stay uptown in Harlem and make such an impression among the Negroes.)

The Braddock Hotel was just up 126th Street, near the Apollo's backstage entrance. I knew its bar was famous as a Negro celebrity hang-out. I walked in and saw, along that jam-packed bar, such famous stars as Dizzy Gillespie, Billy Eckstine, Billie Holiday, Ella Fitzgerald, and Dinah Washington.

As Dinah Washington was leaving with some friends, I overheard someone say she was on her way to the Savoy Ballroom where Lionel Hampton was appearing that night—she was then Hamp's vocalist. The ballroom made the Roseland in Boston look small and shabby by comparison. And the lindy-hopping there matched the size and elegance of the place. Hampton's hard-driving outfit kept a red-hot pace with his greats such as Arnett Cobb, Illinois Jacquet, Dexter Gordon, Alvin Hayse, Joe Newman, and George Jenkins. I went a couple of rounds on the floor with girls from the sidelines.

Probably a third of the sideline booths were filled with white people, mostly just watching the Negroes dance, but some of them danced together, and, as in Boston, a few white women were with Negroes. The people kept shouting for Hamp's "Flyin' Home," and finally he did it. I could believe the story I'd heard in Boston about this number—that once in the Apollo, Hamp's "Flyin' Home" had made some reefer-smoking Negro in the second balcony believe he could fly, so he tried—and jumped—and broke his leg, an event later immortalized in song when Earl Hines wrote a hit tune called "Second Balcony Jump." I had never seen such fever-heat dancing. After a couple of slow numbers cooled the place off, they brought on Dinah Washington. When she did her "Salty Papa Blues," those people just about tore the Savoy roof off. (Poor Dinah's funeral was held not long ago in Chicago. I read that over twenty thousand people viewed her body, and I should have been there myself. Poor Dinah! We became great friends, back in those days.)

But this night of my first visit was Kitchen Mechanics' Night at the Savoy, the traditional Thursday night off for domestics. I'd say there were twice as many women as men in there, not only kitchen workers and maids, but also war wives and defense-worker women, lonely and looking. Out in the street, when I left the ballroom, I heard a prostitute cursing bitterly that the professionals couldn't do any business because of the amateurs.

Up and down along and between Lenox and Seventh and Eighth Avenues, Harlem was like some technicolor bazaar. Hundreds of Negro soldiers and sailors, gawking and young like me, passed by. Harlem by now was officially off limits to white servicemen. There had already been some muggings and robberies, and several white servicemen had even been found murdered. The police were also trying to discourage white civilians from coming uptown, but those who wanted to still did. Every man without a woman on his arm was being "worked" by the prostitutes. "Baby, wanna have some fun?" The pimps would sidle up close, stage-whispering, "All kinds of women, Jack—want a white woman?" And the hustlers were merchandising: "Hundred-dollar ring, man, diamond; ninety-dollar watch, too—look at 'em. Take 'em both for twenty-five."

—1964

Dicky Wells

So I think the real difference between the Basie band and most others was in the way they broke down arrangements the way they wanted them. Sometimes, Benny Carter's bands sounded almost too perfect. That's the funny thing about jazz. You may rehearse until you're hitting everything on the head, and here comes a band like the Savoy Sultans, raggedy, fuzzy sounding, and they upset everything. "What am I doing here?" you wonder. But that's the way it is. That's jazz. If you get too clean, too precise, you don't swing sometimes, and the fun goes out of the music. Like Fletcher's arrangements—they'd make you feel bright inside. You were having fun just riding along. You could almost compare it to a lot of kids playing in the mud, having a big time. When the mother calls one to wash his hands, he gets clean, but he has to stand and just look while the others are having a ball. *He's too clean, and he can't go back.* Same way when you clean up on that horn and the arrangements are too clean: You get on another level. You're looking down on those guys, but they're all having a good, free-going time.

—————

One of the things that keeps tension down in a band is a drummer who plays for the band and for the soloists, rather than for himself. Basie's rhythm section used to be so light and so strong that it was a real inspiration. My idea of a rhythm section is one you feel or sense, one that doesn't disturb you. In the forties, some of the drummers got so technical they spoiled everything. Before he died, Shadow Wilson told me that before he went with Basie he had one way of playing in mind—the latest thing, that was it! Then he got hungry and found out, and began playing with a beat to satisfy the band. He was very versatile and a good drummer, and he played for the musicians on the order of Big Sid. At its best, the Basie rhythm section was nothing less than a Cadillac with the force of a Mack truck. They more or less gave you a *push,* or a *ride,* and they played no favorites, whether you were an E-flat or B-flat soloist.

It was at the Lincoln that Pres got his little bell. If somebody missed a note, or you were a new guy and goofed, you'd hear this bell going— *Dingdong!* If Pres was blowing and goofed, somebody would reach over and ring his bell on him.

"Why, you————," he'd say when he finished.

Jo Jones had another way of saying the same thing. *Bing-bing-bing* he'd go on his cymbal rod. When you first joined, you would take it kind of rough, but later you'd be in stitches with the rest and take it as a joke. They'd ring the bell on Basie, too. And if Pres saw someone getting angry, he'd blow the first bar of "Runnin' Wild."

Harry Edison named himself "Sweets" because he was so rough, always kidding, hiding your hat, and things like that. Sweets, because it was the opposite of what he knew he was. He and Pres just about named everybody, and when Pres named anybody the name stuck.

Basie was "the Holy Main." That meant "tops" in the way you'd apply it to someone you greatly admired. Buck Clayton was "Cat Eye" and Snooky Young was "Rabbit." Ed Lewis was "Big D." George Matthews was "Truce," and Benny Morton was "Mr. Bones." After Benny left, I became "Mr. Bones," but before that I had been "Gas Belly" on account of my troublesome stomach. Freddie Green was "Pep." Walter Page was "Big 'Un" or "Horse." Jo Jones was "Samson." Buddy Tate was "Moon," and Herschel was "Tex." Rush was "Honey Bunny Boo" or "Little Jim."

Earle Warren was "Rev." and Eli Robinson was "Mr. Eli." Jimmy Powell
was "Neat," and Helen Humes "Homey." It was Pres who named Snod-
grass, the manager, "Lady Snar." Everybody had one of those names.

—1971

Leon Forrest

But this sense of personal artistic vision, as a public matter rather than
the reverse, was deep within me, growing up from my mother's interests
in, and intelligence about, the great Negro vocalists and jazz singers—
my parents had gone to high school with Nat King Cole, indeed he was
kind of sweet on my mother, or so I was told—and our apartment at
3704 South Parkway (now King Drive) swung out with the artistry of
the great story-tellers like Billie Holiday (mother's favorite) and Billy
Eckstine, Sarah Vaughan, and Ella Fitzgerald, as well as that of the great
white singers, who were in the great traditions, like Frank Sinatra, Peggy
Lee, and Anita O'Day.

I learned very early, then, that men "much more praise whichever song
comes newest to their ears" from these ethos-bearing, reinventive songsters of the soul. Ironically my father (who was an amateur lyricist) knew
more about what the instrumentalists were doing. And my mother, who
sent off several stories to magazines, but none were published, was close
to the story-telling vocalists. My parents made me aware that in jazz the
vocalist is always trying to get back to the purity of the instrument, and
the instrumentalist is always trying to get back to the purity of the vocalist, like Fitzgerald, Sarah Vaughan, and Lady Day.

—1988

Malcolm X

It was just about time for me to go and pick up Jean Parks, to go downtown to see Billie at the Onyx Club. So much was swirling in my head. I
thought about telephoning her and calling it off, making some excuse.
But I knew that running now was the worst thing I could do. So I went
on and picked up Jean at her place. We took a taxi on down to Fifty-
second Street. BILLIE HOLIDAY and those big photo blow-ups of her
were under the lights outside. Inside, the tables were jammed against the
wall, tables about big enough to get two drinks and four elbows on; the
Onyx was one of those very little places.

Billie, at the microphone, had just finished a number when she saw Jean and me. Her white gown glittered under the spotlight, her face had that coppery, Indianish look, and her hair was in that trademark pony-tail. For her next number she did the one she knew I always liked so: "You Don't Know What Love Is"—"until you face each dawn with sleepless eyes ... until you've lost a love you hate to lose—"

When her set was done, Billie came over to our table. She and Jean, who hadn't seen each other in a long time, hugged each other. Billie sensed something wrong with me. She knew that I was always high, but she knew me well enough to see that something else was wrong, and asked in her customary profane language what was the matter with me. And in my own foul vocabulary of those days, I pretended to be without a care, so she let it drop.

We had a picture taken by the club photographer that night. The three of us were sitting close together. That was the last time I ever saw Lady Day. She's dead; dope and heartbreak stopped that heart as big as a barn and that sound and style that no one successfully copies. Lady Day sang with the *soul* of Negroes from the centuries of sorrow and oppression. What a shame that proud, fine, black woman never lived where the true greatness of the black race was appreciated!

—1964

Billie Holiday

For my money Lester was the world's grates. I loved his music, and some of my favorite recordings are the ones with Lester's pretty solos.

I remember how the late Herschel Evans used to hate me. Whenever Basie had an arranger work out some thing for me, I'd tell him I wanted Lester to solo behind me. That always made Herschel salty. It wasn't that I didn't love his playing. It was just that I like Lester's more.

Lester sings with his horn; you listen to him and can almost hear the words. People think he's so cocky and secure, but you can hurt his feelings in two seconds. I know, because I found out once that I had. We've been hungry together, and I'll always love him and his horn.

I often think about how we used to record in those days. We'd get off a bus after a five-hundred-mile trip, go into the studio with no music, nothing to eat but coffee and sandwiches. Me and Lester would drink what we called top and bottom, half gin and half port wine.

I'd say, "What'll we do, two-bar or four-bar intro?"

Somebody'd say make it four and a chorus—one, one and half.

Then I'd say, "You play behind me the first eight, Lester," and then Harry Edison would come in or Buck Clayton and take the next eight bars. "Jo, you just brush and don't hit the cymbals too much."

Now with all their damn preparation, complicated arrangements, you've got to kiss everybody's behind to get ten minutes to do eight sides in.

When I did "Night and Day" I had never seen that song before in my life. I don't read music, either. I just walked in, Teddy Wilson played it for me, and I did it.

With artists like Lester, Don Byas, Benny Carter, and Coleman Hawkins, something was always happening. No amount of preparation today is any match for them.

In the old days, if we were one side short on a date, someone would say, "Try the blues in A-flat," and tell me, "Go as far as you can, honey." I'd stand up there and make up my words as I went along.

Nowadays you have all this talk and bull and nothing's happening. On a recent date I tried to do it like the old days. I'd never seen the band or the arrangements, and I didn't know the songs they had picked for me, and they wanted me to do eight sides in three hours. We were doing all standards but nobody could read the stuff; the drummer did nothing but sit there grinning; the music had wrong chords; everybody was squawking. We pushed out about nine sides like they wanted. But not a damn one of them was any good.

—1956

Leon Forrest

NEVER-ENDING DREAM OF LADY DAY

I have come to this theatre seeking oracle-like advice from the high priestess. She is standing before the microphone, on a small stage, which is darkened, except for the penetrating spotlight upon her. The high priestess is adorned in her slightly opened secular robe of white mink ermine. Her face is beautifully made up; there is a gardenia in her hair which she wears in an upsweep. She is wearing her high-heel white slippers. She looks exquisite. Not like the directoress of a sanctuary choir either.

But a shift in her stance reveals a little too much, and I suddenly realize that beneath the fur Billie Holiday is gownless, and perhaps even naked. I feel an immediate emptiness in the pit of my soul. I want to rush to her to protect this Lady. Our Lady of Sorrows? Where is your satin gown, Miss Holiday? What do I hunger for? To be her protector? Lover? Father? Brother? Priest? Billie was always so vulnerable, I tell myself. What is that John Donne said: "There is no exquisite genius without some strangeness in the proportion."

Now she is clearing her throat, slowly opening that sensual mouth of hers, but is it to introduce one of her classical offerings, or to sing, in a stripped-down tongue? I don't see any of her side men providing artistic succor for Lady Day. Billie Holiday singing a capella? Oh no. Then I hear a husky-voiced Holiday somewhere between singing, speaking, and sassying, now revealing:

"Ladies and gentlemen, my text for this twilight is the nothingness of nowhereness ..." And then Lady Day launches into: "Please don't talk about me when I'm gone ... though our friendship ceases from now on. And if you can't say anything real nice, just don't talk at all, that's my advice. We parting you go your way, I'll go mine. It's best that we do. Here's a kiss, I hope this brings lots of luck to you. Makes no difference how I carry on ... Please don't talk about me when I'm gone." Which, of course, is the last thing that any Lady wants in the wake of a breakup to be "disremembered." But the cockiness is there. The Jauntiness. The upbeat bounce of rebounding is there. Some of the naughty satirical spirit of slyness, akin to the lady who insisted she had never borrowed her neighbor's pots and had, in any case, already returned them.

—1993

Lester Young

[Lester] YOUNG: Um hm. I just can't take that bull*shit*, you dig, it's all bull*shit*. And they want everybody who is a Negro to be a Uncle Tom or Uncle Remus or Uncle Sam, and I can't make it.

[Francois] POSTIF: Not here, you know, not in France.

YOUNG: Shhi-i-t! Are you kidding? I've been here two weeks, I've been pickin' up on that!

POSTIF: [*Pause.*] [I] don't think so.

YOUNG: No? Well, I won't tell you what I know what jumped off.

POSTIF: Yeah.

YOUNG: Right here. Seeing is believing, and hearin' is a bitch—that's a sound. Right here in Gay Paree. Maybe it wouldn't happen to you, you dig—you're not a colored person like I am, you dig? They'll take advantage of me. But all I can do is tell you what happened. And I'm not gonna tell you that part of it—but it did happen. By somebody you wouldn't believe, too—great person. But it's the same way all over, you dig? It's fight for your life, that's all. Until death do we part, you got it made. But it's the same way ...

POSTIF: Who was the tenor player who made an influence on you?

YOUNG: Oh ... hmm ... he died. Frankie Trumbauer. I had to make a decision between Frankie Trumbauer and—what's the name—Tommy Dorsey, Jimmy, Jimmy Dorsey?

POSTIF: Jimmy Dorsey.

YOUNG: You dig? I wasn't sure which way I wanted to go, you dig? And I had these motherfucking records, and I'd play one of Jimmy's, I'd play one of Trumbauer's, and all that shit. I don't know nothin' about Hawk then, you dig? But I can see the only people that was telling stories that *I* liked to hear were them. So I'd play one of his, one of them, you dig? So I had both of 'em made, you dig?

POSTIF: But do you think your sound is close to the Trumbauer sound?

YOUNG: Yes. . . .

POSTIF: So, it's Trumbauer?

YOUNG: That was my man. I had to pick from two, right?

POSTIF: Did you listen to him on, you know, direct?

YOUNG: Yes. Did you ever hear him play "Singin' the Blues" [a 1927 recording]?

POSTIF: Yeah, nice record.

YOUNG: That tricked me right there, that's where I went.

POSTIF: Oh, by the way, what is your opinion about the blues?

YOUNG: Blues? Great big eyes. Because if you play with a new band, like I have, you know, working around, if they don't know no blues, they can't play shit ... everybody plays the blues, and *have* 'em too! ...

POSTIF: Are you a very easy composer? For example, the ideas, you know, go right down through the sheet of paper?

YOUNG: No, I'll tell you about that, I see what you're saying. You see, when I was coming up playing in the [family] band, I wasn't reading music, I was bullshitting—but I was in the band. And my father got me an alto out of a pawn shop, and I just picked the motherfucker up and just started playing it. And that's the way that went. So he was a musician, he played all the instruments [*laughs*], and all this shit! And my sister, see, she was playing, and I'd get close to her and pick up on the parts, you know? Playing marches, and them shit like that. And finally my father said one day, he say: "Kansas, play your part." I knew goddamn well I'd lose my ass; he knew I wasn't reading. "Play *your* part, Kansas." [*Singing*] "Hup, ta ta lup, da da la da la da lup, boom." He said [to the next person], "Now play *your* part—go!" Say, "Now Lester, play *your* part." I couldn't read a motherfuckin' note, not a goddamn note. He says, "Get up"—you know, he don't curse like I do—"get up and get your fuckin' ass and work you some scales. Get out!" Dig?

The rest of them went rehearsing. Now you know my heart was broke, you dig? I went and cried, and give up my little teardrops and shit, I said, "Well, I'll come back and catch these motherfuckers if that's the way they *want* it." Like that, you know? So I went away and learned how to read the music, *still* by myself, y'dig, and I came back in the band, played this music and shit, and all the time I was copyin' on the records also with the music, so I could fuck these motherfuckers *completely* up. So I went in the band, and they threw the goddamn marches out, and I read the music and shit, and everything was great. But what was in *my* heart, why all the motherfuckers [who] laughed when they put me out, when I *couldn't* read, [and] come up and say, "Won't you show me how this goes? You play like that?" Yeah, sure, I'll show you shit, you rusty motherfucker! So that's the way that went down.... Now, I made that score: I don't like to read music, I don't like to read—

POSTIF: Just play soul?

YOUNG: There you are.

POSTIF: Yeah.

YOUNG: I got a man in New York now [reportedly Gil Evans] writin' some music for me. When I get back, I got bass violin, two cellos and a viola, and a French horn, see what I mean? And the three rhythm, you know what goes with that.

POSTIF: But you know, Pres, your compositions are very easy swing.

YOUNG: Um hm. I'm gonna take my time and gonna just try this, if it don't come out right, fuck it! I'll say no, you know. But this is my first time, and I always wanted to do that. Norman Granz never did let *me* make a record with no strings, you know. Yardbird made millions of records with strings and things....

YOUNG: Well, it's so rough out here, you know? Everybody's so chicken shit, you know? I'm enjoying myself up here by myself, you know, to get away from all that shit and things, and I ain't got a quarter, you know!

[*Laughs.*] But I don't walk around sighing the blues and shit, 'cause my old lady will take care of me, so fuck it. [*Pause.*]

POSTIF: Billie gave you the name of "Pres"?

YOUNG: Um hm.

POSTIF: And you gave her the name of "Lady Day."

YOUNG: [At] her house, see, when I first came to New York in '34 [with Henderson], I used to live there for a long time. She was teaching me about the city, you know, which way to go, you know, where everything is shitty. [*Wistfully*] Yes, she's still my Lady Day.

POSTIF: Oh, yeah, she came here, you know, last fall.

YOUNG: Um hm. [*Long pause, then begins slowly.*] What people do, man, is so obvious, you know. If you want to speak like that, what the fuck, I give a fuck what you do. What he do—what he does—what nobody do—is nobody's business!

POSTIF: No, it's your own business.

YOUNG: So, why you gonna get into it and say: "Oh, he's a old ... Goddamn, I'd go crazy thinking about that shit. [*Laughs, then puts on a hoarse voice.*] "He's a old junky, he's a old funky, he's a old fucky," and all that shit. That's not nice, you know? Whatever they do, let them do that, and enjoy themselves—and get your kicks yourself. Why you envy them because they enjoyin' themselves? Fuck it, you dig? All I do is smoke some New Orleans cigarettes, that's perfect [*Shows arms to prove there are no needle marks.*] No sniff, no shit in my nose, nothing. Still, I drink, and I smoke, and that's all that— ...

But a lot of people think I'm this. [*Perhaps makes a gesture of shooting heroin.*] I don't like that. I resent that like a bitch. If I ever find the motherfucker, [I] would ... ivey-divey, shit, I'd go crazy! Don't put that weight on me; I know what I do.

POSTIF: Anyway, you know, it's your business, it's not my business. My business is the musical thing, you know.

YOUNG: Mine is too—all the way. [*Both laugh.*] *Real* musical thing! ...

YOUNG: But you take a person like me, I stay by myself. So how the fuck do you know anything about me? Nothing. A motherfucker walked up and told me, said, "Pres, I thought you were dead," and all that shit. [*Laughs.*] I'm probably more alive than he is! You dig, from that hearsay shit. Hearing aid. Don't go like that, man. Not with me.

POSTIF: Which way would you like better to play—with a trio, with a quartet, or just with a band?

YOUNG: No. Give me my little three rhythm and me—happiness. [...]

I'm looking for something right now—like a little puff that a lady pout on her pussy when she cleans up, and shit like that—soft eyes for me. I can't *stand* no loud shit. You dig? And the bitches come in a place in New York, and them trumpets be screaming and shit. The bitches put their fingers in their ears, you know? It's got to be sweetness, man, you dig? Sweetness can be funky, filthy, or anything, but which part do *you* want? The funkies about it or the sweet? [*Laughs.*] Shit, what am I talking about?

—1959

Yusef Lateef

WHERE IS LESTER?

I return as if in a dream of a great American musician to New York City and I am standing again on the corner of Broadway and Fifty-second Street. It is always early June and this area is the favorite of many musicians.

Sometimes it is raining on the corner and I'm standing inside the doorway of Birdland. There is always a bandstand in my dream, surrounded by people.

I'm inspired and eager to play my saxophone.

Sometimes I am on the bandstand and I can see myself playing and I can hear the sounds coming from my instrument.

Sometimes I play long intricate passages in triple time. I articulate these passages very carefully and sometimes I play slow melodic phrases just as carefully.

I'm always making sure that these sounds are coming from the core of my heart and soul.

I'm almost like a bodiless being because I'm hardly aware of my physical self.

I'm always alone on the bandstand and there's always an audience.

Sometimes I look both ways on the corner to see who is coming.

Sometimes Lester Young is coming and I just hold tight to my saxophone case and think about music. I have the notion that this is the right thing to do.

I believe I'm right.

Sometimes I don't look to see if Lester is coming. I know I'll just waste my concentration, so I let him pass.

Lester will come by again.

Sometimes I walk through Kansas City and everything is very spiritual because it's so early in the morning and Lester Young is here.

Whenever I walk through Kansas City, I stand and listen to Lester Young. The bandstand is always there and Lester is there alone. The audience is always there and the spiritual atmosphere is never broken because Lester is there.

Sometimes I don't go to Kansas City. I cross over 110th Street and go into Harlem and walk past Dewey Square and follow Seventh Avenue to Minton's Playhouse, hoping to hear Lester.

I always do.

Lester plays very soulfully. I always listen to Lester.

When I can't go inside I stand in the cold or the rain outside of Birdland with my saxophone and listen to Lester.

"What's happenin'?" people say when I get in. I sit beside them with my saxophone in my hand.

I look toward the bandstand. The sounds are vibrating with love—it's beautiful. Lester Young is there.

—1976

Coleman Hawkins

I like most music unless it's wrong. I liked Lester Young the first time I heard him, and I always got along very well with him. We were on a lot of tours together, and I spent a lot of time with him, talking and drinking, in hotel rooms and places like that. People forget that Chu Berry's sound wasn't like mine either.

As for mine, sometimes when people think I'm blowing harder or softer, I'm really blowing with the same power, but the difference is due to the reed. I like my reed to speak. It's supposed to sound just like a voice.

—1961

Red Callender

Art Tatum had been coming to California frequently, dazzling both audiences and musicians. Tatum used to drop by the apartment on Wilton Place that I shared with Eddie Beat before I married. One afternoon Tatum, Oscar Peterson, Benny Carter, and several pianists were there. We had two pianos and everyone sat down to play, even Oscar. Tatum was a listener until all the piano players got through, then he sat down and played "Little Man You've Had a Busy Day." He effortlessly blew everyone away. An unforgettable afternoon. Several people tell this story and have it happening in Chicago or Cleveland or New York. But it happened here in Los Angeles on Wilton Place.

Horowitz was a fan of Tatum's. Art told me a story about the time Horowitz had invited him up to his apartment in New York. Horowitz had just finished working out an elaborate arrangement on "Tea for Two." After he plays it he asks Tatum what he thinks of it. Tatum says, "Fine." Then Art sits down and played *his* arrangement on "Tea For Two" embellished by progressions up and down in thirds.

Horowitz says, "When did you work that out?"

Tatum says, "Just now."

—1985

Al Young

PASSION FLOWER
Billy Strayhorn, composer

Listening to Duke Ellington's band deliver this Billy Strayhorn beauty, how can you not be taken back to the very childhood of spirit by Johnny Hodges's sound?

You know exactly where you are. You don't need no map, no compass, no geography lesson. The men moving around you now are, every last one of them, you. They're all dressed the way you thought, in the forties, you were going to have to look when you grew up, with one of those big-lidded detective hats on your pomaded head, to top it all of. And the women are all you too: lovely, slightly perfumed and fanning themselves, their hair piled high, Lena Horne high, and sloe-eyed.

You know exactly where you are. You're in heaven. And the moon of your return to earth is as full as it'll ever be. Something sails past: a thought, a notion? The peace of mind that's coloring in the spaces on this blissful map of yours is so all-assuring that you can barely make out what it is. Surely it might be there in the breeze by itself; in the magnetic wind of roses that keeps pulling and drawing the soreness from your lopsided sorrow like a kiss or a lyric or a lark.

You can talk about your skylarks and your nightingales and doves, but when it comes to sonic ecstasy, Johnny Hodges will beat a jolly, doleful songbird, wings down, every time.

Listen to the way Hodges plays with time; kneading the years like cookie dough, and making us laugh and weep that they be brought back, but only in the Johnny Hodges/Billy Strayhorn/Edward Ellington fashion. Flowering yet never flowered, and always fragrant with passion.

—1987

Gerald Early

My mother never liked Earl Hines's toupee, a bit of affectation he adopted in the sixties when the thinning of his hair must have reached the plateau of baldness. It was, I suppose, a homely thing; it looked so obviously like a toupee that I wondered why he wore it. I have thought that if a man were vain enough to wear one, he ought to have the decency to buy something that would not call attention to itself, that would not announce to the world its own falseness. Toupees in particular and wigs in general must be subtle; but Hines wore something as shameless and brazen as those leaning towers of horsehair that Diana Ross and her Supremes used to support.

What made Hines's hairpiece so gauche was that it would have looked more suitable perched atop the head of a white man. "He doesn't have straight hair," said my mother, "so why is he wearing a toupee like that?" What my mother meant was that, in the parlance of black folk, Hines did not have "good" hair, that is, hair like a white person. Although the hair may never have been good, it had to be straight, chemically straightened in the old conk style which begat the process which begat the curly perm and the era of wearing a plastic bag to keep the grease in place and the straightening capacity in effect. In short, despite the differences in style, Hines wore his hair in the scam "do" and with the same grease as disco singer Michael Jackson. And the substance that has straightened the hair of black men for generations is lye, the stuff some people used to make soap and others use to open clogged sinks. I remember as a boy seeing young men walking around the street with purple medicine stains on their scalps; they had ruined both their hair and their skin by overapplying the burning, acidlike "conkolene."

I suppose that after all those years of wearing straightened hair, Hines decided that the best way to cover his balding pate was with straight hair, a white man's hairpiece. Of course, Hines's wig revealed the tremendous difference between a black person with straightened hair and the hair of a white person. I think Hines's toupee, much more so than his conked hair, embarrassed a good many black people; to many it symbolized the sort of Sambo inferiority complex that Louis Armstrong's big grin and white handkerchief did. The hairpiece seemingly made apparent what many black people thought Earl Hines always was: a black entertainer from the old school, the school as old as minstrelsy; and the wig may have made him seem like nothing more than a clown. In an odd, paradoxical way, the man known as "Fatha," who, in many ways, was the progenitor of modern jazz, symbolized, in the sixties and seventies, the very sort of jazz musician blacks wanted not only to avoid but actively demythify. Jazz had come full circle, and in the person of Hines the black musician confronted the very essence and origin of his modern self; and, in keeping with the inability of the average American to understand anything about his past, most of the modern cats were distinctly ambivalent about Hines.

I suppose *serious* is the key word here, for Hines always seemed like someone who was never serious about playing, who never quite understood the pose of the *artiste* or even the necessity of that pose. He was, in attitude, an artistic primitive. That is why most people, even musicians, have not really comprehended, would find it almost impossible to appreciate that Hines was one of the greatest piano players in the history of American improvised music. Many of the young jazz musicians are making tribute albums to Thelonious Monk, not only because his music sounds more modern, but because his image seems more modern as well. (After all, bebop was an inchoate form of social protest; is it really an accident that Richard Wright's *Native Son*, the greatest social-protest novel in the history of American literature, and the stardom of Charlie Parker, the greatest iconoclast figure in American art, should have occurred in the same decade?) Hines is the forgotten great man of jazz, and his being forgotten is symbolic of the haphazard way that cultural tradition, black or white, gets passed along to another generation. Tradition in America is characterized by the most intense sort of alienation and by the most intense sense of longing; in the end, we are either hopelessly sentimental or crudely cynical.

Without Hines, Monk would not have been able to evolve as he did; indeed, without Hines, there would have been no Monk, for it is clear to anyone with at least a passing familiarity with the musics of the two men that Hines is the key, the root in Monk's playing. If one listens to Hines playing a piano solo such as "Blues in Thirds" and then listens to Monk's blues originals such as "Functional" or "Blue Monk," the similarity is startling. Anyone who even casually listened to jazz knew that there was plenty of slow blues in Monk's bebop, but it is surprising to realize how much bebop there was in Hines's playing, how much of his best playing anticipated bebop. Perhaps one should have expected this since Hines's famed Grand Terrace band of the thirties had such players as Dizzy Gillespie, Charlie Parker, and Mister B—Billy Eckstine—holding down chairs. And these wound up being associated with the "New Jazz," the modern stuff, in a big way. Yet despite all of this, one still feels that exhilarating sense of new discovery, that special vertigo of aesthetic displacement when one learns that Earl Hines on the piano does not sound like an old fogey.

There was in Hines's playing not only the natural modernity of true genius but the conscious keeping abreast of new things, new happenings, and this is not an easy thing to do in jazz where so much of the newness is simply not worth much; in most cases, it is the novelty of the player coming upon, usually with more luck than daring and always with more daring than logic, a new style. And jazz musicians are obsessed with seeking new styles—which is why that music has evolved more rapidly and often more superficially in sixty years than classical music did in three hundred. For Hines, there were only two requirements for the music: it must swing and it must give pleasure to his listeners.

———

Hines suffered the misfortune of always being overshadowed by jazz's mythic figures: he could have claimed being the most important instrumentalist in the formative years if he hadn't had the ill luck of arriving on the scene at the same time as Louis Armstrong. The waxing of the great *Weatherbird* is symbolic of his relationship with Armstrong. Hines's playing on that record is stunningly alive, rich in easy splendor, yet it will always remain Armstrong's record. Armstrong's great moment of staggering artistic triumph. He might have become known as jazz's greatest bandleader if Duke Ellington and Count Basie had not come along. His reputation as a pianist was overshadowed first by Art Tatum, then by Bud Powell, then by Oscar Peterson. When the young moderns such as Bill Evans, Herbie Hancock, and Chick Corea arrived on the scene during the late fifties and early sixties, Hines was a respected figure but hardly revered. He was also no longer recording music and seemed to have been forgotten by the public at large. He was rediscovered in the late sixties, and the dozen or so years before his death in 1983 were quite productive. He probably recorded more than fifteen albums during this period. Hines, in this way, did prove one point before his death: He put out more consistently good music than Armstrong and remained active for more years than either Armstrong or Ellington.

When Hines says in his autobiography, "I've never been what is commonly termed an Uncle Tom," it seems a strangely distressing plea. Anyone with feeling for his music is made more than a little uncomfortable that a man of his stature should be forced to make it. It is the keen and bitter demand—keen because it is so deeply wrought and bitter because it is so undeniably petty—that black people make of their artists—that they must be great in their art and somehow always "current" in their politics—that engenders such a plea. One would find this sort of demand more bearable if blacks were not so quick to condemn their artists for being out of style, so easily able to disengage themselves from engagements of awesome worth. In the end, black people relate to their artists in a way that is both ardently romantic and profoundly nihilistic. And perhaps what we have always thought of as penetrating engagement is, in truth, a most complex alienation. It may very well be the process of manipulating their collective alienation that has enabled black artists to overcome and survive their adversity. Many people did not know this fact: Earl Hines, like most great black artists, outran and outrode the out-of-style all of his life.

—1987

Bebop

*Two bopsters who had never been in the country be-
fore saw a cow in a pasture one day. At the sight of
her tits both of them cried at once, "Dig those crazy
bagpipes!"*

Langston Hughes

Somebody upstairs in Simple's house had the combination turned up loud with an old Dizzy Gillespie record spinning like mad filling the Sabbath with Bop as I passed.

"Set down here on the stoop with me and listen to the music," said Simple.

"I've heard your landlady doesn't like tenants sitting on her stoop," I said.

"Pay it no mind," said Simple. "Ool-ya-koo," he sang. "Hey Ba-Ba-Re-Bop! Be-Bop! Mop!"

"All that nonsense singing reminds me of Cab Calloway back in the old *scat* days," I said, "around 1930 when he was chanting, 'Hi-de-*hie*-de-ho! Hee-de-*hee*-de-hee!'"

"Not at all," said Simple, "absolutely not at all."

"Re-Bop certainly sounds like scat to me," I insisted.

"No," said Simple, "Daddy-o, you are wrong. Besides, it was not *Re*-Bop. It is *Be*-Bop."

"What's the difference," I asked, "between *Re* and *Be?*"

"A lot," said Simple. "Re-Bop was an imitation like most of the white boys play. Be-Bop is the real thing like the colored boys play."

"You bring race into everything," I said, "even music."

"It is in everything," said Simple.

"Anyway, Be-Bop is passé, gone, finished."

"It may be gone, but its riffs remain behind," said Simple. "Be-Bop music was certainly colored folks' music—which is why white folks found it so hard to imitate. But there are some few white boys that latched onto it right well. And now wonder, because they sat and listened to Dizzy, Thelonius, Tad Dameron, Charlie Parker, also Mary Lou, all night long every time they got a chance, and bought their records by the dozens to copy their riffs. The ones that sing tried to make up new Be-Bop words, but them white folks don't know what they are singing about, even yet."

"It all sounds like pure nonsense syllables to me."

"Nonsense, nothing!" cried Simple. "Bop makes plenty of sense."

"What kind of sense?"

"You must know where Bop comes from," said Simple, astonished by my ignorance.

"I do not know," I said. "Where?"

"From the police," said Simple.

"What do you mean, from the police?"

"From the police beating Negroes' heads," said Simple. "Every time a cop hits a Negro with his billy club, that old club say, 'BOP! BOP! ... BE-BOP! ... MOP! ... BE-BOP! ... MOP!'

"That Negro hollers, 'Oool-ya-koo! Ou-o-o!'

"Old Cop just keeps on, 'MOP! MOP! ... BE-BOP! ... MOP!' That's where Be-Bop came from, beaten right out of some Negro's head into them horns and saxophones and piano keys that plays it. Do you call that nonsense?"

"If it's true, I do not," I said.

"That's why so many white folks don't dig Bop," said Simple. "White folks do not get their heads beat *just for being white*. But me—a cop is liable to grab me almost any time and beat my head—*just* for being colored.

"In some parts of this American country as soon as the polices see me, they say, 'Boy, what are you doing in this neighborhood?'

"I say, 'Coming from work, sir.'

"They say, 'Where do you work?'

"Then I have to go into my whole pedigree because I am a black man in a white neighborhood. And if my answers do not satisfy them, BOP! MOP! ... BE-BOP! ... MOP! If they do not hit me, they have already hurt my soul. *A dark man shall see dark days.* Bop comes out of them dark days. That's why real Bop is mad, wild, frantic, crazy—and not to be dug unless you've seen dark days, too. Folks who ain't suffered much cannot play Bop, neither appreciate it. They think Bop is nonsense—like you. They think it's just *crazy* crazy. They do not know Bop is also MAD crazy, SAD crazy, FRANTIC WILD CRAZY—beat out of somebody's head! That's what Bop is. Them young colored kids who started it, they know what Bop is."

"Your explanation depresses me," I said.

"Your nonsense depresses me," said Simple.

—1953

Acklyn Lynch

The age of minstrelsy was over. Black artists confident of their creative sensibilities joined the assertiveness of Black people in the lengthening of the urbanization process. Interestingly, however, the art critics and historians who have written about this particular period have emphasized the technical breakthroughs in the so-called "Jazz" arena, which were made by Kenny Clarke, Max Roach, Thelonious Monk, Jimmy

Blanton, Charlie Christian, Tadd Dammeron, Bud Powell, Charlie Parker, and Dizzy Gillespie as they executed the "changes" from "swing" to "bop." Yet, they have rarely examined the creative and political milieu from which this important music emerged.

Generally, these critics have examined the harmonic, rhythmic, and conceptual advances made by the musicians, as though this creative work was simply the logical result of musical experimentations. Actually, the development was part of the maturation process that influenced the creative sensibilities of Black people, in general—who were dealing not only with the migratory process, but the technological advancement of urban society and war economies. Black artists recognized that the "changes" in American society's dominant structures were authoritarian and autocratic in form. More specifically, Black musicians realized that the centralization of power in the music industry, as well as the cultural apparatus, provided them with little room for creative expansion. Even the important seminal music of Count Basie with Lester Young and Herschel Evans, Jo Jones, and Duke Ellington with Ben Webster, Jimmy Blanton, and Billy Strayhorn found itself contained within the dictates of John Hammond, Joe Glaser, and Irving Mills. Irving Mills never wanted Duke Ellington to change the directional focus of his music. Likewise, Joe Glaser and John Hammond kept Louis Armstrong, Count Basie, and Billie Holiday in a traditional cast.

Young musicians were yearning for new ways to express themselves that were consistent with the continuum of creative Black music, but reflective of the social forces in motion. Henry Minton, the first Black delegate to Local 802, reconverted the dining room in the Hotel Cecil on West 118th Street, reopened it as Minton's Playhouse in 1941, and eventually brought in Teddy Hill as manager. Teddy Hill hired Kenny Clarke to put together a house band and Kenny Clarke encouraged Joe Guy, Thelonious Monk, and Nick Fenton to join him. Soon, they instituted after-hours jam sessions, where musicians came to explore and examine new ideas. It was a continuation of a tradition, which evolved in New Orleans, Chicago, Memphis, St. Louis, Kansas City, New York, etc., that allowed a musician to demonstrate that he had absorbed complex ideas, as well as developed the ingenuity to bring his individuality and musical personality to the forefront. These "jam" sessions engaged both audience and musicians in a free exchange of creative spontaneity. They became legendary in Black communities across the country.

During this period within the fraternity of musicians, everyone was familiar with each other's work and there was a cross-fertilization of ideas. The musicians lived in the Black community and drew their creative sustenance from their daily experiences. This was reflected, for example, in Billy Strayhorn's "Take the A Train," "Things Ain't What They Used to Be," and Duke Ellington's "Harlem Airshaft." In addition, Duke Ellington wrote the music for a series of annual concerts starting with *Jump For Joy* (1941), *Black, Brown, and Beige* (1943), *New World A-Coming* (1943), *Deep South Suite* (1946), *Liberian Suite* (1947), and *The Beautiful Indians* (1946), all of which reflected the mood of the times and were socially relevant. *Jump For Joy* premiered in Los Angeles, while the other concerts were done at Carnegie Hall in New York.

Jump for Joy was an attempt by Duke Ellington and a group of Hollywood writers to make a statement on the contemporary racial situation. Duke wrote a very controversial piece in which he attempted to eliminate the stereotype images of Blacks fashioned by Hollywood and Broadway. He included such titles as "Rent Party," "The Sun Tanned Tenth of The Nation," "Uncle Tom's Cabin is in a Drive-In Now," "I've Got a Passport from Georgia (and I'm Going to the U.S.A.)," and "Mad Scene from Woolworth's." The show was a success during its three-month run, and Duke described the audiences as "including the most celebrated Hollywoodians, middle-class ofays, the sweet-and-low, scuffling-type Negroes and dicty Negroes as well (doctors, lawyers, etc.). The Negroes always left proudly with their chests sticking out." In a later interview he was asked, "Is there any achievement, outside the realm of music, that you are proud and happy about?" He replied promptly, "The first social significance show, *Jump for Joy* in 1941, and its various successors continually since."

This sense of deep social concern was expressed in many other major compositions during this period, all of which became extremely popular among the masses of Black people. The following, among others, represented this trend: The Golden Gate Quartet ("No Segregation in Heaven"), Sally Martin ("Just a Closer Walk with Thee"), Thomas A. Dorsey ("Precious Lord"—as sung by Mahalia Jackson), Ira Tucker and the Dixie Hummingbirds ("I Don't Know Why and Move Up a Little Higher"). R.H. Harris and the Soul Stirrers ("I Am Gonna Tell God How You Treat Me"), Muddy Waters ("Rolling Stone, I'd Rather Drink Muddy Water"), Huddie Ledbetter ("The Midnight Special" and

"Goodnight Irene"), Billie Holiday ("Lover Man," "Traveling Light," "Strange Fruit," and "God Bless the Child [who has got his own]"), Erskine Hawkins ("After Hours"), Jerry Valentine ("Blitzkrieg"), Bud Powell ("Echoes of Harlem," "Reverse the Charges" and "Do Some War Work Baby"), and Tadd Dammeron ("A Hundred Years From Today"). All of these compositions dealt with the concrete social reality of the Harlems of America. Simultaneously, they expanded our musical palette by introducing new conceptions of rhythm, harmony, and melody.

—1992

Anatole Broyard

Then, just when I needed something to do, my friend Milton Klonsky asked me to collaborate with him on a piece he had been asked to write for *Partisan Review.* The piece was on modern jazz, a subject neither Milton nor the editors of *Partisan Review* knew anything about. Since I had always been interested in jazz, Milton suggested that I write the first draft and he would rewrite it. What he meant was that I'd supply the facts and he'd turn them into prose.

It never occurred to me to resent this arrangement—I was awed by *Partisan Review* and flattered by Milton's offer. I had never written anything but notes to myself. I was always scribbling on little pads I carried around, jotting down ideas, phrases, images. Half of the young men in the Village were writing such notes. They wrote them in cafes, in the park, even on the street. You'd see them stop and pull out their pads or notebooks to jot down something that had just struck them—the color of the sky, the bend of a street, an incongruity. These notes were postcards to literature that were never mailed.

I took Milton's proposal very seriously. I would go upstairs in my parents' house and listen to jazz for hours, playing records over and over. It suited my mood, which was like the lyrics of a blues song. I had always liked old jazz—from Louis Armstrong to Lester Young—but I hadn't made up my mind about Charlie Parker, who was everybody's hero at that time. While he could be brilliant, I found in Parker's style a hint of the garrulousness that would soon come over black culture.

Also, it seemed to me that jazz relied too much on improvisation to be a full-fledged art form. Nobody could be that good on the spur of the moment. And there was too much cuteness in jazz. It stammered and strained. It took it sentimentality for wisdom.

I tried to imagine what Meyer Schapiro would say about jazz. Was it like *Les Demoiselles d'Avignon*, a fracturing of music, like the splitting of the atom? But there was something momentous, something world-shaking about the Demoiselles that jazz didn't have. It seemed to me that jazz was just folk art. It might be terrific folk art, but it was still only local and temporary.

I found a parallel for jazz not in Schapiro's class but in Gregory Bateson's. Bateson loved to tell stories, and he told them very well. He was in New Guinea, he said, living with the Iatmul tribe, sleeping in a thatched hut on tall stilts, when one morning he was awakened at daybreak by a sound of drumming. He got up and looked out and saw a lone man walking beneath the clustered huts of the village, beating a drum. He walked in a curious way, this man, in a sawtooth pattern—not turning around to keep his pattern but stepping backward, heels first. And in counterpoint to his drumming, he chanted a sad, staccato recitative.

Bateson learned that this man had suffered a grievance that he could not get settled. The tribe had rejected his plea for redress and so he got up every morning and rehearsed his complaint to the village. He tried to wake them, to disturb their rest, invade their dreams. Thinking about jazz, I remember this man and I thought that jazz musicians were something like that.

—1989

LeRoi Jones / Amiri Baraka

If R&B was the basic contemporary Afro-American urban blues, what was bebop? And what were its roots? Various kinds of bourgeois-oriented chauvinist and otherwise flawed music and art and social critics had unkind words to say about bop, and by now these are well documented. (See: *Blues People* or *Bird Lives!* or *Jazz: A People's Music*.) The unhep, then unhip, then corny music magazine *DownBeat* actually had to re-review the bop classics because they had torn their ass so bad when they reviewed the records when they first came out—demanding, as the bourgeoisie always does, that any expression in the society be accountable to and controllable by it. Why Did The Music Have To Sound Like That? was the question. Why didn't it sound like something quiet and invisible and nice or dead and respectable or at least European? (And this is not to make the case that jazz is something that is exclusively black, that there are no white or Asian &c players. That is nonsense. A nationalist friend of mine was genuinely embarrassed but enlightened when he found out from me that a record he admired, "I Can't Get Started," and the dude who composed and played and sung it, Bunny Berigan, was a tragic Irishman with a derby.) But the heaviest sources of jazz and blues are Afro-American folk sources, and it has been Afro-American people who have been the principal innovators. And this has shaped the peculiar strengths and weaknesses of the music.

Just as the monopoly music manipulators had succeeded in flooding the country with inferior imitations of real big-band swing, the most creative musicians broke away from this sterile form in rebellion, and using small groups as laboratories produced a new music that raised the level of jazz, of Afro-American music, of American music, of "popular" music, and of world music in general. Sidney Finkelstein in his important book tells us how the immigrants, "Jewish, Italian, Irish ... who came to these shores with a cultural heritage that could have added much to American life were discouraged from using this heritage and instead had given not a better culture, but the phony contrived and synthetic 'popular' culture that is good business but bad art. They have nevertheless made a contribution." (*Jazz: A People's Music*, 270–71.) For the Afro-American people, however, the basic foundation of the exploitative capitalist society is built on the fundamental and historical exploitation and oppression of black people, based initially on slavery, and then and now on imperialist control of the Afro-American nation in the Black Belt South. [...]

Bebop rebelled against the absorption into garbage, monopoly music; it also signified a rebellion by the people who played the music, because it was not just the music that rebelled, as if the music had fallen out of the sky! But even more, dig it, it signified a rebellion rising out of the masses themselves, since that is the source of social movement—the people themselves! [...]

In Afro-American music, the rebellion and protest became an actual reaching back to go forward, a reassertion of the elemental and the essential. It was felt in all aspects as the R&B shook off its older Tin Pan Alleyisms in the burst of the shouters and the electricity and took it back to basic rhythm and blues. But out of this basic blues environment, which itself is constantly changing, the so-called jazz expression also takes its shape. This expression always begins by trying to utilize the fundamental Afro-American musical impulse, blues, and extend it, in all the ways it can: instrumentally (blues was basically a vocal music), technically and emotionally and philosophically. The harmonic, melodic, and of course rhythmic innovations that jazz has made upon the blues impulse had produced some of the most exciting music of the twentieth century anywhere in the world. But this kind of Afro-American music utilizes a much broader musical palette with which to express itself than blues does. Jazz, so called, calls upon everything in the American experience it is aware of. It has borrowed more widely than blues (it is, in its best aspect, the blues doing the borrowing!). It has made use of and makes use of the music of the white national minority in the Black Belt homeland (called country and western), "classical," semi-classical, quasi-classical, Latin, the American "popular" song—which it promptly transformed. Not to mention that it has continually gone back farther to where the blues came from to the shores of Africa, or when it wants to the Middle and Far East. It is intellectual and internationalist (but deeply emotional and with a a national form), a working and oppressed people's music; it has nevertheless affected every class in society!

Jazz is by its nature *ambitious.* It has succeeded in being the fullest expression of American life. At its most expressive it is exactly that, not just an expression of the Afro-American's life but, with its borrowings and wanderings, it pretensions and strengths of character, it sums up the U.S. in a thousand ways. While blues is more specifically a *black music!*

—1979

Dizzy Gillespie

Around 1946, jive-ass stories about "beboppers" circulated and began popping up in the news. Generally, I felt happy for the publicity, but I found it disturbing to have modern jazz musicians and their followers characterized in a way that was often sinister and downright vicious. This image wasn't altogether the fault of the press because many followers, trying to be "in," were actually doing some of the things the press accused beboppers of—and worse. I wondered whether all this "weird" publicity actually drew some of these way-out elements to us and did the music more harm than good. Stereotypes, which exploited whatever our weaknesses might be, emerged. Suable things were said, but nothing about the good we were doing and our contributions to music.

Time magazine, March 25, 1946, remarked: "As such things usually do, it began on Manhattan's Fifty-second Street. A bandleader named John (Dizzy) Gillespie, looking for a way to emphasize the more beautiful notes in 'Swing,' explained: 'When you hum it, you just naturally say bebop, be-de-bop ...'

"Today, the bigwig of bebop is a scat named Harry (the Hipster) Gibson, who in moments of supreme pianistic ecstasy throws his feet on the keyboard. No. 2 man is Bulee (Slim) Gaillard, a skyscraping zooty Negro guitarist. Gibson and Gaillard have recorded such hip numbers as 'Cement Mixer,' which has sold more than 20,000 discs in Los Angeles alone; 'Yeproc Heresay,' 'Dreisix Cents,' and 'Who Put the Benzedrine in Mrs. Murphy's Ovaltine?'"

The article discussed a ban on radio broadcasts of bebop records in Los Angeles where station KMPC considered it a "degenerative influence on youth" and described how the "nightclub where Gibson and Gaillard played" was "more crowded than ever" with teen-agers who wanted to be bebopped. "What bebop amounts to: hot jazz overheated, with overdone lyrics full of bawdiness, references to narcotics, and doubletalk."

Once it got inside the marketplace, our style was subverted by the press and music industry. First, the personalities and weaknesses of the in people started becoming more important, in the public eye, than the music itself. Then they diluted the music. They took what were otherwise blues and pop tunes, added "mop, mop" accents and lyrics about abusing drugs wherever they could, and called the noise that resulted bebop. Labeled bebop like our music, this synthetic sound was played heavily on commercial radio everywhere, giving bebop a bad name. No matter how bad the imitation sounded, youngsters and people who were musically untrained liked it, and it sold well because it maintained a very danceable beat. The accusations in the press pointed to me as one of the prime movers behind this. I should've sued, even though the chances of winning in court were slim. It was all bullshit.

Keeping in mind that a well-told lie usually contains a germ of truth, let's examine the charges and see how many of those stereotypes actually applied to me.

Lie number one was that beboppers wore wild clothes and dark glasses at night. Watch the fashions of the forties on the late show, long coats, almost down to our knees, and full trousers. I wore drape suits like everyone else and dressed no differently from the average leading man of the day. It was beautiful. I became pretty dandified, I guess, later during the bebop era when my pants were pegged slightly at the bottom, but not unlike the modestly flared bottoms on the slacks of the smart set today.

We had costumes for the stage—uniforms with wide lapels and belts—given to us by a tailor in Chicago who designed them, but we didn't wear them offstage. Later, we removed the wide lapels and sported little tan cashmere jackets with no lapels. This was a trendsetting innovation because it made no sense at all to pay for a wide lapel. *Esquire* magazine, 1943, America's leading influence on men's fashions, considered us elegant, though bold, and printed our photographs.

Perhaps I remembered France and started wearing the beret. But I used it as headgear I could stuff into my pocket and keep moving. I used to lose my hat a lot. I liked to wear a hat like most of the guys then, and the hats I kept losing cost five dollars apiece. At a few recording sessions when I couldn't lay my hands on a mute, I covered the bell of the trumpet with the beret. Since I'd been designated their "leader," cats just picked up the style....

Lie number two was that only beboppers wore beards, goatees, and other facial hair and adornments.

I used to shave under my lip. That spot prickled and itched with scraping. The hair growing back felt uncomfortable under my mouthpiece, so I let the hair grow into a goatee during my days with Cab Calloway. Now a trademark, that tuft of hair cushions my mouthpiece and is quite useful to me as a player; at least I've always thought it allowed me to play more effectively. Girls like my goatee too....

Number three: that beboppers spoke mostly in slang or tried to talk like Negroes is not so untrue. We used a few "pig Latin" words like "ofay." Pig Latin as a way of speaking emerged among blacks long before our time as a secret language for keeping children and the uninitiated from listening to adult conversations. Also, blacks had a lot of words they brought with them from Africa, some of which crept over into general usage, like "yum-yum."

Most bebop language came about because some guy said something and it stuck. Another guy started using it, then another one, and before you knew it, we had a whole language. "Mezz" meant "pot," because Mezz Mezzrow was selling the best pot. When's the "eagle gonna" fly, the American eagle, meant payday. A "razor" implied the draft from a window in winter with cold air coming in, since it cut like a razor. We added some colorful and creative concepts to the English language, but I can't think of any word beside *bebop* that I actually invented. Daddy-O Daylie, a disc jockey in Chicago, originated much more of the hip language during our era than I did.

We didn't have to try; as black people we just naturally spoke that way.

People who wished to communicate with us had to consider our manner of speech, and sometimes they adopted it. As we played with musical notes, bending them into new and different meanings that constantly changed, we played with words. . . .

Number four: that beboppers had a penchant for loose sex and partners racially different from themselves, especially black men who desired white women, was a lie.

It's easy for a white person to become associated with jazz musicians, because most of the places we play are owned and patronized by whites. A good example is Pannonica Koenigswater, the baroness, who is the daughter of a Rothschild. She'll be noticed when she shows up in a jazz club over two or three times. Nica has helped jazz musicians, financially. She saw to it that a lotta guys who had no place to stay had a roof or put some money in their pockets. She's willing to spend a lot to help. There's not too much difference between black and white women, but you'll find that to gain a point, a white woman will do almost anything to help if it's something that she likes. There's almost nothing, if a white woman sees it's to her advantage, that she won't do because she's been taught that the world is hers to do with as she wants. This shocks the average black musician who realizes that black women wouldn't generally accept giving so much without receiving something definite in return.

A black woman might say: "I'll love him . . . but not my money." But a white woman will give anything, even her money, to show her own strength. She'll be there on the job, every night, sitting their supporting her own goodies. She'll do it for kicks, whatever is her kick. Many white women were great fans and supporters of modern jazz and brought along white males to hear our music. That's a secret of this business: Where a woman goes, the man goes.

"Where you wanna go, baby?"

"I wanna go hear Dizzy."

"Okay, that's where we go." The man may not support you, but the woman does, and he spends his money.

As a patron of the arts in this society, the white woman's role, since white males have been so preoccupied with making money, brought her into close contact with modern jazz musicians and created relationships that were often very helpful to the growth of our art. Some of these relationships became personal and even sexual but not necessarily so. Often, they were supportive friendships which the musicians and their patrons enjoyed. Personally, I haven't received much help from white female benefactors. All the help I needed, I got from my wife—an outspoken black woman, who will not let me mess with the money—to whom I've been married since 1940. Regarding friendships across racial lines, because white males would sometimes lend their personal support to our music, the bebop era, socially speaking, was a major concrete effort of progressive thinking black and white males and females to tear down and abolish ignorance and racial barriers that were stifling the growth of any true culture in modern America.

Number five: that beboppers used and abused drugs and alcohol is not completely a lie either. They used to tell jokes about it. One bebopper walked up to another and said, "Are you gonna flat your fifths tonight?"

The other one answered, "No, I'm going to drink mine." That's a typical joke about beboppers....

Dope, heroin abuse, really got to be a major problem during the bebop era, especially in the late forties, and a lotta guys died from it. Cats were always getting "busted" with drugs by the police, and they had a saying, "To get the best band, go to KY." That meant the "best band" was in Lexington, Kentucky, at the federal narcotics hospital. Why did it happen? The style of life moved so fast, and cats were struggling to keep up with it. It was wartime, everybody was uptight. They probably wanted something to take their minds off all the killing and dying and the cares of this world. The war in Vietnam most likely excited the recent upsurge of heroin abuse, together with federal narcotics control policies which, strangely, at certain points in history, encouraged narcotics abuse, especially among young blacks.

Everybody at one time or another smoked marijuana, and then coke became popular—I did that too; but I never had any desire to use hard drugs, a drug that would make you a slave. I always shied away from anything powerful enough to make me dependent, because realizing that everything here comes and goes, why be dependent on any one thing? I never even tried hard drugs. One time on Fifty-second Street a guy gave me something I took for coke and it turned out to be horse. I snorted it and puked up in the street. If I had found him, he would have suffered bodily harm, but I never saw him again.

With drugs like benzedrine, we played practical jokes. One record date for Continental, with Rubberlegs Wilson, a blues singer, I especially remember. Somebody had this date—Clyde Hart, I believe. He got Charlie Parker, me, Oscar Pettiford, Don Byas, Trummy Young, and

Specs Powell. The music didn't work up quite right at first. Now, at that time, we used to break open inhalers and put the stuff into coffee or Coca-Cola; it was a kick then. During a break at this record date, Charlie dropped some into Rubberlegs's coffee. Rubberlegs didn't drink or smoke anything. He couldn't taste it. So we went on with the record date. Rubberlegs began moaning and crying as he was singing. You should hear those records! But I wouldn't condone doing that now, Rubberlegs might've gotten sick or something. The whole point is that, like most Americans, we were really ignorant about the helpful or deleterious effects of drugs on human beings, and before we concluded anything about drugs or used them and got snagged, we should have understood what we were doing. That holds true for the individual or the society, I believe. [...]

Number six is really a trick: that beboppers tended to express unpatriotic attitudes regarding segregation, economic injustice, and the American way of life.

We never wished to be restricted to just an American context, for we were creators in an art form which grew from universal roots and which had proved it possessed universal appeal. Damn right! We refused to accept racism, poverty, or economic exploitation, nor would we live out uncreative humdrum lives merely for the sake of survival. But there was nothing unpatriotic about it. If America wouldn't honor its Constitution and respect us as men, we couldn't give a shit about the American way. And they made it damn near un-American to appreciate our music.

Music drew Charlie Parker and me together, but Charlie Parker used to read a lot too. As a great reader, he knew about everything, and we used to discuss politics, philosophy, and life-style. I remember him mentioning Baudelaire, I think he died of syphilis, and Charlie Parker used to talk about him all the time. Charlie was very much interested in the social order, and we'd have these long conversations about it, and [about] music. We discussed local politics too, people like Vito Marcantonio, and what he'd tried to do for the little man in New York. We liked Marcantonio's ideas because as musicians we weren't paid well for what we created.

There were a bunch of musicians more socially minded who were closely connected with the Communist Party. Those guys stayed busy anywhere labor was concerned. I never got that involved politically. I would picket, if necessary, and remember twice being on a picket line. I can't remember just what it was I was picketing for, but they had me walking around with a sign. Now, I would never cross a picket line.

Paul Robeson became the forerunner of Martin Luther King. I'll always remember Paul Robeson as a politically committed artist. A few enlightened musicians recognized the importance of Paul Robeson, amongst them Teddy Wilson, Frankie Newton, and Pete Seeger—all of them very outspoken politically. [...]

Within the society, we did the same thing we did with the music. First we learned the proper way and then we improvised on that. It seemed the natural thing to do because the style or mode of life among black folks went the same way as the direction of the music. Yes, sometimes the music comes first and the life-style reflects the music because music is some very strong stuff, though life in itself is bigger. Artists are always in the vanguard of social change, but we didn't go out and make speeches or say, "Let's play eight bars of protest." We just played our music and let it go at that. The music proclaimed our identity; it made every statement we truly wanted to make.

Number seven: that "beboppers" expressed a preference for religions other than Christianity may be considered only a half-truth, because most black musicians, including those from the bebop era, received their initial exposure and influence in music through the black church. And it remained with them throughout their lives. For social and religious reasons, a large number of modern jazz musicians did begin to turn toward Islam during the forties, a movement completely in line with the idea of freedom of religion. [...]

Number eight: that beboppers threatened to destroy pop, blues, and old-time music like Dixieland jazz is almost totally false.

It's true, melodically, harmonically, and rhythmically, we found most pop music too bland and mechanically unexciting to suit our tastes. But we didn't attempt to destroy it—we simply built on top of it by substituting our own melodies, harmonies, and rhythms over the pop music format and improvised on that. We always substituted; that's why no one could ever charge us with stealing songs nor collect any royalties for recording material under copyright. We only utilized the pop song format as a take-off point for improvisation, which to us was much more important. Eventually, pop music survived by slowly adopting the changes we made.

Beboppers couldn't destroy the blues without seriously injuring themselves. The modern jazz musicians always remained very close to the blues musician. That was a characteristic of the bopper. He stayed in close contact with his blues counterpart. I always had good friendships with T-Bone Walker, B.B. King, Joe Turner, Cousin Joe, Muddy Waters— all those guys—because we knew where our music came from. Ain't no need of denying your father. That's a fool, there were few fools in this movement. Technical differences existed between modern jazz and blues musicians. However, modern jazz musicians would have to know the blues. . . .

The squabble between the boppers and the "moldy figs," who played or listened exclusively to Dixieland jazz, arose because the older musicians insisted on attacking our music and putting it down. Ooooh, they were very much against our music, because it required more than what they were doing. They'd say, "That music ain't shit, man!" They really did, but then you noticed some of the older guys started playing our riffs, a few of them, like Henry "Red" Allen. The others remained hostile to it. [. . .]

Number nine: That beboppers expressed disdain for "squares" is mostly true.

A "square" and a "lame" were synonymous, and they accepted the complete life-style, including the music, dictated by the establishment. They rejected the concept of creative alternatives, and they were just the opposite of "hip," which meant "in the know," "wise," or one with "knowledge" of life and how to live. Musically, a square would chew the cud. He'd spend his money at the Roseland Ballroom to hear a dance band playing standards, rather than extend his ear and spirit to take an odyssey in bebop at the Royal Roost. Oblivious to the changes which replaced old, outmoded expressions with new, modern ones, squares said "hep" rather than "hip." They were apathetic to, or actively opposed to, almost everything we stood for, like intelligence, sensitivity, creativity, change, wisdom, joy, courage, peace, togetherness, and integrity. To put them down in some small way for the sharp-cornered shape of their boxed-in personalities, what better description than "square?" . . .

Number ten: that beboppers put down as "commercial" people who were trying to make money is 50 percent a lie, only half true. [. . .]

People with enough bucks and foresight to invest in bebop made some money. I mean more than just a little bit. All the big money went to the guys who owned the music, not to the guys who played it. The businessmen made much more than the musicians, because without money to invest in producing their own music, and sometimes managing poorly with what they earned, the modern jazz musician fell victim to the forces of the market. Somehow, the jazz businessman always became the owner and got back more than his "fair" share, usually at the player's expense. More was stolen from us during the bebop era than in the entire history of jazz up to that point. They stole a lot of our music, all kinds of stuff. You'd look up and see somebody else's name on your composition and say, "What'd he have to do with it? But you couldn't do much about it. Blatant commercialism we disliked because it debased the quality of our music. Our protests against being cheated and ripped off never meant we stood against making money....

Beboppers were by no means fools. For a generation of Americans and young people around the world, who reached maturity during the 1940s, bebop symbolized a rebellion against the rigidities of the old order, an outcry for change in almost every field, especially in music. The bopper wanted to impress the world with a new stamp, the uniquely modern design of a new generation coming of age.

—1979

Bob Kaufman

Hawk Lawler was born in Kansas City in a charity ward where his father was also born, perhaps in the same bed. His early childhood was that of any Negro child of his town in the 1930s. Regular—attendance at a seedy rundown school, daily salutes to the flag, solemn morning pledges of allegiance, and standard Beard Geographies. A special interest in history led him to build a makeshift log cabin in his backyard in preparation for the presidency, which his father tore down for firewood as soon as his discovered what motivated Hawk. His favorite friends were those with whom he traveled to the relief depot to collect the family ration of potatoes and dried prunes—these boys he trusted; others just happened to be boys, too. In school, he was good in mathematics but hated to do figures on paper. He usually worked out arithmetic problems in his head long before the rest of the class rested their pencils.

He attended church each Sunday at the Rising Sun Baptist Church where he secretly sang hymns in numbers, because he did not like hearing the same words all the time, yet could offer no resistance to the music. His first personal contact with music as an independent act was when he played triangle in the school band and discovered that when he pinged his instrument at the wrong times he could feel its tingle separate and distinct from the other instruments—at which times he would smile inside his mouth—while apologizing to the leader who was an ex–New Orleans musician that jazz had passed by, yet secretly enjoyed the hardhead. He discovered the saxophone while listening to the band tune up and found that this gilded pipe could play free of the mob; at that instant, he became a saxophone player for life and never touched another triangle. The only possession of which he was proud was an aging Elgin bicycle he received at Christmas from the Afro-American Doll and Toy Fund sponsored by the local Negro paper and provided for by all good white people of the town. It was given to him during a bleak Roosevelt Christmas for winning the school's annual composition contest. The subject was "Why I want to be President," and he was proudest when the bike was presented to him by a snow-bearded colored Santa Claus, whom he recognized as the Mayor's chauffeur. This cherished trophy he surrendered to Horton, son of the family his mother washed for, in return for one battered saxophone which he slept with three nights before feeling intimate enough to try it, and when he did finally find sufficient courage to blow it, his die was cast—he and horn were one, world blotted out.

The only two courses available to him outside of regular studies were the Bible and music, and since he preferred playing the saxophone to being God, his choice was preordained. Before long he was being heard in small local clubs with largely blues clientele. Often experiencing that same feeling about words he had once felt in church, he began to blow numbers; he was fired over and over, yet could not stop blowing numbers. He was hired as second-chair man with the Bat Bowles orchestra, with the provision that he refrain from blowing numbers, which he did, until the band's dilapidated bus pulled up in front of the Theresa Hotel on Harlem's busiest corner ... where, without a word, he picked up his horn case and disembarked. For no reason at all, he walked and wandered. He had never seen so many Negroes at one time in his whole life. He wondered if some big dam had burst in Africa and spilled its contents, or laughed at the crazy thought that they were all white and this was some special holiday when they all wore black and brown faces for some religious Mardi Gras. This speculation was soon replaced by sounds smacking into his eardrum which dispelled any notions of masquerade, causing him to finger his case and peer into doorways for that big hidden jazz womb, oozing blues and down warmth, welcome as new shoes but still emptied of his embryonic numbers.

Strange melodic numbers whose sum total was the blues and so personal no Arab would have acknowledged inventing them—his numbers, each one a fragment of a note. In lieu of finding a room, he found a girl, which was easier in a place where there were more girls than rooms, and while he waited the chance to blow his lover horn again, he blew numbers with his body, which left him sperm-poor and brain-pained, longing to give wind to numbers and breathe life into them. One night his girl-mother-sister-lover-whore had a five-dollar date at one of the better after-hours spots with a leading writer of detective stories, and since this writer was a favorite of his, he went along, taking his horn as always, like some tubular security blanket. Five minutes after he enters the place, God created earth, Christ was born, and Gabriel exchanged his trumpet for a saxophone. For there in this headquarters of black revolution sat these long-sought comrades, blowing numbers. Illegal notes floated in the air as though they had a right to, floated right into his suddenly blossomed ears, followed him up to the bandstand, crept into his pores as he deceased the horn, placed it to his parched lips, and sighed, for without willing it they came—numbers, notes, songs, battle cries, laments, jazzy psalms, tribal histories in cubist and surrealist patterns, and an unmistakable call to arms, to jazz, to him, as others put down their horns in silent thanks that he had come, as the drums promised he would come, come to lead into lead, with his pumping, grinning throat. Let us not go into it, we all know he led, though we don't all know how—some of us are more familiar with the intermissions, aware of the passions, privy to the junk, witnesses to the uprising when the handkerchief was cast off; some of us were counters of madhouse excursions, and a few of us have withstood the silence, wondering from where it came. Some of us have to know.

—1996

Babs Gonzales

By this time, the happenings had all moved to Fifty-second Street. Coleman Hawkins and Lady Day were the king and queen. Dizzy and Oscar Pettiford had a band in the Deuces, and Clark's Monroe the only colored owner had his joint and was featuring Bud Powell and Max Roach. Miles Davis had just come to study at Julliard and was the envy of everyone because his father sent him $75 a week, which was as much as the guys working were getting. The new sound got to me so I found myself there every night. I began to get gigs on weekends going up to Bridgeport and New Haven.

The street was really something in those days. The war was on and there were always loads of sailors and soldiers who wanted to and did fight every time they saw a Negro musician with a white girl. I'd seen a whore uptown beating her man with her shoe heel and him just holding his eyes screaming. When it was all over I asked her why the guy didn't fight back. She answered, "Just get a box of red pepper for a dime and throw it in his eyes and you'll win."

I took her advice and until today, I've never been without one.

The guys all laughed at me at first but after I saved Oscar [Pettiford] and Bird's life with it, quite a few more colleagues copped some. There was one Irish bar on the corner of Sixth Avenue and Fifty-second Street that wouldn't serve colored even though the law said so. One night four of us went in with our white girls. After refusing us, the girls ordered. The owner called them all kinds of tramps, bitches, for being with niggers, etc. There were about thirty ofays there so we left. At 4:30 that morning, we took trash cans and broke out all his windows. We did this five times in a year before he finally got the message.

Another incident involved Ben Webster. At that time Ben weighed two hundred forty pounds and was always ready to fight. Baby Lawrence, the greatest jazz tap dancer that ever lived, ran into the Downbeat and yelled "the sailors are beating up Bud Powell." We all rushed around the corner to the White Rose bar and there was Bud in the street unconscious and bleeding. Ben grabbed two sailors, one in each hand by the backs of their necks. He ran them both from the curb straight through the plate glass windows and the rest took off like track stars.

—1967

David N. Baker

The seeds of jazz were firmly planted by 1931. Great strides had been made in instrumental technique, giving the soloist an equal footing with the ensemble. The harmonic framework had been enriched and expanded. Vertical and horizontal structure was evidenced and the emotional latitude went from hot to cool. There developed two camps: those musicians who wanted as few restrictions on their music as possible and those who wanted to absorb various European ideas.

The big bands reflected the hope of recovery from the Depression,

but the big band concept had other social implications. Factory production lines suggested a certain kind of efficiency, perhaps akin to the written arrangement that predestined some musical effects with a degree of
security. The liberalism of the Roosevelt administration was mirrored in
the increasing number of bands with players from both races. They had
existed in the 1920s, but for recordings not for public appearances. Concert music was looked up to by many jazzmen, many of whom accepted
some values as their own. Leroi Jones called swing and ragtime "the de-
bris of vanished emotional references," meaning they were White realizations of a music that began as emotional music.

The wind players of the time were fleet fingered. The performances
tended toward eight- and sixteen-note patterns in place of ternary beat
subdivisions. Phrases were larger and harmony became more important
than melody (one of the first really beautiful examples of this was Coleman Hawkins's "Body and Soul").

—1973

David N. Baker

The early development of bop is not documented on recordings because
of the musicians' union ban on recording from 1942 to 1944. Bird and
Diz, to some people, popped out of a shell like Venus because of this
ban. We miss things like the experimentation which took place in Earl
Hines's band, and it looked as if a new music appeared all of a sudden in
1945 or 1946 which had no roots or past at all. People like Louis were really up in arms. Boppers were guys who flatted their fifths and one cat
said, "I don't flatten my fifths, I drink them." With bop, harmony gained
equal footing with melody and rhythm. The players needed a good technique, finely developed ears, and the ability to construct music at a fast
tempo. It was multi-metered, rich in syncopation. The wind players imitated the pianists. Phrase lines were asymmetrical, and the soloists had a
wide choice of notes from what I call the chord and melodic referentials.
Drummers let the bassists keep time and became freer in their own expressions.

Rootlessness was a way of life for many people at this time, just after
the war. The past was gone, and society was in an upheaval. The first
boppers were young Blacks, sensitive to the fact that Black music had
been exploited by the Whites and that it had been debased as a result.
Some sought to make their styles too difficult to imitate. They thought

of themselves as artists, not as entertainers. The days of second-class citizenship for music were over, and there was a significant departure from the aesthetic of New Orleans. Increased consideration was given music's artistic quality, its form, and its harmonic and thematic development. Though most of the young musicians were not from large metropolitan areas, they were nevertheless big city men and their speech, dress, and mannerisms were urbane, sometimes even flamboyant. But they were pure musicians for the most part, unwilling to compromise their art to the expediencies of commerce. They would not hesitate to offend bourgeois tastes.

The new jazz retained the collectivism of the old, but now the collective improvisation was exclusively between soloists and the rhythm section. Ensemble work was usually unison, and intensity was at an explosive level.

Despite the aura of revolution, and notwithstanding the high artistry of some of its practitioners (Charlie Parker, for example, was to prove as influential as Armstrong had been a decade or two earlier), bop was a more restrictive music than jazz had been in its earlier days. Playing within the demanding harmonic framework called more for clever minds and nimble fingers than for true creativity. From the sociological viewpoint, by its emphasis on harmony and instrumental facility and the use of European concepts, bop was considerably more White than Black, despite the social stance of the beboppers, and yet the effect of bop on jazz was great. It led to a significant rise in basic musicianship (according to European standards), it increased the number of rhythmic and metric choices open for expressive reasons, its best players served as reference points for more than a generation, and the seeds for further evolution of jazz as an artistic expression were planted.

The big bands generally served more as synthesizers, rather than innovators. As is true with Western music, innovations took place in the chamber-like ensembles ten or twenty years before these ideas really reached the bigger groups.

—1973

Ortiz M. Walton

The bebop musician was often the subject of jokes and stories during the early stages of the movement. (One of the functions of the joke is to conceal or mask fear and anxiety over an otherwise socially taboo subject.) One of the frequent themes of these jokes was "way out" Jazz musicians perched on "cloud 9" smoking reefer. This supposed obliviousness to reality was reinforced by the usage of bop-derived terms such as *crazy, cool, swinging, cat,* and *dig,* which, when taken out of cultured context, came to connote meanings other than those intended by the musicians. *Dig* had meant to look beneath the surface, uncover the esoteric rather than rely solely on external appearance. Words like *crazy* were a subtle challenge to the conviction that rationality, logic and conventional morality, the backdrops of apparent sanity, were indeed the ultimate standard. *Crazy* was conceptualized as a complimentary adjective rather than a put-down. The term was not diagnostic or clinical, but connoted clarity and profundity of vision. It was a cryptic term of acceptance, intimating a sense of understanding, professional fraternity, and appreciation of performance skills. In the hands of the jokesters, *crazy,* like other bop terms, came to have confused implications, relegating the value changes that were taking place to the realm of the absurd.

Soon after whites from upper middle-class families began to imitate the new sounds and behavior, the jokes became sour and the punch lines turned into narcotics arrests. The artistic underground was spreading to the disillusioned sector of society, the sons and daughters of prominent families, who welcomed the new, refreshing culture. Herein we see the precursor of the present-day "hippie," the "beat" generation.

Certainly, the invention of heroin cannot be attributed to Jazz or, more specifically, to bop musicians. The same holds true for its manufacture and distribution. Nor, one can be sure, were a few black bebop artists the only members of society who sometimes partook of the drugs between the early forties and mid-fifties. Yet to judge by the number of arrests, convictions, and widespread publicity given to bop musicians for alleged possession of "horse," as it was called, one would conclude that the above statements were true. For practically all of the outstanding players of bop were arrested during this period, some, like Sonny Rollins and Gen Ammons, receiving long jail terms. When narcotics could not be found, they were either planted by policemen or other charges were preferred. For example, Miles Davis was incarcerated for nonsupport, having to serve over a year's time at the notorious Sing Sing prison in New York. Billie Holiday, though not a part of the bop movement, was hounded from one city to the next, detectives even breaking down her hotel-room door during a Philadelphia engagement in the early fifties. Detectives somehow always managed to find what they were looking for in such operations, and the media, particularly the newspapers and magazines, embellished the stories with morbid details. However, one circumstance that media never discussed was the wholesale dissemination of opiates into black communities during and following World War Two, the Korean War, and the present war in Vietnam.

Now that the white middle-class addicts are greatly increasing in number, a great humanitarian concern is being shown by many of the same authorities who made life miserable for the black bop musician. The terminology has conveniently changed from *dope fiend* and *junkie* to *acid head* and *user of mind-expanding drugs.* It also might come as a surprise to some that during the bop period, and since, an array of symphony conductors and "classical" musicians have been the users of "hard" drugs, especially cocaine. They, however, were not, in society's eyes, musical outlaws. They maintained the society's values. Their reward from society was immunity from punishment for their legal transgressions. One conductor, who shall remain anonymous, could not, for reasons that became clear later, begin his Sunday afternoon concert at Tanglewood. Just before the concert, he drooped into the green room, head bowed, a look of agony on his face. The general manager seemed furious at the delay and intent on hiding the spectacle from general purview. A few minutes later, an expensive car sped from the main entrance to the stage door. Out came a dignifed-looking man carrying a little black bag, the type that doctors use. He immediately went to the green room and in a few seconds out came the maestro, this time full of zest and with smiling countenance. The concert went splendidly, with the conductor's arms thrashing wildly as he beat the tempo up to a frenzy. We in the orchestra knew that he had gotten his fix.

The point is that for bebop musicians a blatant form of *cultural suppression* was taking place, a suppression not restricted solely to black musicians, since white players such as Art Pepper and Stan Getz were also arrested for narcotics violations.

Like Ragtime, bebop was a system which could absorb and transform other musical genres. While Ragtime transformations occurred through syncopated rhythmic structure, bebop not only enhanced the latter but succeeded in a distillation of harmonic structure from American popular standards with a highly original, individualized treatment of melody. By systematic alteration, substitution, and extension of chord structure to standards like "I Got Rhythm" or "How High the Moon," infinite melodic permutations could be composed. This was true both for the initial melodic statement, or "head," as well as subsequent solo choruses....

For the first time, black musicians were in the position to turn the game around and use "white" elements of that which had been originally borrowed from black culture. [...]

Through the use of ingenious coding techniques having evolved from New Orleans "head arrangement," entire songs could be reduced to a few inches of space, with only chord symbols and the melody or head. This format largely replaced the customary "long hand" sheet music, or written-out arrangements, which had evolved from the days of the big bands. For the white bands, arrangements had been a necessity on two counts. First, reading from arrangements precluded the need for improvisation, an artistic mode virtually intrinsic to Afro-American music culture. Second, elaborate, expensive arrangements resulted in white competitors gaining ascendancy in the industry during the twenties. They were combined with large personnel, elaborate costumes and music stands, managers, band boys, and valets, the effect of which was to seriously disadvantage Afro-American musicians without the financial wherewithal to compete against such "show biz" models. In New York during this era a successful Afro-American orchestra on the order of Vincent Lopez or Paul Whiteman was an exception.

The advantage accorded by the shorthand code system so frequently employed during the bop era was the creation of a musical language that could be understood by both those who could read music as well as those who played by "ear." [...]

Unlike the so-called swing era, when Jazz had been an adjunct of the dance and therefore required the continuous pulsation of the bass drum and guitar, bop was solo-oriented. For this reason, standards chosen for bop composition contained as a rule fewer chord changes per measure, allowing a greater space for melodic invention and heightened possibilities for harmonic alteration and substitution.

The drums and guitar, no longer confined to a strict rhythmic function, swiftly evolved into melodic instruments, with the basic impulse or beat shifting from bass drum to the shimmering, lighter-sounding cymbal. Off-beat syncopation, or "bombs," replaced the previous steady 4/4 beat of the bass drum, increasing musical feedback (by making the musical structure more elastic) and providing inspiration to the soloist. The "elasticized" musical universe gave more and more varied perspectives from which to begin and provided more varied paths along which to travel for both soloist and rhythm section.

The African concept of drums involving both rhythm and melody was being reasserted more than a hundred years after its banishment during slavery. Art Blakey studied drums in Africa. Dizzy Gillespie employed the Afro-Cuban drummer Chano Pozo in one of his early 1940 bands. As in the days of slavery, some white listeners began to express fears over the verbal-like qualities reasserting themselves. Some, for example, saw bop drumming as indicative of hate, and portending revolution and violence....

Bop was a major challenge to European standards of musical excellence and the beginning of a conscious black aesthetic in music. Since the twenties, when the term "sweet" was created to imply that a new style had arisen among the white imitators of New Orleans Jazz, a sort of orthodoxy had become manifest in terms of tone production. "Sweet" came to describe, not an innovation in content or style, but tonal production that was characterized by a wide vibrato. Although vibrato had been employed in African and Afro-American music for expressive effect or nuance, under the European-influenced imitators in the twenties it had been used continuously, in accordance with traditional European canons of style. Therein, tone without continuous vibrato was considered to be indicative of inferior playing. As with other "new" periods of Afro-American music, the originators were forced, out of commercial necessity, to imitate their imitators. The latter, by inculcating such European aesthetic criteria, were then able to give the appearance of innovation and thus force commercial models on black musicians.

Shock waves throughout the industry were felt with the advent of vibrato-less tones in the forties. The iconoclastic figures of Lester Young, Charlie Parker, Dizzy Gillespie, and Miles Davis suddenly altered the European conception by tonal production that was unarguably beautiful, even though based on non-European standards ... which are to a great extent based upon speed or frequency of continuous vibrato within a carefully circumscribed range. Vibrato that is "too fast" or "too slow" is judged as productive of "bad" tone. Vibrato in Afro-American music has not been subjected to this degree of stylization, being dependent on expressive mood and therefore capable of greater variation in terms of speed or frequency.

Other serious challenges to the uniform European aesthetic concerned the outcropping of personalized methods of playing. Breaking away from European notions of the "correct" way to play, men like Gillespie experimented with methods that had heretofore been considered wrong. The puffed cheeks of Gillespie defied notions that the diaphragm must be the sole source of air production. Later he was to turn the bell of his trumpet from the accustomed horizontal position to a sixty-degree angle. Babs Gonzales wrote, sang, and recorded bop compositions such as "Oop-Pop-A-Da" which replaced conventional lyrics with those of his own invention. Commenting on the music industry's tendency to credit whites with black developments, Gonzales remarked: "Charlie Ventura was the first to emulate our style and in two months of constant plugging by this snake (a radio disc jockey) *he* became the ORIGINATOR of the bop vocals."

Finally, even though European music had employed dissonance, it was conventional and prescribed that a composition end on a consonance. Bop pieces, however, frequently defied this rule by ending on dissonances.

With the sudden barrage of innovations and deviations from European musical norms, would-be white imitators were, as never before or since, thrown off the path to easy accessibility.

The total effect of this barrage was that Afro-American musicians gained a measure of control over their product, a situation that had not existed since the expansion of the music industry in the Twenties. Even though whites still controlled radio and the phonograph industry, they could no longer dominate the performance field. The constant drive of the bop rhythm section, coupled with an inscrutable Afro-American ethos in soloistic playing, sharply delimited white competition. If one compares the recordings of whites with those of black players, musical differences are immediately recognizable ...

—1972

Mary Lou Williams

Two other pianists I met in Kaycee during the mid-thirties were Tadd Dameron and Thelonius Monk. I was to get to know both of them well in New York years later. Tadd, who came from Cleveland, was just starting out playing and writing for a band from Kansas. Though very young, he had ideas even then that were way ahead of his time. Thelonius, still in his teens, came into town with either an evangelist or medicine show—I forgot which.

While Monk was in Kaycee he jammed every night; really used to blow on piano, employing a lot more technique than he does today. Monk plays the way he does now because he got fed up. Whatever people may tell you, I *know* how Monk can play. He felt that musicians should play something new, and started doing it. Most of us admire him for this. He was one of the original modernists all right, playing pretty much the same harmonies then that he's playing now. Only in those days we called it "Zombie music" and reserved it mostly for musicians after hours.

Why "Zombie music"? Because the screwy chords reminded us of music from *Frankenstein* or any horror film. I was one of the first with these frozen sounds, and after a night's jamming would sit and play weird harmonies (just chord progressions) with Dick Wilson, a very advanced tenor player.

—1954

Milt Hinton

The personality and color of Beefsteak's seemed to change once a day. During the daytime the customers were mostly white. Lunchtime was very popular with truck drivers and service guys from the neighborhood office buildings and hotels. Like many other bars in those days, they'd set up a steamtable and you could buy a beer and get a sandwich and condiments—pickles, macaroni, salad, beets, sardines—free.

By late afternoon the customers were mostly blacks, which was somewhat unusual for a midtown bar at that time. I think I know why it happened. Right above Beefsteak's, in the same building, was a ballroom dancing place where guys would go and pay ten cents a dance. The clientele was white but the band was black. Every intermission, they'd go downstairs and drink in the front section of the bar near the big windows, where they were easily seen by people walking by. It didn't take long before a couple of guys from our band walking through the neighborhood on a break noticed them and went in for a drink. Word spread quickly and soon more and more black musicians were spending time in there.

It really didn't happen because other neighborhood bars refused to serve blacks. It's that we felt more comfortable in places where there was a good-sized group of us. Besides, Beefsteak's was really cheap. Even in the mid-fifties a glass of beer cost fifteen cents and a shot of scotch was half a dollar.

For a while Beefsteak's became a place where a few musician junkies hung out. It was safe because cops never seemed to look for them in bars and the bartenders never knew what was going on. I remember being in there when I'd see a couple of well-known guys standing at one end of the bar or sitting in a booth sipping a Coke. They'd hang around for an hour, maybe more. Then somebody told me these guys were coming in and waiting for their connection. I became more observant and it didn't take long before I was able to identify the dealer. He always carried a trombone case, but I never saw him on a gig. A couple of minutes after he'd arrive, his customers would go off to the bathroom, one by one, to make their buy.

I still remember an afternoon when one of the bartenders asked if I'd help him pull out a guy who'd slid down onto the floor in one of the front booths. He told me he couldn't understand what had happened because, even though the guy had been in the bar a couple of hours, he'd only had one or two Cokes. I crossed the aisle to the booth and when I looked down I saw it was Charlie Parker. He was conscious, but slobbering all over himself and nodding the way junkies do. I told the bartender the guy was a friend of mine and was feeling sick. We walked him to a booth in the back and laid him across one of the benches so he could sleep it off.

—1988

Dizzy Gillespie

We took modern jazz out to the land of enchantment, California. When I was playing with Charlie Parker for those eight weeks out in California, every moment was like magic, almost. Hollywood, we gave some golden magic, never fully appreciated moments. I've often wondered where that element comes from that makes a phrase or a note coherent, spiritual, and meaningful to someone else besides yourself. How does it trip that valve in the listener? It could come from the audience, or from the musicians you're playing with, but sometimes it just hits and everything is just right. If you're lucky, that happens once in your lifetime, maybe.

Every bit if not *all* of the magic during that engagement came from the guys on the bandstand. That little band we had was very skillfully assembled. Charlie Parker I hired because he was undeniably a genius, musically, the other side of my heartbeat. Milt Jackson, on vibes, was someone new and coming up fast in our music, very rhythmic, soulfully deep, and definitely my most prized pupil. Ray Brown, on bass, played the strongest, most fluid and imaginative bass lines in modern jazz at the time, with the exception of Oscar Pettiford. People noticed I had two white guys in the group—Al Haig, piano, and Stan Levey on drums. I guess because it seemed strange during the time of segregation. Almost everyone disregarded the fact that both cats were excellent musicians and devotees of the modern style. I didn't hire them because of their color but because they could play our music. All those guys, white boys, like Shelly Manne, Irv Kluger, Jackie Mills, Stan Levey were drummers in the drawer behind Max Roach and they knew all the licks Max played. There wasn't that much money in the gig either, so Kenny Clarke had gone with Red Allen and Max went with Benny Carter. Both of them had better jobs than playing for peanuts with me.

Lay to rest any rumors that Charlie Parker resented working for me. Hell no! Yard was glad not to have that responsibility because he might not be there. I actually took six guys to California instead of five I had contracted for because I knew—them matinees, sometimes he wouldn't be there and I didn't want the management on my back. Yeah, Charlie Parker was such a great musician that sometimes he'd get lost and wouldn't show up until very, very late. Then the guy would look up on the stand and tell me, "You got a contract for five guys, and only four guys on the stand, deduct some money." So I hired Milt Jackson as an extra musician when I went to Billy Berg's to be sure that we had five musicians on the line, according to the contract. Sometimes, when Charlie Parker wouldn't make a matinee, Billy Berg would come up to me and say, "Where's Charlie Parker?"

I'd say, "Look, you don't have Charlie Parker's name on the contract, and you want five guys. You've got five guys on the stage." So he'd get outta my face, you know what I mean, and then Charlie Parker would come up later. But it was my group, the Dizzy Gillespie Quintet, and Charlie Parker was just a prominent member of that. I paid all the bills and made the major decisions.

We hit some grooves on the bandstand at Billy Berg's that I'll always remember, but the audience wasn't too hip. They didn't know what we were playing, and in some ways, they were more dumbfounded than the people were down South. Just dumbfounded. There were a lotta dumbfounded people because a lot of them came to see us. We were on the bill with Slim Gaillard and Harry "the Hipster" Gibson, big stars on the West Coast.

I had a big fight with Slim Gaillard. Somebody asked me in the club one night, "How do you like California?"

"I'll be glad when this eight weeks is over with," I said. "I don't like this place."

"What about it—?"

"Man, it's a whole lotta 'Toms' and musical nothings and all that."

Slim Gaillard's wife heard me say that. She heard me use the word "Tom," and went and told her husband that I called him a "Tom," and he accosted me in the men's room.

"Man, I ain't even mentioned your name since I been out here. What are you talking about?"

"Don't tell me you didn't!" he said. And he wanted to get bad about it.

I was just oozing over to the place in the bathroom where they sell all the bottles of cologne, and he was just oozing up on me. Finally, he hit at me, and I ducked, and he missed. I hit him and he went down, and I was getting ready to walk through him. The fight spilled outside, and his wife must have seen the scuffle; she went in the kitchen and got a butcher knife and was getting ready to stab me in the back with it.

"Look out—!" somebody said. So I grabbed a chair, an iron chair. I was getting ready to crown her with that iron chair because she had this knife in her hand, but before I could hit her somebody grabbed both of us and that was the end of it.

I cold-cocked Slim Gaillard, just one lick, a big lick, but since that time we were great friends. I made some records with Slim Gaillard after that, Charlie Parker and I. We had all the Hollywood crowd there trying to get "in." Naturally, anything new that comes out, people want to be "in" on it, but they didn't begin to understand our music until a little later on. They were much more interested in singers out in California.

—1979

Red Callender

It was around this time that Charlie Parker was in Camarillo State Hospital getting his head together. After he came out, the Dial series of recordings was made. Ross Russell was on the scene, he was one of the forward-looking guys on the West Coast who recognized the greatness of Parker and players like Wardell Gray, Joe Albany, Dodo Marmarosa, Chuck Thompson, Dexter Gordon. He set up the sessions at MacGregor's Studio on Western. The tunes are all classics now: "Stupendous," "Carvin' the Bird," "Relaxin' at Camarillo," "Pastel." Bird liked the singer Earl Coleman, brought him to the date, insisted that Ross Russell record him. Earl sang on "Dark Shadows" and "This is Always." They both became hit tunes, they sold far more than the instrumentals.

To most people Parker would have seemed a trifle remote because he was always preoccupied with his thing, music. He could sit and write out a chart in a matter of a few minutes. Anything he played he could put on manuscript. Charlie Parker was actually a brilliant man who was unfortunate enough to be into drugs. When he was straight, he was a beautiful person to talk to, he was well versed, even erudite on many topics. Bird would talk Stravinsky or Bartok, he'd talk politics too. Often he'd discuss what was happening with President Truman, who was from his home state, Missouri. He was very articulate, had opinions on everything, especially the structure of the capitalist system and racism in America. Bird wasn't at a loss on any subject, particularly when his head was together. When he was strung out he became another person.

People were misguided about his drug use. Bird would advise people to leave it alone. But they thought that's what made Bird play. That's not what made Bird play; Bird played better when he was straight, like when he came out of Camarillo and we did those Dial sessions, before the hustlers got to him again. He was like Lady Day in that respect, a little weak for it. When Bird was straight he was a demon player. Charlie Parker was so far ahead of his time that now, thirty years after his death, there's still a group called Supersax led by Med Flory playing all his music. By now he would have been doing something entirely different....

I can remember how Howard McGhee more or less kept Bird in line, just like you would lead a small child around and make him behave. See, Bird would do so much and then he'd get a jug. Because he was trying to be straight. However, he drank. I guess when you're trying to kick a habit ... well, he drank and we'd record all we could until Bird got loaded. Howard McGhee, a guy of short stature, curly light-brown hair, had a very strong influence over Bird. He took care of business. By the time Bird would get loaded the session would be over anyway, though Bird could always play, even if he was loaded. I've never seen him when he couldn't play except when he was so drunk he couldn't stand up.

MacGregor Studio was a big roomy studio and a lot of people would come down and watch the sessions. One guy named Shifty Henry hung out all the time. He was an aspiring bass player who died way before he should have. Many ladies were present also, though during the recordings my mind wasn't on ladies. To me, playing me, playing music is utter concentration.

Bird would explain to me how most of the things he wrote at that time were based on standard changes. For instance, "Stupendous" was based on "It's Wonderful," and another thing was based on "Whispering," a jam tune. He'd explain, really break it all down; it wasn't that hard, I understood it, it was pretty obvious. Like he'd call a tune and say, "Just play 'Honeysuckle Rose' and we'll change the bridge."

Bird was a guy like this—he knew he had something different going but he wasn't an egotist. He knew he had something going but I don't think he knew how great his music was. The new sounds weren't making the heavy bread. Dizzy was much more aware of what was going on in that sense than Bird, and Dizzy was a better businessman. Bird never jammed on and on. He would state what he had to say in three or four choruses and that was it. Bird used to say, "If you can't say it in two or three choruses, you're not saying anything." I wholeheartedly agree with him to this day. Playing a million choruses doesn't make you more eloquent. Course, a guy can get wound up and extend himself sometimes, but most of the time guys just take advantage of a good rhythm section and never stop blowing.

That pisses the rhythm section off, that's why I used to get literally angry. We used to have jam sessions at a place over on Santa Monica. I remember Lucky Thompson being there, Dexter, Wardell Gray, Teddy Edwards, and some other cats, can't think of their names. We'd play tunes like "Indiana" way up, fast tempo. One guy took over thirty choruses, then someone would turn to the bassist, which happened to be me, and say, "Okay—you got it." Then they'd light cigarettes, go over in the corner to have a conversation. Well, this would get any bass player pissed. You want some respect, you've been breaking your butt making them sound good. Then, you don't even get the courtesy of them listening to your solo. . . .

Bird never did that, he had great respect for the rhythm section. I loved Bird, I was so sorry he got himself messed up. There are people who have kicked the habit, people who are still around. I never shot anything in a needle in my arm. A trumpet player who shall remain nameless at the YMCA in Dayton, Ohio, said to me once, "Hey—try this . . ."

"No way," I said. I'd never seen any funny-looking brown stuff before and I wasn't about to shoot it in my vein. I did sniff some of it and was sick for a week. I thought it was cocaine; later I discovered it was heroin. Frequently I've thought about the whole drug thing, but never could understand why anybody would want to feel that way. Personally, I like to be aware of what's happening. I've seen guys nodding and thought, "How can anybody enjoy life when they don't know what's going on, when they get so far out of it they can't even hold their heads up?" To me it was ridiculous. How can anybody get hooked unless they want to?

That's my opinion. I've been around all kinds of people all my life but I never wanted to get hooked on anything but music.

Some musicians thought it made them play better, got rid of their inhibitions. *Thought* they got rid of their inhibitions. There were a few bass players that got hooked on junk; they didn't live very long either. My contention was, and is, that I need all the energy and awareness I have to play the instrument. Therefore when I go to play I go to play straight-life, like Lester used to say, with no assistance but feeling good inside.

—1985

Charles Mingus

There was a man named Fats Navarro who was born in Key West, Florida, in 1923. He was a jazz trumpet player, one of the best in the world. He and my boy met for the first time on a cold winter night in 1947 in Grand Central Station in New York City. Lionel Hampton's band had just got off the train from Chicago and Benny Bailey gaily said good-bye and split: he was leaving for Paris, France. The guys all stood around in their overcoats by the clock, waiting for the new man joining the band. A big, fat fellow walked up carrying a trumpet case and asked in the oddest high squeaky voice "This the Hampton crew?" and Britt Woodman introduced Fats Navarro.

Charles felt embarrassed as the band walked out. There were strangers, women and children, all around, and the guys were laughing too loudly and joking and words like *motherfucker* and *cocksucker* echoed through the station. They took the shuttle to Times Square and another subway to Pennsylvania Station and boarded the train for Washington, D.C. It was my boy's first trip in the Apple, but all he saw of it was underground.

Next day they rehearsed at the Palace Theatre in Washington. Hamp had a nine-brass book. The trumpets were Wendell Cully, Duke Garret, Walter Williams, and the high-note player they all called "Whistler." Navarro just sat there placidly with his horn on his lap waiting for his solos while the rest of the band played arrangements. When Hamp pointed to him, Fats stood up and played, and played, and played! played! played! One of the other trumpet players became resentful of this new star in their midst and started muttering, "Schitt, this guy can't even read!" Fats laughed, grabbed the musician's part, eyed it and said, "Schitt, you ain't got nothin' to read here!" And he sight-read from the score impeccably for the entire last show.

Fats was featured all that week in Washington and then they went on the road. The trumpet player whose parts Fats had read with such scornful ease couldn't forget what had happened. He was a man who carried a gun and he was convinced that he had been insulted. He was lipping a lot about how he would kill Fats one of these days.

They traveled by bus. The small instruments were in the luggage racks, the basses lay cushioned in the back row. Seats were assigned by seniority and the one next to my boy was vacant and was given to Fats Navarro. Mingus and he hadn't talked much up to now. The first night out the whole band was tired and they settled down to rest as the bus headed west. Later Mingus woke up feeling uneasy. It was past twelve midnight and everything was still, the men were sleeping, but the seat beside Mingus was empty. He heard a voice in the dark, someone pleading. "No ... nooo ... nooooo ..." Then a familiar little high-pitched voice squeaked, "Don't you *ever* say you gonna cut or shoot somebody 'less you do it, hear? Now if you don't be quiet I might cut you too deep to hold still while I makes you bleed a little 'cause when Theodore Navarro says *he's* gonna cut you that's what he's gonna do." My boy felt the others waking and listening too but nobody made a sound.

Later Fats came quietly back to his seat. After a silence he said, "That wasn't no way to treat a new member, that was old-fashioned jealousy schitt. Me and Miles and Dizzy and little Benny Harris played together and didn't never have no old-fashioned jealousy schitt. Why should any old member of the band be so uncourteous as to uncourteously threaten a new member?"

Nothing was said afterwards about the cat who got scratched and nothing more was heard from him about shooting Fats.

The band played thirty or forty one-nighters in a row, usually arriving in a town just in time to check into their dingy hotel rooms and wash up. Fats and my boy liked to talk to each other and began to room together. It was cheaper that way anyhow.

So this bus rolled on and on across the country, sometimes by day and sometimes at night. And in the crummy hotel rooms with big old-fashioned brass beds that sagged under Fats's enormous weight like hammocks they began a dialogue that continued off and on until the time it had to end.

"You like all kinds of music, Mingus? I was born in Key West, Florida. My family's Cuban. You play Cuban music?"

"I'm not hip to that, Fats. I know some Mexican tunes."

"Hang out with me and I'll take you to some of the joints. You can sit in, blow some. Do you play any other than bass?"

"I try my best not to but I get my chops up on piano sometimes when I'm scoring long enough. I love to hear it on piano."

"Who'd you work with before, Mingus?"

"Illinois Jacquet ... Alvino Rey ..."

"Yeah? I played with Jacquet too. You play with Diz or Bird when they was in California? See, I knowed of you before you knowed of me. Talk to Jacquet or someone else—you ain't so undiscovered. Miles played once with you. He used to tell about the band you guys had."

"He did? He hardly said a word except with his horn. How cool can you get when a cat don't even say hello. That's the system, Fats, the system that keeps the blacks apart."

"I see what you mean—so busy worrying how to make a dime with your horn, ain't got time to make a race. Gotta go downtown and see the man, ain't got time to shake your hand. So we play jazz in its place."

"Where's the place, Fats?"

"Right in their faces. They know we know where it's at. Aw, they own us, Mingus. If they don't own us, they push us off the scene. Jazz is big business to the white man and you can't move without him. We just work-ants. He owns the magazines, agencies, record companies and all the joints that sell jazz to the public. If you won't sell out and you try to fight they won't hire you and they give a bad picture of you with that false publicity."

"Sell out, Fats? To who? Look at Ellington, Armstrong, Basie—look at Hamp. All big famous band leaders. You can't tell me that agents and bookers own guys like that!"

"Mingus, you a nice boy from California, I don't want to disillusion you. But I been through all that schitt and I had to learn to do some things to get along. I learned better than to try to make it just with my music out on these dirty gang-mob streets 'cause I still love playing better than money. Jazz ain't supposed to make nobody no millions but that's where it's at. Them that shouldn't is raking it in but the purest are out in the street with me and Bird and it rains all over us, man. I was better off when nobody knew my name except musicians. You can bet it ain't jazz no more when the underworld moves in and runs it strictly for geetz and even close out the colored agents. They shut you up and cheat you on the count of your record sales and if you go along they tell the world you a real genius. But if you don't play they put out the word you're a troublemaker, like they did me. Then if some honest club owner tries to get hold of you to book you, they tell you're not available or you don't draw or you'll tear up the joint like you was a gorilla. And you won't hear nothin' about it except by accident. But if you behave, boy, you'll get booked—except for less than the white cats that copy your playing and likely either the agent or owner'll pocket the difference."

"But Fats, I know a lot of guys with managers taking a fair cut—fifteen, twenty, maybe thirty per cent."

"Who told you that? Mingus, *King Spook* don't even own fifty per cent of himself! His agent gets fifty-one, forty-nine goes to a corporation set up in his name that he don't control and he draws five hundred a week and don't say *nothing*—but he's famous, Mingus, hear, he's famous!"

"Nobody didn't hold no gun on King Spook to sign no contract like that."

"You sure about that? One time he got uppity and they kicked him out of the syndicate joints. He had to break up his band out in California. He tried to buck it on his own with nobody but his old lady to help him beat the system. Mingus, that's the biggest gun in the world to stick in a man's ribs—*hunger*. So he sold out again. Now he's got a club named after him but it ain't his. Oh, it's a hard wrinkle, Mingus. Haw haw! I'm thinking when Peggy Lee be appearing in some East Side club. Her biggest applause comes when she says, 'Now I'm going to do the great Billie Holiday,' and Billie be out in the street and they all be saying she's a junkie. They had Billie so hung up they wouldn't pay the right way, they just put a little money in her hand every night after work, just enough so she come back tomorrow. They drives ya to it, Mingus. They got you down and they don't let you up."

"If you're right, why don't some of the big Negro businessmen step into the picture?"

"'Cause they ain't caught on it's a diamond mine and they too busy scufflin' in their own corn patch and maybe scared. You breaking into Whitey's private vault when you start telling Negroes to wake up and move in where they belong and it ain't safe, Mingus. When the day comes the black man says I want mine, then hide your family and get yourself some guns. 'Cause there ain't no better business for Whitey to be in than Jim Crow business."

"I guess you got something here, Fats. I notice you and me staying in hotels like this one for twice what the white man pays."

"Well, if things don't change, Cholly, do like I tell you, get yourself some heat, guns, cannons, and be willing to die like *they* was. That's all I heard when I was a kid, how bad they was and not 'fraid to die—to arms, to arms, and all that schitt, give me liberty or give me death! Show me where the atomic power button is and I'll give them cocksuckers some liberty!"

"You said money shouldn't matter to musicians, Fats. What if we all gave up on fame and fortune and played 'cause we love to, like the jazzmen before us—at private sessions for people that listened and respect the players? Then people would know that jazz musicians play for love."

"I thought you had some children, Mingus. Don't they need no ends out there in California?"

"I'm going to write a book and when I sell it I'm not gonna play any more for money. I'll compose and now and then rent a ballroom and throw a party and pay some great musicians to play a couple of things and improvise all night long. That's what jazz originally was, getting away from the usual tiddy, the hime, the gig."

"But Mingus, how about them crumb-crushers of yours when their little stomachs get to poppin' and there ain't nothin' in their jaws but their gums, teeth, and tongue, what you gonna do? Play for money or be a pimp?"

"I tried being a pimp, Fats. I didn't like it."

"Then you gonna play for money."

———

The tour continued and Fats began to complain that he didn't feel good, he hurt all over and he wanted out. My boy thought it was just an excuse because they were tired of the strenuous one-nighters. One day on the bus Fats began coughing up blood. When they got to Chicago he quit the band and left for New York. But my boy and he were to meet and talk again many times before the day in July 1950 when Fats Navarro died in New York City of tuberculosis and narcotics addiction. He was twenty-six years old.

—1971

Martin Bauml Duberman

Bach and Mozart, yes; they stood apart for [Paul Robeson]; the *Art of the Fugue* he found "intoxicating." But henceforth his chief concern would be "trying to find an Art that is purely Negro, that is not dependent on Western and European influences."

In this regard, he rejected jazz as well as Wagner. Jazz "reflects Broadway, not the Negro. It exploits a Negro technique, but it isn't Negro. [It] has something of the Negro sense of rhythm, but only some ... The rhythmic complications of [African dialects] ... make Duke Ellington's hot rhythms seem childish." He elaborated further the following year [1933]: "Jazz, which is admittedly negroid in its rhythmical origin, is no longer the honest and sincere folk-song in character ... Jazz songs like 'St. Louis Blues' or 'St. James's Infirmary' ... are actually nearer to their folk-song origin than they are to Tin Pan Alley, but ... most of it isn't genuine negro music any longer"—and as for a jazz piece like "High Water," it was merely "a vulgarized form of 'Roll, Jordan, Roll.'" ("I would rather get together half a dozen African drummers and listen to them. Their rhythm is so much more complicated.") In dismissing jazz as having "no spiritual significance," and in saying it would have no "serious effect on real music," Robeson was expressing an opinion shared by most "serious" composers and critics of the day. The early explorations of the jazz idiom on the part of Copland, Stravinsky, Milhaud, Weill, Kreneck, and others, these critics argued, had just about exhausted its possibilities. Robeson was also echoing an attitude that had existed in the twenties among the black bourgeoisie and some of the Harlem elite—though for very different reasons. Whereas the black upper crust denigrated jazz as the music of their Southern peasant antecedents (an attitude they applied as well to spirituals), Robeson came to disdain it because it was not a *pure enough* expression of those folk origins. However, just as the Harlem elite had eventually succumbed to the mania for jazz in the late twenties, Paul also seems in later years to have been able to set aside his theoretical arguments with it and to enjoy it for what it was. Throughout the forties, he frequented such legendary jazz joints as the Apollo and Café Society to hear big bands and some of the jazz greats, like Chick Webb and Ella Fitzgerald. In the fifties he would go "up to the Savoy Ballroom very often to hear Count Basie ... downtown to hear Don Shirley and back up to Manhattan Casino to hear Charlie Parker and get 'twisted around' trying to dance to those 'off beat riffs,' down to the Apollo to hear Dizzy Gillespie take flight ... And Thelonious Monk really floored [him]." And much later, in 1958, Robeson would come around to saying, "For my money, modern jazz is one of the most important musical things there is in the world."

—1988

Michele Wallace

During the fifties in Harlem, Charlie Parker's trickster alto sax provided the catalyst for bebop and for the counter-cultural scene that developed around it. By the time cultural nationalism and Black Power rolled around in the sixties, Bird had become a cultural icon among black intellectuals and artists, equaled in stature only by Billie Holiday and John Coltrane, not only for his art but for his political anger. Even when his music, his natty style in dressing, his existential alienation, and his troubling addiction to drugs seemed to fade into the margins as irrelevant to Black Power's affirmation, Bird's shadow lingered still to remind us of black creativity's crucial element, its profound deformation of white cultural hegemony.

The beauty of the movie *Bird*, directed by Clint Eastwood, is, of course, the music. The heresy of bebop in concert with fellow conspirators Dizzy Gillespie, Bud Powell, Thelonious Monk, Kenny Clarke, and Max Roach (other artists embellished the original recordings for the film) still rattles the corpses that customarily assail our ears in movie houses and elsewhere. The horror, which the film sublimely advances, is the notion that this tortured black artist, played by Forest Whitaker, could have sprung full grown from the head of a white Zeus, issuing, he seems to, from no black community, no black family, no black woman that he wouldn't have been better off without.

If it is true, as Parker himself claimed, that he was addicted to heroin from the age of twelve, this is perhaps the most important fact we can know about him after we know that he was what's called in the West "a musical genius." Yet in *Bird*, no more substantial reason seems to emerge to explain Parker's precipitous decline and death from drug addiction at thirty-five than that he is a black man trapped in a white man's movie. Parker as rootless, alienated from the black community, family, and bourgeois existence, which he undoubtedly was, might have made a fascinating film. It is not really these issues that are explored in *Bird*, however, rather the parasitic concept that Parker's life is only significant to the degree that it illustrates the antithesis of what it means to be white, male, and privileged. (The same seems true of the Bud Powell/Dexter Gordon character in *'Round Midnight*.) On the other hand, because we view the film through the body of Parker's music—awesome, lush, and on an entirely different trajectory—our objections are silenced.

—1989

Arthur Brown

THE ASSASSINATION OF CHARLIE PARKER

bird does not live
charles christopher parker is dead
is dead in marbled legends
of a bronze benin faced boy with patch-work horn
          and mama-made macoute
a jazz-juba muse
watching down lester's hands
from kansas city balconies
tracing with bird's eye feather fingers melodic pantomime
          of syncopated braille
bluing a new cartography of flight
at the ear's horizon's deepest touch

is dead whose soul's-song was dust roads was goat paths
          was brooming from gold coast to stoop-down
          to git-back to guinea to harlem
was shuffle blue-black bottom and whoa back buck up
comin down and lord child now's the time and catch up
and huckle buck a stop and double time kalinda
through the four four and misty
          of tin pan alley
was sugar rum molasses sweet back and back
in lockstep in coffle and in harvest of heart-drought
is dead in chili parlors and cherokee
in the recycled but unresurrected riff
in turn your money green
is dead in the elegant laps of hip debutantes
dead to tommy dorsey's horn-rim
          glasses
as bennygood man and the wrong note
is dead in taxicabs
          nodding to everywhere
out in the out chorus
          and the vamp is dead
          to smack

to smacked back
screeching A Train subway and so soon and bye baby the obscene solo
come shitty come yuk yuk come tee hee come mellow
      fucked up and over
funny phoenix orgasmic out of the asshole of he gone
        is dead
in all the bop visioned and bop spent
        stations of the breath
is dead
      to BE
bop charles christopher parker is yardbird-dead
       o-rooney

—1981

Arthur Brown

ERRATA:

change RE to BE bop. RE BE BOP.
p. 1 change st francis the sissy to st elmo hope.
p. 2 change bud to power. change bird's madness to a method book
for the young (you dont have to play). see bop run bop come bop
come bop. change parker to a directional sign. bop can be a book to
live as well as die by. change the beauty of the dead to the beauty of
the living. telephone the generations. bop reconstruction for the un-
reconstructed. for the freed man. bop mules. bop acres. bop signatures on bop votes and boplicity. walk parker gently home. catch
trane. reclaim bop territory. show your blues tattoo.
p. 3 change loneliness into onliness. change self to selves.
p. 4 change into. change into. swallow the gold sardine walk parker
boppily home.
p. 5 change into. you know
we could call it ornithology

—1980

Postbop, Free Jazz and Onward

David Henderson

HANGING OUT IN THE MUSIC

1
he breathed the hot room
alive with jass and vivid colors
breathed in and out
faces raptured towards the light
made of jass playing towards the light
brilliant faces facing

he felt sparks of energy along his back
the wingspread within without
his eyes opened wider
he saw everything in the room at once
and there was so much
the trumpet hit a trill
his stomach fluttered

he sat upon his stomach
the seat of wind
he felt the energy possessed by the electric wind
the energy of atoms

sensitized to open the eyes
a tickling occurring
twinkle of brilliance in the room
high yellows and cosmic blues
going into Shango reds—a *fireness*

sensitized
like a kiss upon the eye
tender lips brushing
enhance consciousness of respiration
of a coming in and out
with life and the death is exhaled
enhance the respiration
deepen the ears to the room containing all

2
jass they play
you hear at it
it be a part of you
alive
it be alive
like when you alone in the house
maybe a little lonely
you put on some bad jass
and they be company

you hear them grow
you see them play
the musicians
they be going thru changes
in the music
like you be going thru changes
like the jass tunes.

3
hubbard and his ghetto beaus
getting down the batty
popping the tune down
like slaps of five
or shafts of blades
or good reefer
going in and out yo head
we partake of the jammers
the jammers
we partake of them
they lay it out
they got it to give

—1980

LeRoi Jones / Amiri Baraka

Most jazz critics have been white Americans, but most important jazz
musicians have not been. This might seem a simple enough reality to
most people, or at least a reality which can be readily explained in terms

of the social and cultural history of American society. And it is obvious why there are only two or three fingers' worth of Negro critics or writers on jazz, say, if one understands that until relatively recently those Negroes who *could* become critics, who would largely have to come from the black middle class, have simply not been interested in the music. Or at least jazz, for the black middle class, has only comparatively recently lost some of its stigma (though by no means is it yet as popular among them as any vapid musical product that comes sanctioned by the taste of the white majority). Jazz was collected among the numerous skeletons the middle-class black man kept locked in the closet of his psyche, along with watermelons and gin, and whose rattling caused him no end of misery and self-hatred. As one Howard University philosophy professor said to me when I was an undergraduate, "It's fantastic how much bad taste the blues contain!" But it is just this "bad taste" that this Uncle spoke of that has been the one factor that has kept the best of Negro music from slipping sterilely into the echo-chamber of middle-brow American culture [...]

There were few "jazz critics" in America at all until the thirties and then they were influenced to a large extent by what Richard Hadlock has called "the carefully documented gee-whiz attitude" of the first serious European jazz critics. They were also, as a matter of course, influenced more deeply by the social and cultural mores of their own society. And it is only natural that their criticism, whatever its intention, should be a product of that society, or should reflect at least some of the attitudes and thinking of that society, even if not directly related to the subject they were writing about, Negro music.

Jazz, as a Negro music, existed, up until the time of the big bands, on the same socio-cultural level as the subculture from which it was issued. The music and its sources were *secret* as far as the rest of America was concerned, in much the same sense that the actual life of the black man in America was secret to the white American. The first white critics were men who sought, whether consciously or not, to understand this secret, just as the first serious white jazz musicians (Original Dixieland Jazz Band, Bix, etc.) sought not only to understand the phenomenon of Negro music but to appropriate it as a means of expression which they themselves might utilize. The success of this "appropriation" signaled the existence of an American music, where before there was a Negro music. But the white jazz musician had an advantage the white critic seldom had. The white musician's commitment to jazz, the *ultimate concern,* proposed that the subcultural attitudes that produced the music as a profound expression of human feelings could be *learned* and need not be passed on as a secret blood rite. And Negro music is essentially the expression of an attitude, or a collection of attitudes, about the world, and only secondarily an attitude about the way the music is made. The white jazz musician came to understand this attitude as a way of making music, and the intensity of his understanding produced the "great" white musicians, and is producing them now.

Usually the critic's commitment was first to his *appreciation* of the music rather than to his understanding of the attitude which produced it. This difference meant that the potential critic of jazz had only to appreciate the music, or what he thought was the music, and that he did not need to understand or even be concerned with the attitudes that produced it, except perhaps as a purely sociologcial consideration. This last idea is certainly what produced the reverse patronization that is known as Crow Jim. The disparaging "all you folks got rhythm" is no less a stereotype, simply because it is proposed as a positive trait. But this Crow Jim attitude has not been as menacing or as evident a flaw in critical writing about jazz as has another manifestation of the white critic's failure to concentrate on the blues and jazz attitude rather than his conditioned appreciation of the music. The major flaw in this approach to Negro music is that it strips the music too ingenuously of its social and cultural intent. It seeks to define jazz as an art (or folk art) that has come out of no intelligent body of socio-cultural philosophy. [...]

Strict musicological analysis of jazz, which has come into favor recently, is also limited as a means of jazz criticism or as a strict sociological approach. The notator of any jazz solo, or blues, has no chance of capturing what in effect are the most important elements of the music. (Most transcriptions of blues lyrics are just as frustrating.) A printed musical example of an Armstrong solo, or of a Thelonius Monk solo, tells us almost nothing except the futility of formal musicology when dealing with jazz. Not only are the various jazz effects almost impossible to notate, but each note *means something* quite in adjunct to the musical notation. The notes of a jazz solo exist in a notation strictly for musical reasons. The notes of a jazz solo, as they are coming into existence, exist as they do for reasons that are only concomitantly musical. Coltrane's cries are not "musical," but they *are* music and quite moving music. Ornette Coleman's screams and rants are only musical once one understands the music his emotional attitude seeks to create. This attitude is real, and perhaps the most singularly important aspect of his music.

Mississippi Joe Williams, Snooks Eaglin, Lightnin' Hopkins have different emotional attitudes than Ornette Coleman, but all of these attitudes
are continuous parts of the historical and cultural biography of the
Negro as it has existed and developed since there was a Negro in America, and a music that could be associated with him that did not exist anywhere else in the world. The notes *mean something;* and the something is,
regardless of its stylistic considerations, part of the black psyche as it
dictates the various forms of Negro culture.

Another hopeless flaw in a great deal of the writing about jazz that
has been done over the years is that in most cases the writers, the jazz
critics, have been anything but intellectuals (in the most complete sense
of that word). Most jazz critics began as hobbyists or boyishly brash
members of the American petit bourgeoisie, whose only claim to any understanding about the music was that they knew it was *different;* or else
they had once been brave enough to make a trip into a Negro slum to
hear their favorite instrumentalist defame Western musical tradition.
Most jazz critics were (and are) not only white middle-class Americans,
but middle-brows as well. The irony here is that because the majority of
jazz critics are white middle-brows, most jazz criticism tends to enforce
white middle-brow standards of excellence as criteria for performance of
a music that in its most profound manifestations is completely antithetical to such standards; in fact, quite often is in direct reaction against
them. (As an analogy, suppose the great majority of the critics of Western formal music were poor, "uneducated" Negroes?)

—1963

Walter De Legall

PSALM FOR SONNY ROLLINS

This vibrant, all-embracing, all-pervading
Sound which bleeds from the vinylite veins
Of my record, steals into the conduits of my heart
Forces entrance into the sanctuary
Of my soul, trespasses into the temple
Of my gonads. In a lifespan-while, I am
Absorbed into the womb of the sound.
> I am in the sound
> The sound is in me.
> I am the sound.

I am your tears that you shed for forty days
And forty nights, Theodore. I am
Your pain who you accepted as
Your bedfellow. I am your hunger and
Your thirst, which purified your
Soul, Theodore. I am your sorrow that
You won in a raffle. Pick up your axe
And let us blow down the Chicago citadels
Of convention. "You just can't play like that in here."
Let us blow down the Caucasian battlements
Of bigotry. "But we don't hire Colored musicians."
Open your tenor mouth and let
Us blow into oblivion the insensible
Strongholds of morality.
"And I'm sure he's an addict."
Blow down thunder and lightning
And White People!! Blow down moons
And stars and Christs! Blow down
Rains and trees and Coltranes! Blow down
Shirleys and Star-eyes and West Coasts!
Walk naked into a 52nd street basement
And show Them the "Bird" in your thighs.
Open your Prestige mouth and let them see
The "Hawk" in your voice. Recite ten
Stanzas of blackeyed-pead Bluing. Sing
A hundred choruses of South Street
Solid. Paint a thousand canvases of Dig
For Joe White. Lead us you Harlem
Piper with a Selmer pipe. The black
Boned children of tomorrow follow
You through space and time
                    Lead us to truth,
                    To order, To Zen.
                    Lead us to Poetry,
                    To love, to God.

        Ring halleluiahs from a sombre past.
        Roll halleluiahs to a buoyant dream.
        Breathe hallleluiahs for a solemn few.
        Halleluiah! Halleluiah! Halleluiah!

LeRoi Jones / Amiri Baraka

[Thelonius] always had a strong reputation among musicians, but perhaps his wider acceptance began during his stay at the old Five Spot the late spring and summer of 1957, with that beautiful quartet consisting of John Coltrane, Wilbur Ware, and Shadow Wilson. Anyone who witnessed the transformation that playing with Monk sent Coltrane through (opening night he was struggling with *all* the tunes), must understand the deepness and musical completeness that can come to a performer under the Monk influence. It is not too far out to say that before the Monk job Trane was a very hip saxophonist, but after that experience, he had a chance to become a very great musician and an ubiquitous influence himself.

When Monk opened at the new Five Spot, the owners said that he would be there "as long as he wanted." Monk also went out and bought a brand-new piano, though after the long stay there were hundreds of scratches, even gashes, on the wood just above the keyboard, where Monk, slashing at the keys, bangs the wood with his big ring, or tears it with his nails.

"No one," said Joe Termini, co-owner with his brother, Iggy, of the Five Spot, "draws crowds as consistently as Monk." And it seemed very true during the six months Monk spent at the new sleek version of the old Bowery jazz club. Most evenings there was a crowd of some proportions sitting around the club, and the weekends were always swinging and packed, the crowds stretching, sometimes, right out into the street. The crowds comprised of college students ... by the droves, especially during the holidays ... seasoned listeners, hippies, many musicians, tourists, explorers, and a not so tiny ungroupish group of people immediately familiar to each other, if perhaps obscure to others, Monkfans. For certain, a great many of the people who came and will come to see Monk come out of a healthy or unhealthy curiosity to see somebody "weird," as the mystique of this musician and his music, even as it has seeped down distorted, to a great extent, by the cultural lag into the more animated fringe of the mainstream culture, has led them to believe he is.

Of course many of Monk's actions can be said to be strange ... they are, but they are all certainly his own. He is a very singular figure, wearing a stingy brim version of a Rex Harrison hat every night I saw him for the whole stretch of the date. All the old stories about Monk coming hours late for a job and never being able to hold a gig dissipated at the Five Spot to a certain extent. Certainly a six-month stand [...] ought to prove he can hold a job. And after a while Monk kept adjusting his employers and his audience to his entrance times, and while someone might think, if it were his first time in the Spot, that the music should begin a little earlier, anyone who had been through those changes before, and gotten used to the schedule, knew that Thelonius never got there until around eleven. But he was very consistent about that.

Monk's most familiar routine at the Five Spot was to zoom in just around eleven and head straight back for the kitchen, and into some back room where he got rid of his coat and then walked quickly back out into the club and straight to the bar. Armed with a double bourbon "or something," he would march very quickly up to the bandstand and play an unaccompanied solo. This would be something like "Crepuscule With Nellie," or "Ruby My Dear" or a very slow and beautiful "Don't Blame Me," the last finished off most times with one of his best "James P. Johnson" tinkles.

After the solo, Monk would take the microphone and announce (which surprised even the Monk fans, who by now have grown used to the pianist's very close-mouthed demeanor on the stand). But the announcements, for the most part, were very short: something like, "And now, Frankie Dunlop will play you some tubs." Then Monk would disappear out into the alcove, and a few fans who had waited for a long time, say a couple of hours, to hear Thelonius, would groan very audibly, but would still have to wait for a little while longer until the rest of the program was finished. After Dunlop's unaccompanied drum solo Monk would return to the stand, but only to say, "Butch Warren will play a bass solo," and gesturing toward Warren as he left the stand, returning to the alcove to walk back and forth or dance with the solo, he'd add, "You got it!" "Softly as in the Morning Sunrise" was what Warren usually played. . . .

Monk's playing is still remarkable. The things he can do and does do almost any night, even when he's loafing, are just out of sight. Even when he's just diddling around the keys looking for a chord to shake somebody . . . the rest of his group most times . . . up, he makes a very singularly exciting music. Critics who talk about this pianist's "limited technical abilities" (or are there any left?) should really be read out of the club. Monk can get around to any place on the piano he thinks he needs to be, and for sheer piano-lesson brilliance, he can rattle off arpeggios and brilliant sizzling runs that ought to make even those "hundred finger" pianists take a very long serious look.

While the other musicians solo, Monk usually gets up from the piano and does his "number," behind the piano, occasionally taking a drink.

The quick dips, half-whirls, and deep pivoting jerks that Monk gets into behind the piano are part of the music, too. Many musicians have mentioned how they could get further into the music by watching Monk dance, following the jerks and starts, having dug that that was the emphasis Monk wanted on the tune. He would also skip out into the alcove behind the bandstand and continue the dance, and from the bar it was pretty wiggy digging Monk stepping and spinning, moving back and forth just beyond the small entrance to the stand. You'd see only half a movement, or so, and then he'd be gone off to the other side, out of sight.

One evening after the last tune of the set, Monk leaped up from the bench, his hands held in the attitude he had assumed as he finished the number, and without changing that attitude (hands up and in front of him as he lifted them from the keys) he wheeled off the stand and did a long drawn out shuffle step from the stand completely around the back of the club. Everyone in the club stopped, sort of, and followed him with their eyes, till he had half circled the entire club. Monk brought the semicircle to a stop right at the center of the bar, and without dropping his attitude or altering his motion he called out to the bartender very practically and logically, "Give me a drink." Somebody next to me said, to no one in particular, "Now, you get to that."

—1963

Thomas J. Porter

It is very important to understand that music, like all art regardless of its form, is ideological. That is, it reflects or transmits certain political, class, and national interests. A creative and revolutionary music, however, is more than just reflective, but criticizes the very social substance of the society, and ultimately contributes towards giving direction to the social reconstruction of that society.

There is no abstract black music. There is black music reflecting different political positions of the Black people. Ramsey Lewis's music is not the same as Cecil Taylor's. So when we talk about black music, we mean the most advanced, the most socially conscious music which historically has been the music called "jazz."

Because of the critical nature of black music by 1960, it became increasingly dangerous to the keepers of the nightmare, and quite possibly, has led to spiritual and physical deaths (John Coltrane, Albert Ayler, Eric Dolphy, Booker Little, Booker Ervin) of some of its major forces.

Despite the horrors of the McCarthy period (an attempt to stifle all progressive political and social thought in America), the Robesons and DuBoises had maintained the continuity of the struggle, regardless of the price. As a result, Blacks emerged seemingly more determined than ever to press forward. This determination can, perhaps, best be explained by certain fundamental changes in the material condition of Blacks.

———

Charlie Parker's "Another Hairdo" ushered out the konk (a backyard process) and all it symbolized. However it was his musical heirs such as Clifford Brown, Miles Davis, Fats Navarro, Horace Silver, Wardell Gray, John Coltrane, etc., through their hard driving, aggressive music who captured the mood of the masses in the mid-fifties. No wonder this music became known as "hard bop."

While the Miles Davis Quintet of the mid-fifties, which included John Coltrane, instinctively reflected the crystallization of a Black proletariat, it was Mingus ("Fables For Faubus," *Scenes of the City*), Max Roach (*We Insist: Freedom Now*, "Garvey's Ghost," "Mendacity"), and Rollins (*Freedom Suite*) in the late fifties who stated it very clearly. Needless to say, neither Mingus nor Max Roach is recorded with any frequency, or is regularly available in clubs. The album which contains "Fables For Faubus" immediately became unavailable for ten years (it was re-released in 1971). Roach's album *We Insist: Freedom Now* is still unavailable. Rollins's *Freedom Suite* has since been retitled twice without the original liner notes written by Rollins.

Musicians began to free themselves from the chains of musical orthodoxy, and the limits of worn-out forms. The changes in the form and substance of the music were very similar to the motion in the political and social spheres. The major innovators were Ornette Coleman, John Coltrane, and Cecil Taylor.

Ornette Coleman's music, almost as if he were setting the pace for the cadences counted off by the marchers, the sit-ins, and freedom riders, added a new rhythmic concept which was complex in its simplicity, not unlike the early New Orleans jazz music in its emphasis on freedom and group improvisation. Coltrane's contributions are many, but his major one was in his further development of the harmonic nature of the music. Coltrane's wide-open, go-for-broke solos, played dialectically against a chordal substance, were very similar to the movement's reliance on the religious substance of our historical tradition passed down from the Nat Turners, David Walkers, to Dr. King and Malcolm. Coltrane's uniting of certain elements of music, heretofore considered dissonant, was very reflective of the emergence of a group cohesiveness of the masses. Cecil Taylor was primarily interested with "ordering the music" as he called it. He was concerned with getting beyond tunes to the construction and organization of new sounds. [...]

Black music through Coltrane, Taylor, Coleman, and the young musicians who followed them such as Archie Shepp, Andrew Hill, Bobby Hutcherson, Benny Maupin, Wayne Shorter, Joe Henderson, Grachan Moncur III, Joe Chamber, Tony Williams, Richard Davis, Cecil McBee, Freddie Hubbard, the late Booker Little, and Eric Dolphy became the Achilles heel, the weak link (and dangerous) in Western culture. The music, like the people, was immersed in Western culture, yet digested the forms without becoming overwhelmed by them. Thus by 1964, Afro-American music, in its fully developed form, had moved beyond critical realism (criticism of the forms), the high point of Western music, to a music which was both critical and analytical of the social substance of society. By 1964, it became increasingly evident that efforts were being made to formalize or cool-out *both the music and the movement which had produced it.* (...)

—1970

Wanda Coleman

BLUES FOR THE MAN ON SAX

the horn the horn *blows*

green moving thru undertow this sea these eyes promise soft
lights and lips pursed in sweet-hot tomorrows. his heart wavers
for a bit, shivers, "suppose she says no." a whine, a
flicker, something is wrong, but he doesn't know what, a
certain odor. a certain note off key.

the horn the horn *toots*

upstairs thighs drop in misconception. but this isn't the
right number. she's black like cobalt and her eyes rise over him
a serpent; teeth sharp as needles, a tongue thick with smoke winds
its way throatward. and the venom numbs his dick. death at
$3.33 per minute

the horn the horn *soars*

leaving a sour aftertaste. a skullcap of roses. stale doobies clutter the
table top. nose full of coke boogers needed, a hot shower across
town. sunday morning his soul is ripped open. bleeds love. and she
was never even there

—1987

Al Young

NOSTALGIA IN TIMES SQUARE
Charles Mingus, 1958

In this Charles Mingus version of urban renewal, you can hear truck
rumbling and traffic moaning and somebody's heart that seems to have
gotten run over in the scramble. For me it's all so clear, not unlike the
way life is when you've just turned draft age in a world laid out for one-
way wandering.

No wonder I respond to the power of this music by letting my shoulders shake ever so vibrantly, and by letting my boodie move while my
ears pick up the huffy he-bump and the shadowy she-bump that's busy
dislodging itself in there. And like that crazy feeling my ears are picking
up, I too refuse to grind to any halt that a city runner of red lights
wouldn't. This means: There comes a time to sit down and recall in slow
motion all this one-wayness, a process that seems to see each moment as
one of a kind.

Even my deepest confusion back when this record came out often
sounded so delicious it threw me. Take the days I was reading the New
York papers in Spanish and hungering for the only friend I had in Manhattan at that point: a London-born undergrad I'd met at a gig in Ober-
lin. She was sophisticated, beautiful, and spoke in lilac. Afternoons I'd
drop by her East Seventies digs (her girlfriend's uncle's triple-decker
townhouse) and, madly jabbering the only kind of jive I knew to put
down—I'd land with her in the lovesick hotseat of their bottom-most
deck and we'd pet like mink until the sky turned ink and we never bothered checking whether the stars came out.

One night we were walking to her place through Times Square—back
before genitals and orifices were being packaged—and she turned to me
and, letting go of my hand, shaped her lips to say something I sensed
was going to be urgent and deep, but changed her mind.

It is this remembered silence of hers that has hovered for decades in a secret part of me that would come out sounding—were it ever orchestrated—like Mingus's subway-grounded, wounded slash-and-burn landscape of love. Sometimes, standing at the edges of "Nostalgia in Times Square" and listening to it without regard for history or time, this piece sounds to me the way God might've described how it might feel to go spirit-slumming and wind up sidetracked and unheard from on some festive backstreet. But I know I can always pull out of this mood because those choo-choo strains in the background of this blues come right out of Jimmy Forrest's "Night Train." I know I can always hop that load of freight and bum a ride home. Besides—and even Mingus will you this— it all started back there at the roundhouse with Duke Ellington's "Happy-Go-Lucky Local."

Love, where are you now? And what was it that you were about to say before we were so hauntingly interrupted?

—1987

Herbie Nichols

NEPTUNE OFF JAMAICA

Ten dimensions of pleasure
are mine in a treasure trove,
Bobbing to all degrees
to the nonaccompaniment of trees—
The usual electricity of
sun and clouds and foam . . .

Funny cockroach, tugging at the shrouds
of a hoodoo saucer,
Fascinated by the mystic saucepan,
awash in a giant zinc . . .
What chance damned such ecstasy?

An abstract sort of bash,
spiced with a little finity!
Initial chordal splash,
hence, a wee infinity!
Sweet breakfast of causality,
forgive my search for suppertime.

Charles Ellison

I think that with John Coltrane's *A Love Supreme, Ascension Meditations,* and the albums that followed, with the general projection of Coltrane's charisma, many Black people who had previously been only marginally interested in Black music, in their own personal life style, and conditions in general, changed their life styles immensely. The reason for this rests in the tremendous spiritual reservoir which is found in Coltrane's music and that of his various disciples. When I was in high school, people started listening to Coltrane and liked what he was doing but, beyond that, they began to get into his spiritual philosophy and the philosophy of the life style in general. They saw that what he was projecting was very valuable, that it was a model which required us to follow and made us change our attitudes and manner of thinking. It was an event analogous to the Black man who had not been particularly conscious politically before coming under the influence of Malcolm X, or before discovering the political and social validity of things W.E.B. DuBois had to say. Coltrane's music made us reevaluate ourselves, see ourselves more objectively, more clearly, and place ourselves in a position within society.

With the event of a personal feeling of ethnic-nationalistic consciousness, there is a highly enthusiastic devotion which comes along as part of this new awareness, almost like an over-reaction. The political or musical message has to be lived with for a while, because it is impossible in most cases to understand the total impact of the implications. You have to deal with it from where you are and to the extent you understand it at that particular moment. As you get into it, you begin to grow and see more, your horizons expand, and the growth continues. I've seen junkies, hustlers, and people who had been taking advantage of their own brothers who came under the influence of Coltrane or Malcolm who were changed accordingly.

Coltrane's music is a guideline in terms of consciousness that leads our people into something very spiritual and cosmic. In essence, it transcends the immediate needs and talks of Utopia, of real brotherhood. [...]

If you really understand the music of Coltrane and his disciples, your life will change. The kind of thing he was into before he died was not concerned with traditional form, or the framework of "jazz." It is the music which Pharaoh Sanders terms high energy, where the vibrations (the music) are self defining. It's highly emotional music, and it brings you closer to the Creator and the marrow of being itself.

The effects of Miles Davis is entirely different. From the general time of Coltrane's *A Love Supreme,* we see evidence of his whole spiritual religious sense. On the other hand, Miles Davis has always been extremely individualistic, as if to say "I really don't need anybody; I do my own thing." That philosophy is important because it plants the seed for another Miles to keep pushing. His ideas reflect what we as a people have had to go through since being brought here in chains. The music of Miles is very strong and defiant, but it can be subtle, it can be bittersweet, it can be swinging, and it reflects his own strength. In terms of the overall plan, it is just as valid as Coltrane's music because it takes all kinds of individuals to mold a strong and durable body in the final analysis.

—1973

Sonia Sanchez

a / coltrane / poem

my favorite things
        is u / blowen
               yo/favorite/things.
stretchen the mind
        till it bursts past the con/fines of
solo / en melodies.
            to the many solos
of the
     mind / spirit.
        are u sleepen   (to be
        are u sleepen   sung
        brotha john   softly)
          where u have gone to.
     no mornin bells
     are ringen here. only the quiet
aftermath of assassinations.
        but i saw yo/murder/
the massacre
    of all blk/musicians. planned
in advance.

yrs befo u blew away our passsst
and showed us our futureeee
screech screeech screeeeech screeech
a / love / supreme. alovesupreme a lovesupreme.
    A LOVE SUPREME
scrEEEccCHHHHH screeeeEEECCCHHHHHHH
 sCReeeEEECHHHHHHH SCREEEECCCCHHHH
 SCREEEEEEEECCCHHHHHHHHHHHH
a lovesupremealovesupremealovesupreme for our blk
people.
        BRING IN THE WITE / MOTHA / fuckas
        ALL THE MILLIONAIRES / BANKERS / ol
MAIN / LINE / ASS / RISTOCRATS (ALL
THEM SO-CALLED BEAUTIFUL
PEOPLE)
    WHO HAVE KILLED
WILL CONTINUE TO
        KILL US WITH
THEY CAPITALISM / 18% OWNERSHIP
OF THE WORLD.
      YEH. U RIGHT
THERE. U ROCKEFELLERS. MELLONS
 VANDERBILTS
      FORDS.
            yeh.
GITem.
   PUSHem / PUNCHem / STOMPem. THEN
LIGHT A FIRE TO
        THEY pilgrim asses,
TEAROUT THEY eyes.
        STRETCH they necks
till no mo
     raunchy sounds of MURDER/
POVERTY / STARVATION
         come from they
throats.
screeeeeeeeeeeeeeeeeCHHHHHHHHHHHH
SCREEEEEEEEEEEEEEECHHHHHHHHHH
screeEEEEEEEEEEEEEEEEEEEEEEEEE
EECCCCHHHHHHHH
SCREEEEEEEEEEEEEEEEEEEEEEEEEEEEEEE

EEEEEEECHHHHHHHHHHH

BRING IN THE WITE / LIBERALS ON THE SOLO

SOUND OF YO / FIGHT IS MY FIGHT

                        SAXOPHONE.

                              TORTURE

THEM FIRST AS THEY HAVE

                      TORTURED US WITH

PROMISES /

          PROMISES, IN WITE/AMURICA. WHEN

ALL THEY WUZ DOEN

               WAS HAVEN FUN WITH THEY

ORGIASTIC DREAMS OF BLKNESS.

                  (JUST SOME MO

CRACKERS FUCKEN OVER OUR MINDS.)

                    MAKE THEM

SCREEEEEEAM

          FORGIVE ME. IN SWAHILI.

DON'T ACCEPT NO MEA CULPAS.

                DON'T WANT TO

                    HEAR

BOUT NO EUROPEAN FOR / GIVE / NESS.

DEADDYINDEADDYINDEADDYINWITEWESTERN

           SHITTTTTT

(softly   da-dum-da da da da da da da da /da-dum-da

till it   da da da da da da da da da da

builds   da-dum- da da da

up)   da-dum. da. da. da. this is part of my

             favorite things.

             da dum da da da da da da

             da da da da

                da dum da da da da

                da dum da da da da - - - - -

(to be   rise up blk / people

sung   de dum da da da da

slowly   move straight in yo / blkness

to tune   da dum da da da da

of my   step over the wite / ness

favorite   that is yesssss terrrrrr day

things.)   weeeeeeee are toooooooday.

(f   da dum

a   da da da (stomp, stomp) da da da

s   da dum
t   da da da (stomp, stomp) da da da
e   da dum
r)   da da da (stomp)   da da da dum (stomp)
          weeeeeeeee (stomp)
              areeeeeeeee (stomp)
                    areeeeeee (stomp, stomp)
          tooooooday   (stomp.
                day   stomp.
                day   stomp.
                day   stomp.
                day   stomp!)
(soft   rise up blk / people. rise up blk / people
chant)   RISE. & BE. what u can.
          MUST BE. BE. BE. BE. BE. BE. BE-E-E-E-E-
                         BE-E-E-E-E-
              yeh. john coltrane.
my favorite thing is u.
                   showen us life /
                       liven.
alove supreme.
        for each
      other
    if we just
lisssssssSSSTEN.

                           —1969

A. B. Spellman

DID JOHN'S MUSIC KILL HIM?

in the morning part
of evening he would stand
before his crowd. the voice
would call his name &
redlight fell around him.
jimmy'd bow a quarter hour
till Mccoy fed block chords
to his stroke. elvin's thunder
roll & eric's scream. then john.

then john. *little old lady*
had a nasty mouth. *summertime*
when the war is. *africa* ululating
a line bunched up like itself
into knots paints beauty black.

trane's horn had words in it
i know when i sleep sober & dream
those dreams i duck in the world
of sun & shadow. yet even in the day john
& a little grass put them on me clear
as tomorrow in a glass enclosure.

kill me john my life eats
life. the thing that beats out of
me happens in a vat enclosed
& fermenting & wanting to explode
like your song.

    so beat john's death words down
    on me in the darker part
    of evening. the black light issued
    from him in the pit he made
    around us. worms came clear
    to me where i thought i had been
    brilliant. o john death will
    not contain you death
    will not contain you

—1969

Ornette Coleman

Harmelodics really means that the lead concept expressing ideas and sequences is made into the kind of logic that has to do with making a musical idea work on any instrument. Harmelodics is a system that will allow the person to lead or to extract any part of an idea in order to enhance the particular philosophy they feel will allow the composition to develop or the ingredients that have been performed for the betterment of the collectivity ... or the total sound. In other words, Harmelodics is a philosophy based upon all forms of concepts or ideas being equal in the status of matter. The time, the rhythm, the speed, the harmonics are all equal. The technical term means having to use the basic clef sign as the unisons for the lead of any particular instrument, then you have the tenor clef, the soprano clef, bass clef and the alto clef as one unison representing the total idea for all those particular voicings. [...]

Well for instance, in traditional forms the harmonic structure in most songs is basically the tonic to the fourth, or either the tonic to the relative minor. Most song forms have a harmonic structure known as II-V-I in Western music. Well in harmelodic structure, the II-V-I structures are spread out in three basic changes, the major 7th, the minor 7th, and a minor sound. In other words, in music you have a major sound, a minor sound, and a dominant sound. But in harmelodics those sounds are three individual chords that consist of the whole total of 12 pitches in Western musics.

—1982

Archie Shepp

I asked a group of young people recently in a class of black and white students—Who was Sidney Bechet? None of them knew who he was. Neither Negroes or Whites. And then in my lecture, I asked: Who was Paul Robeson? And none of them knew who he was ... well, *one*, a white student. So at that point I reflected on the need for the professional at the level of academia to say: Does the artist have a role to play, particularly the black artist? And I say: *You damn well right! He's got to have.* Because if I go to France, say I go to the town of Nancy. They built a big statue there to Sidney Bechet, one of the greatest clarinetists, soprano saxophonists, and proponents of the blues this country has ever known. In France, they built a statue to him—every schoolkid knows who this man is. Here in the place of his birth, knowledge of him has completely disappeared. We may look at these people somewhat as role models as well. Role models are not only successful TV personalities or successful musicians. They represent the entire spectrum of our people who achieve some degree of success in whatever their life endeavor is. In this case Bechet was a musician, but I think he represents something important to black youth they should be hip to. So what's the need for me at that level, what is the need to proliferate people like me? I'd say we are *essential* to raise the level of consciousness in respect to Culture. I think also of people like Harold Cruse, who teaches at the University of Michigan. He is a very essential person because he is a *critic of culture.* Negroes know nothing about their culture. They just boogeying, baby. That's why you have the present administration in Washington. Sad, man ...

The challenge [Cruse] raises to the intellectual and the artist is to forge a dialogue, a *critique* of American Culture. At a certain level it cannot be left to the musician. I don't think we can just rely on B.B. King or Muddy [Waters] to begin to form those kind of slick, sophisticated alliances: Neo-Quasi Marxist-Post Socialist-Renaissance ideas that really don't belong to their chain of experiences. Or musicians, per se. Musicians of course have their role to play, but you see I've often challenged young students, black students. Why haven't you studied and organized? The Chinese have discussed Black Culture, the Russians have talked about it. They say it's decadent, they say we play the Blues because of slavery. And a lot niggas believe that!! That's how ignorant they are. They've never really even thought about the fact that the blues is the basis of their identity. The basis of the identity of their music, of their *Being;* it's a *metaphor* if we understand it. So first the Black youth, the students, etc., they have to come together and say: What is it to be Black? How do we *define* that? First, they would have to go to their Music. After all, Nat Turner is the reputed author of the song called "Steal-Away," one of the Negro Spirituals. So it shows us that there is an intrinsic alliance between our Politics and our music, because Turner also forged one of the great rebellions in our history. There is an intrinsic relationship between our Politics and our Culture, specifically our Music. Sojourner Truth and Harriet Tubman were very close to music and used music to help people escape from slavery. This is part of the whole African "Song of Allusion," if we get into some musical history. This is how our people carry on these various forms and spin them off into certain kinds of meaningful political statements.

So first the black youth must begin to forge a dialogue and discuss exactly what is their culture—what does it *mean* to be black? What are the essential components of our culture? What is the Blues? What is "Jazz"? Should we describe these realities with these old terms that have been handed down to us from slavery? The Africans changed the names of their countries, can't we change the names of our cultural experiences? We're still relating to our music through slave symbols: Disco, Rock 'n Roll. All this is done to keep Negroes from realizing that their music represents the whole (African) Diasporic entity. If they could *understand* that what they're doing down in those places, in Haiti and Brazil and Cuba, Condomble, Lucimi ... is very close to the syncretism of Afro-

Christianity, which is the source of so called "Jazz" music. So first of all
what do we say as an "intellectual-academic" constituency? We should
confab and dig what it is we are. Maybe when we're listening to Stevie
Wonder we're also listening to a Shango rhythm ...

—1982

Donald L. Graham (*Dante*)

POEM FOR ERIC DOLPHY

Then
        i was ten and layed in the grass
        with mattie and let her call me
        nasty
and snot dripped on the rag
            then
        12 with a sling shot for birds
        i didn't know charlie
                in three
        i 15ed my way thru another year
        chasing foxes and ragging down
        cause that was a hip thing
and blood dripped on the sheet
        but 17 years creased my ass before
        i could ask who's eric.

II
        I didn't know eric
i didn't know i didn't know

you sang for black babies in apartment
buildings, drunks pissing in the halls
and black chicks doing the back-bends for
pink men with slimy lips

I didn't know, i didn't know you or malcolm
or patrice or trane or me
had i known
i would have said
scream eric scream
you're a bad muthafucka

—1967

Haki Madhubuti/Don L. Lee

blackmusic/a beginning

pharaoh sanders
had
finished
playing
&
the whi-
te boy was to
go on next.

him didn't

him sd
that
his horn
was
broke.

they sat
there
dressed in
african garb
& dark sun glasses
listening to the brothers
play. (taking notes)
we
didn't realize
who they
were in
til their
next recording
had been
released: the beach boys play soulmusic.

real sorry about
the supremes

being dead,
heard some whi
te girls
the other day—
all wigged-down
with a mean tan—
soundin just like them,
singin
rogers & hart
& some country & western

—1969

Anthony Braxton

Pee Wee Russell, I just love his music and I don't ... see music like the
way a lot of people see music. I mean it's like he played his music and he
played with whop he played with. And I'm fortunate to have a chance to
be able to experience it on record. As far as your question is concerned,
have I been influenced by Pee Wee Russell ... I've been influenced, man,
from every piece of music I ever listened to. I have *not* put him under the
microscope to the extent where I see myself coming from some of his
solutions, I've learned from his music—but that's not to say that I don't
appreciate his music, or anything like that. But, wow, I would say Louis
Armstrong, even before Louis Armstrong, the music was "avant-garde"
... I think there's a wrong conception of what contemporary music's
about, expressly as far as ... "avant-garde" and what [it] really means ...

What I'm saying is that if we look at the whole of creative music as it is
through the black aesthetic, I don't think the term "avant-garde" can
apply because what we're really dealing with is an aesthetic which has
defined the way to be creative dealing with real time, moment-time, and
like however different the vibrational arena is in any given period the
music adheres to what it is, manifests what that is through its music ...
so Pee Wee Russell's music, however we deal with it, in my opinion only,
cannot be talked about as being "avant-garde" because nobody was playing any time-zone outside their time-zone ... whatever he played was,
really ... how can I say it? whatever he played was really played in that
time-zone ... it could only be talked of in terms of its vibrational envi-

ronment to that time-zone, which doesn't have anything to do with
Louis Armstrong's time-zone because he is equally in the time-zone he
played in which what I'm only trying to do in my time-zone. So it's like
how can you be more "avant-garde" than to be in the moment, you know
... I imagine "avant-garde" has something to do with being able to be
outside of the moment and I'm saying ... that music is always in the
moment. [...]

———

In the late sixties and early seventies whenever I would read a *Down Beat*
magazine someone would talk of communication and how they love the
people and they love the music the people could relate to, and I find myself thinking that what was happening here was the word *communication*
was going to be the vehicle for the next spectacle or diversion cycle to
happen. And I think that I'm right in that regard. I think that Cecil Taylor was very correct when he said that the artist's first responsibility was
to establish communication with himself. As for me it's like *of course* I
would like the people to be able to hear the music and I *don't* believe in
the idea of "art" [...] But I *have* to believe in what I'm doing or at least
my activity has to be meaningful for me and I have to ... there has to be
something in there that I agree with, *first,* and then I try and present it in
a way where hopefully people might be able to get into it or people
might be able to experience it. But I'd prefer for them to hate it and at
least really hate something which is happening as opposed to presenting
something which I don't believe in, where it doesn't really mean anything
even if they dig it. Now as far as the idea of "art" and what's happening
there: I disagree completely with the idea of "art" ... I think "art" is a
notion which is and has been perpetrated and defined by white people
having to do with completely different vibrational forces as far as what
creativity is supposed to be about. [...] I think the responsibility of any
person trying to be cognizant or any person ... trying to develop or understand the planet and would have to do with trying to realign people
with creativity and the spirit—in terms of the implications of what creativity's really about and hopefully what that might mean to the forming
of the world-cultural community. [...]

   As far as the responsibility of the creative person I imagine it would
have to do with more than playing the saxophone or whatever. I mean,
for me, like I'm trying to finish three books I've been writing. And Leo
Smith and I have been talking about putting together a school, you

know, like I'd like to be able to help form a school in the black communities where children can come and learn about music and not have to pay any money, but there's a real need to, in this time-zone, establish some kind of understanding of young black children in the music because there's another separation happening there because of the economic, racial, social, and political factors moving towards separating black people. But I don't mean to be exclusively talking about black people because—I'm black and I'm coming from there and I have an affinity there—I also have an affinity with people on the planet which is to say white people, poor white, poor green, black, or even rich who need the music as much as everybody else and, now, I'm trying to answer the question … I'd say the responsibility doesn't end on the drawing board or in some theoretical notion or even in some hip intellectualism of being able to rap about the people, what Cage does and at the same time he sees himself quite separate from the people. I'd say ultimately it'd have to be about organizing on the grass-roots level and trying to bring in some real, true understanding of what creativity is all about and hope, hopefully on the cultural level it would have to do with, you know, like opening centers for people to be able to deal with the music—on the way towards forming an alternative-spiritual essence where we can being to move towards the spiritualization, the *real* spiritualization of the music as opposed to walking around talking about much I "love" you or if you drink KRAML MILK you'll be redeemed or all this shit which went down in the sixties, having to do with musicians walking around like they know everything and "We're gonna *teach* you something" when in fact I'm in a position in my life where I'm struggling trying to *learn* something like everyone else about what is happening. In other words, it's not about me *teaching* anybody anything. It's about hopefully me learning so I can help myself and if I can do that it implies in *my* understanding of things then I can be able to be of service.

—1976

Sun Ra

I'm not a human. I never called anybody *mother*. The woman who's supposed to be my mother I call *other momma*. I never call nobody *mother*. I never call nobody *father*. I never felt that way. You have to realize this planet is not only inhabited by humans, it's inhabited by aliens too. They got the books say they fell from heaven with Satan. So, in mixed up among humans you have angels. The danger spot is the United States. You have more angels in the country than anywhere else. You see, it was planned.

I'll tell you something fantastic. It's unbelievable. They say that truth is stranger than fiction. Never in this history of the world has there been a case where you take a whole people and bring 'em into the country in the Commerce Department. Never before has that happened. It happened here. They bringing 'em in through the Commerce Department. It was possible for aliens and angels and devils and demons to come in this country. They didn't need no passport. So then they'd come as displaced people. Perfect setup. So they come right on into the United States. They could come here and act like poor people, they could come here and act like slaves because they didn't keep up with what was happening. They just brought some people in ... and said *Oh you, they is nothing, they beastly*. They brought 'em in here and doin' that, they allowed anything to come here.

If someone has the authority from the one who's causing the problem, it's no problem. It is not the nature of the human being to be self-destructive. So someone is causing it—there's a lot of confusion. But the Bible says God is the cause of confusion, that he confused the languages at the Tower of Babel. That's what it says. He did it, that's what they teach. So if he confuses, how do you do it? That's the point. If you find out how he did it, you can unravel the whole thing.

Well I found out how he did it. He did it with phonetics. Still telling the truth, but phonetics goes two ways. Like I just told you the words *virgin,* and *version,* it's like sun/son, *son* or *sun;* you got a lot of words spelled just alike, like *live* and *live,* and they go separate directions.

I don't really deal with life. I feel that life is death, you know. That it's a curse according to the Bible ... Paul said, *Oh, who would deliver me from this body of death.* He said, *If a man is led to life he is led to death* ... Another place in the Bible it says, *Their whole life through is nothing else but death.*

I understand English, you see, from a basic point of view, not from the American point of view, but from the Old English point of view which is very necessary if you get an old Bible. You start back there, this Bible translated by Englishmen, and you can find out they made a few mistakes. They made a few mistakes in the setters and the printers, too. And those are some problems you have in this country. Slight mistakes. Good ideas, but you can't even make the slightest mistake 'cause everything will move that way.

In Egypt we played at the German Embassy over in Helipolis, which I didn't even know was the headquarters of the priests who dealt with Ra. I didn't know 'til I got to the United States and that's where I played. This big house. The Germans invited the Egyptians there and that's how the Egyptians knew I was in town 'cause they had never heard the band. So the cultural ministry wanted us to play so bad—*Our children need you and you have to go on* TV*! Don't ask us how much we're going to pay you. We pay our musicians so little; I can't even tell you what we will pay you, but it'll be after the program. That's the way we do things over here. Please play for our children.* The Egyptians don't seem to worry about time. They said we're gonna pick you up at three o'clock—send the bus out. Four o'clock—no bus; five o'clock—no bus; six o'clock I said, Well, we'll just get cans and go down there. I called up and they said, Well, the bus left at three o'clock. So here we go down to the TV station and we set up maybe about six o'clock or six thirty and they said, *Well, you'll go on soon.* Seven o'clock came—the band is set up. Eight o'clock came—the band, nobody went to the washroom, nobody asked for no water. Nine o'clock came—we're still not on. Ten o'clock came. By eleven o'clock all at once, *Oh, we got to put the band on!* So we went on then. But now nobody went to the restroom. Nobody asked for no water and they saw some discipline. They can appreciate that. I'm going back to Egypt.

—1984

Sun Ra

THE OUTER DARKNESS

Intergalactic music is of the outer darkness
Therefore it is of the greater Void-Blackness
And from that point of view:
. . . . It is Black-Infinity:
. . . . And from that point of view:
. . . . It is Cosmo-Nature's music . . . . . .
. . . . It is the music of natural-spontaneous Infinity
. . . . . It is unlimited in scope . . . .
Immeasurable in its multiplicities and potentialities,
Natural dark-black music projects the myth of ever Is
And he who is not dark in spirit will never know That these
words are true and valid forever.

I speak of a different kind of blackness,
The kind that the world does not know . . . .
The kind that the world will never understand.
. . . . . . It is rhythm against rhythm in kind dispersion,
. . . . . It is harmony against harmony in endless coordinate
. . . . It is melody against melody in dark-enlightenment
. . . It is Nature's voice in Cosmo-Sound
. . It is the everything and the subtle nothing
                Of Omni-All
. . . . It is the ever quickening-presence of the Living Spirit
. . . It is the Cosmo-bridge to the Dark Unknown Eternal,
. . . .
. . . .
. . . .
. . . .
. . . .
. . . .
. . . .
. . . .
. . . .
. . . .
. . . .
. . . .

                                —1985

Lorenzo Thomas

By 1966, Baraka had framed the message much more concisely: "The music you hear (?) is an invention of Black lives." What was at stake, of course, was a cultural hierarchy explicit in American society. As a visiting African student once expressed it, "They love your music—but they don't love you." The Black Arts Movement asked, basically, what's love got to do with it?

In the area of music, the prevailing cultural hierarchy assigns value to the European symphonic tradition at the expense of indigenous American musical conventions. Compared to jazz, classical music has been assigned a higher cultural value which—of course—has very little to do with music per se.

In 1948 Sidney Finkelstein noted that "the man who listens to jazz, whether 'New Orleans' or bebop, is hearing as unstandardized a set of musical scales as is he who listens to Copland or Ives." Finkelstein logically concluded that "the artificial distinction between 'classical' and 'popular' has been forced upon our times by the circumstance that the production of both ... has become a matter for financial investment instead of art." (*Jazz: A People's Music.*)

There is, however, a definite political rationale involved that touches on aesthetic questions. The Black Arts Movement tried simply to dismiss the problem along with the European tradition. The critics of an earlier generation, however, attempted to elevate jazz by developing it as a "classical" music. A close examination of the reasoning behind each position suggests that the dynamics of assimilation and resistance in African American culture involve a dialectical movement that reflects a general tendency in American society's unresolved search for a national cultural identity.

Just as the African American is on a continuing quest to learn what is African about him, so America seems persistently clueless about what makes it American.

—1993

LeRoi Jones/Amiri Baraka

Social consciousness in jazz is something again because it is largely a purely instrumental music ... though there have always been musicians who have been deeply conscious of their exact placement in the social world, or at least there was a kind of race pride or consciousness that animated the musicians and their music (again, here, Ellington is a giant. "Black Beauty," "Black, Brown, and Beige," "For My People," and so many many others).

In recent times musicians like Charles Mingus (dig "Fables of Faubus," etc.), Max Roach, and some others have been outspoken artists on and off the stage, using their music as eloquent vehicles for a consciousness of self in America. The new musicians have been outspoken about the world through their music and off the stage as well. Archie Shepp has perhaps been the most publicized of the new socially conscious musicians. And some of his music is self-consciously socially responsive, e.g., "Malcolm," but this so-called consciousness is actually just a reflection of what a particular generation is heir to, and their various responses from wherever they (are) find themselves.

Also, of course, the music is finally most musicians' strongest statement re: any placement of themselves socially. And the new music, as I
have stated before about Black music, is "radical" within the context of
mainstream America. Just as the new music begins by being free. That is,
freed of the popular song. Freed of American white cocktail droop, tin-
kle, etc. The strait jacket of American expression *sans* blackness ... it
wants to be freed of that temper, that scale. That life. It screams. It
yearns. It pleads. It breaks out (the best of it). But its practitioners
sometimes do not. But then the vibrations of a feeling, of a particular
place, a conjunction of world spirit, some of everybody can pick up on.
(Even imitate, which is Charlie McCarthy shouting freedom! or white
snick workers going back to Jumpoff Manor after giving a few months to
"The Problem.") It is an ominous world all right. You can say *spiritual.*
You can say *Freedom.* But you do not necessarily have to be either one. If
you can dig it. White, is abstract. A theory. A saying. A being ... the verb
... the energy itself, is what is beautiful, is what we want, sometimes, are.

Music as the consciousness, the expression of where we are. But then
Otis Redding in interviews in *Muhammad Speaks* has said things (or Shakey
Jake, for that matter) more "radical," Blacker, than many of the new musicians. James Brown's screams, etc., are more "radical" than most jazz
musicians sound, etc. Certainly his sound is "further out" than Ornette's. And that sound has been a part of Black music, even out in them
backwoods churches since the year one. It is just that on the white man's
instrument it is "new." So, again, it is just life need and interpretation.

Sun-Ra speaks of evolution of the cosmic consciousness; that is future, or as old as *purusa.* Where man will go. "Oh you mean space ships?"
Which is like the Zen monk answering the student's question about
whether or not dogs have souls ... i.e., "Well, yes ... and no."

And the social consciousness displayed in that music. Pharaoh
Sanders will say OMMMMMMMMMMMMMMMMMMMMMMMMMMMMM-
MMMMMMMMMMMMMMMMMMMMMMMMMMMMMMMMMMMMM-
MMMMMMMMMMMM. Which is more radical than sit-ins. We get to
Feel-Ins, Know-Ins, Be-Ins.

But here is a theory stated just before. That what will come will be a
Unity Music. The Black Music which is jazz and blues, religious and secular. Which is New Thing and Rhythm and Blues. The consciousness of
social reevaluation and rise, a social spiritualism. A mystical walk up the
street to a new neighborhood where all the risen live. Indian-African
anti-Western-Western (as geography) Nigger-sharp Black and strong.

The separations, artificial oppositions in Black Music resolved, are the ditty strong classic. (Ditty bop.) That is, the New Black Music and R&B are the same family looking at different things. Or looking at things differently. The collection of wills is a simple unity like on the street. A bigger music, and muscle, for the move necessary. The swell of a music, of action and reaction, a seeing, thrown in swift slick tone along the entire muscle of a people. The Rhythm and Blues mind blowing evolution of James-Ra and Sun-Brown. That growth to include all the resources, all the rhythms, all the yells and cries, all that information about the world, the Black ommmmmmmmmmmmmmmm, opening and entering.

—1967

Faruq Z. Bey

ALBERT AYLER: 1936 1970

they did not need you, Albert
they did not need an
we could not bear
the awful weight of
your song ... Albert
of Ancient Dynasties
of occult stellar
communities, of Ausars
insistant transmigration
& cosmic parody they
prefer to stare blank-eyed
into the god-damned maw
of intransigence, we
could not hold not pro-
tect you, Albert
we who are raw &
debauched would not
suffer for your
brutally olympian sweet-
ness, the invocation of power
ghosts, your untimely
candor, the burden of your
martyrdom

and so they come.
loudspeakers in the nite
with jarring angular
voices comes red mists
& sulphiric yellow rains
so we sweat pus &
languid oils from the east
comes prophets unacquainted
with sin
comes the anti-cristo
comes in halting
arhythmic steps, & we're
to assume them dangers
they come with stones
& equations they claim
to love the brilliant imago
if you are the dali lama
then your light is dis-
pursed among raggedy-assed
saxophonists under the
evasive streetlights of
tomorrow

As for me I must forage

—1981

Joseph Jarman

J[OSEPH] J[ARMAN]: Certainly media has a great deal to do with the pro-
gramming that goes down, but more than media, program directors, and
the concept of capitalist enterprise, and the concept of mind control.
These entities become realities when we talk about media. If I'm going
to sell a bar of soap, I'm going to have to package that bar of soap so it
will appear to be the best thing, to the widest group. And I'm going to
shoot at the bottom for the widest group. I mean, there's an assumption
that people are stupid and dumb, and it's not that people are stupid and
dumb, it's that the bosses—whoever they may be—want to increase their
bank accounts. So they construct a situation where creativity at *every* level
is mashed out. When people witness and experience a creative act of any

kind, it reinforces the consciousness of the possibility of creativity in their own life. One doesn't have to be an "artist" to be creative, one can be a floor sweeper, and select the kind of wax that would go best on the floor. This, to me, is also a creative act. So the media has to control the population, and in the capitalist society these methods for controlling the population are different from any other kind of form, because the emphasis is always on increasing some budget, rather than enlightening the people in any kind of way, with any kind of substance.

P[ETER] K[OSTAKIS]: In the front of *Black Case* you wrote "In reality all the words are music themselves." In what way, do you think, has the writing of poems and plays served as a source of enrichment for your music?

JJ: Well, for me, and for a certain kind of aesthetic approach that seems to be being realized, there is no difference between any of these forms we employ to express ourselves. For example, I always had the notion that music, and movement … and the voice being, language being music. I mean, when we speak, we speak in timbre, in rhythm, in sound, we speak in silence, we speak loud, we speak soft, we speak music. The words are like notes to me, that is, I can make a phrase with a musical instrument that will have the same density and everything else as I can with words. But what I want to say is that I had this idea, but recently I had the opportunity to witness the Moroccan National Folk Festival, and that experience was the confirmation for these ideas I had. Because all of the performers were actors, and dancers, and singers, and poets, and everything. It was just one entity. So for me at this point it's impossible to separate … It all goes together. For me now, to say a music with my voice and body is the same as saying a music with a traditional musical instrument. Also for me now the body has become a musical instrument as well as a movement instrument. The dynamics of the whole unit now, for me … I am a sound. But that sound contains all these parts. The body is a machine and it can be a well-defined machine or it can be a non-functional machine. But when we coordinate our minds with our bodies, then whatever expression is there will be able to come out very clearly.

———

I don't know what the advantages of (our) musical approach is, but again, we create problems to make life interesting. And whether we create them in the creation of music, or the creation of a poem, or creation of a play, or the creation of a hot date, it's all the same. So that technique has been around for a long time, and you were talking about synthesizers earlier, and that's one of the basics for that kind of music, this overlay. But we can find the bottom of it in many cultures—that's the same type of thing, basically, as a "call and response." Before the "call" is completely out, the "response" begins to come in. That's the same thing as a canon. One voice starts and another starts immediately behind it. That's the same thing as the reading of the sutras in Tantric Buddhist practices. They'll start to read one part of the sutra and that will be followed by the same part immediately at a different tone. So that, that's nothing extraordinary. What we were trying to do was create the circle that was included. And it become a spiral, a collage, density there. That's what it is, it's a spiral, of all this. In actual performance, that situation should be accompanied by a movement scenario as well. And, yes, I plan on using this technique again [...] What we must remember when we talk about music with musicians is that there is always a tremendous backlog of work to be realized. Always. I know musicians that have music, like piles, never heard, and maybe one day it'll happen and maybe it won't. But that's Braxton, Mitchell, Abrams, everybody, Threadgill, Ewart, anybody. Doesn't even matter. I mean everybody. [...]

I don't want them to be like me. I want them to be like whatever they are. I don't really want anything from the audience except that they consider themselves in this experience. I mean, if someone pours water over your head, and if it's nice refreshing water, then it'll be a pleasant experience and you'll want it again. But if it's scalding hot water, you'll remember that. And if it's freezing water, you'll remember that as well. So in this music, you can feel the spirit come over you, and that's what keeps people coming back. Because it feels good. It might sometimes be grotesque or bizarre, but even in that grotesqueness and that bizarreness, it's giving something vital, and people understand that. Whatever it is they get out of it, I don't even know what it is, really. But it's a vital thing, a healing, helpful force. And their presence gives vitality to the practitioner's life as well. So it's on that level that the interchange is happening. Don Cherry called it "complete communion." It's a kind of touching that has been so far away from human beings that we forgot it existed. But it's beginning to come up again, and enter into the psyche. But it's not new. It's been going on ever since the first two beings communicated without language. Just "chuk-pow," like that. So it's about that to me.

—1977

Michael S. Harper

EFFENDI

The piano hums
again the clear
story of our coming,
enchained, severed,
our tongues gone,
herds the quiet
musings of ten million
years blackening the earth
with blood and our moon women,
children we loved,
the jungle swept up
in our rhapsodic song
giving back
banana leaves and the incessant beating
of our tom-tom hearts.
We have sung a long time here
with the cross and the cotton field.
Those white faces turned
away from their mythical
beginings are no art
but that of violence—
the kiss of death.
Somewhere on the inside
of those faces
are the real muscles
of the world;
the ones strengthened
in experience and pain,
the ones wished for in one's lover
or in the mirror
near the eyes
that record this lost, dogged data
and is pure, new, even lovely
and is you.

   for McCoy Tyner

Bill Dixon

My initial attraction to Archie [Shepp] was because he was a playwright in addition to being a musician and had other interests. I don't really have that much of an affinity for most musicians simply because they are much too monochromatic. But then in recent years I've had to tell myself, and thus realize, that one cannot stay in a room learning to play an instrument literally all of your life and then be expected to know anything else. Archie had an alert mind; rehearsals were a pleasure; we started work together and that was it. A lot of dues were paid for that but a lot of good and interesting music and musical situations evolved. Archie, however, immediately marshaled his forces. Recently, much to my surprise, he did acknowledge in print that I was the one that advised him to speak to John Coltrane about possibly helping him get a record date for the Impulse label. And prior to Shepp's becoming a rather "valuable artistic force" for Impulse neither Bob Thiele nor anyone else of the record moguls would speak to me or Shepp. It's amazing how soon people forget where they once were. But we did discuss his speaking to John Coltrane, who was then recording with regularity for Impulse. At the time, all of these musicians were using Coltrane. Trane was probably, of all the significant musicians, the most sensitive and the most kind. It seemed to me that no matter what they did he could manage to see and hear some significant musicological point trying to be expressed or at least being in existence. A lot of those people I don't think dug him at all; they saw themselves as getting somewhere so they would, irrespective of their musical qualifications at that time, sit in with him. I know that to some of those musicians sitting in with Trane had little to do with their even attempting to understand why he was allowing them on the bandstand anyway. They were more concerned with doing their own individual thing, if it could be called that. And it must have literally drove the regular members of the band up the wall.

But John's music and direction had such an inner strength to it that his musical point of view could sustain what was or wasn't happening. To my way of thinking he represented the epitome of being an art musician. Very strong with the relevant amount of sensitivity and compassion. And if you want to really understand that, listen to the Ascension album where none of them understood why John Coltrane had them there. As a classic of the New Music it sustains the theory that the cream does finally come to the top.

—1981

Yusef Lateef

The flute is in his hands. His hands are strong and reveal the scars that age and labor have produced. The fingers are long and thick; the wrinkled fingertips caress the flute with a determined and delicate passion.

The flute is made of nickle-silver. Twenty-seven keys of various shapes sparkle as they are apprehended by the light.

In his hands are only the flute, the nervous sweat of tension and the marks that time and activity have brought about.

To the left sits New York's favorite critic.

There is a huge gray velvet curtain behind the man who holds the silver flutes. Hanging directly from the ceiling is a maze of cylindrical lights.

Light reflecting from the flute onto the curtain offers playful designs.

Between the man who holds the flute and New York's favorite critic are a microphone, a row of seats, and a distance of twenty feet.

The air is charged with impending decisions and expectations as the faithful hands raise the flute to a horizontal position.

Behind the velvet curtain can be heard the footsteps of strangers and friends rushing to their positions.

The lights above the curtain slowly diminish and the man who holds the flute moves quietly to the center of the stage.

The unresolved sounds behind the curtain are suddenly gone; the scars on the hands disappear with the dimming of the lights. The surrounding atmosphere is vibrating with thoughts of love and peace.

The twenty-seven keys respond in obedience as the thick fingers manipulate the keys.

Listen to the silent voices saying: "How soothing the music sounds."

A legacy of well-being and brotherhood pervade the hearts of those who hear the summons of the flute.

Tense bodies relax. Dull minds become enlightened and attitudes of indifference reverse their direction.

The lights above the curtain are slowly returning to brightness. The flute has completed the gospel that penetrates the soul.

The flute moves from the horizontal to a vertical position, aided by the hands. The scars, no longer concealed, reappear.

The flute is in his hands. The hands are strong.

—1976

LeRoi Jones / Amiri Baraka

Hip band alright
sum up life in the slick
street part of the
world, oh,
blow,
If you cd
nigger
man

Miles wd stand back and negative check
oh, he dug him—Trane
But Trane clawed at the limits of cool
slandered sanity
with his tryin to be born
raging
    shit
    Oh
    blow,
        yeh go do it
        honk, scream
        uhuh yeh—history
            love
            blue clipped moments
            of intense feeling.
"Trane you blows too long."
Screaming niggers drop out yr solos
Bohemian nights, the "heavyweight champ"
smacked him
  in the face
his eyes sagged like a spent
dick, hot vowels escaped the metal clone of his soul
fucking saxophone
tell us shit tell us tell us!

There was nothing left to do but
be where monk cd find him
that crazy
mother fucker

duh duh-duh duh-duh duh
duh duh
duh duh-duh duh-duh duh
duh duh
duh duh-duh duh-duh duh
duhduh
duh Duuuuuuuuuhhhhhh
Can you play this shit? (Life asks
Come by and listen

& at the 5 Spot Bach, Mulatto ass Beethoven
& even Duke, who has given America its hip tongue
checked
checked
Trane stood and dug
Crazy monk's shit
Street gospel intellectual mystical survival codes
Intellectual street gospel funk modes
Tink a ling put downs of dumb shit
pink pink a cool bam groove note air breath
a why I'm here
a why I ain't
& who is you - ha - you - ha -you - ha
Monk's shit
Blue Cooper 5 Spot
was the world busting
on piano bass drums & tenor

This was Coltrane's College. A Ph motherfuckin d
sitting at the feet, elbows
& funny grin
Of Master T Sphere
   too cool to be a genius
he was instead
Theolonius
with Comrades Shadow
on tubs, lyric Wilbur
who hipped us to electric futures
& the monster with the horn.

—1979

Oliver Lake

WORKIN' ON SOMETHIN'
dedicated to Cecil Taylor

darting quickly thru
the ivories, strings and grunts
tapest-ring the air lobes
possessed

charted chanced vibrations
arrowed to our sensors
propelling his energy 'round notes

audience
spongin'
this translator's mode
strong strong strong
"workin' on somethin'"

—1979

Miles Davis

Some of the things that caused Bill [Evans] to leave the band hurt me,
like that shit some black people put on him about being a white boy in
our band. Many blacks felt that since I had the top small group in jazz
and was paying the most money that I should have a black piano player.
Now, I don't go for that kind of shit; I have always just wanted the best
players in my group and I don't care about whether they're black, white,
blue, red, or yellow. As long as they can play what I want that's it. But I
know this stuff got up under Bill's skin and made him feel bad. Bill was a
very sensitive person and it didn't take much to set him off. Then a lot of
people were saying he didn't play fast enough and hard enough for them,
that he was too delicate. So on top of all this shit was the thing about
traveling and wanting to form his own group and play his own music,
which was where Coltrane and Cannonball [Adderly] were moving.

We were playing the same program every night and a lot of it was
standards, or my music. I know they wanted to play their own stuff and
establish their own musical identity. I didn't blame them for feeling that
way. But we had the best group in the business and it was *my* band and so

I wanted to keep it together for as long as I could. That was a problem, but it happens with most bands after a while. People just outgrow each other, like I did with Bird, and they have to move on.

Bill left the band in November 1958 and went down to Louisiana to live with his brother. Then he came back after a while and formed his own group. After a while he got Scott LaFaro on bass and Paul Motian on drums and he became very popular with that group, winning a number of Grammy Awards. He was a great little piano player, but I don't think he ever sounded as good after that as he did when he played with me. It's a strange thing about a lot of white players—not all, just most— that after they make it in a black group they always go and play with all white guys no matter how good the black guys treated them. Bill did that, and I'm not saying he could have gotten any black guys better than Scott and Paul, I'm just telling what I've seen happen over and over again.

—1989

Albert Murray

Similarly, though few students of American culture seem aware of it, but as those who are truly interested in promoting "black consciousness" in literature should note, what makes a blues idiom musician is not the ability to express *raw* emotions with primitive directness, as is so often implied, but rather the mastery of elements of esthetics peculiar to U.S. Negro music. Blues musicians do not derive directly from the personal, social, and political circumstances of their lives as black people in the United States. They derive most directly from styles of other musicians who play the blues and who were infinitely more interested in evoking or simulating raw emotion than in releasing it—and whose *"primitiveness"* is to be found not so much in the *directness* of their expression as in their prounounced emphasis on stylization. In art both agony and ecstasy are matters of stylization.

Currently popular social science conditioned interpretations notwithstanding, U.S. Negro singers, for example, are influenced far more directly and decisively by Bessie Smith and Louis Armstrong, among others, and by the sonorities of various down-home church rituals than by any actual personal experience of racial oppression, no matter how traumatic. Indeed, what is most characteristic of the black American lifestyle is infinitely more closely related to an orientation to African-derived dance and work rhythms and to the rich variety of music which Afro-

Americans have heard in the United States than to any collective reaction to the experiences of slavery and segregation as such.

The actual working procedures of such blues-oriented arrangers, composers, and conductors as those who provided the scores for the orchestras of Fletcher Henderson, Chick Webb, Earl Hines, Jimmie Lunceford, Count Basie, Lionel Hampton, and numerous others can hardly be explained by references to oppression or even economic exploitation. When viewed in the context of artistic creation, however, such procedures can be as immediately understood and as fully appreciated as those of the playmakers who supplied the scripts for the Elizabethan stage companies.

As a matter of fact, the Elizabethan playmakers suggest an historical frame of reference within which Duke Ellington, the most masterful of all blues idiom arrangers-composers, becomes the embodiment of the contemporary artist at work. The Ellington orchestra is frequently booked for recitals in the great concert halls of the world, much the same as if it were a fifteen-piece innovation of the symphony orchestra—which in a sense it is. Nevertheless, by original design and by typical employment as well, Ellington's is still an itinerant song and dance band. Moreover, its repertory clearly reflects the fact that over the years most of its performances have been in night clubs, theaters, dance halls, and at popular music festivals. However, it is largely because of, not in spite of, such show business affiliations that the image Ellington the artist so closely resembles is that of the Elizabethan playmaker, whose productions, it must not be forgotten, also began as popular entertainment. Show business motivation underlies Ellington's construction of numbers for the special solo talents of, say, Cootie Williams, Johnny Hodges, and Ben Webster, no more nor less than it underlies Shakepeare's composition of soliloquies for the actor Burbage. This similarity is perhaps at least as important to an understanding of Ellington's aesthetics about black experience, by which is usually meant black misery.

—1973

Oliver Lake

SEPARATION

first it's the salad
then the meat
    then the vegetables ...
                "WAIT"
bring all my food at one time on the same plate!

dixieland, be-bop, soul, rhythm & blues, cool school,
swing, avant-garde, jazz, free jazz, rock, jazz-rock

WHAT KINDA MUSIC U PLAY?
                    "GOOD KIND"
Aretha Franklin & Sun Ra is the same folks,
Coltrane & the Dixie Hummingbirds same folks
Miles & Muddy Waters same. there is no ... there is no ...
             LABELS DIVIDE! SEPARATE
             THE ORAL AND THE LITERARY

One music—diff feelings & experience, but same ... the total
sound—mass sound—hear all the players as one

THE HISTORY OF AFRICA WAS MEMORIZED, LIVED,
EXPERIENCED, NOWED!
"WE DIDN'T READ IT. WE DID IT!"

ORAL-LITERARY:
                oral -
                    do
                        experience
                                improvise
                                      adjust
                                            create
literary—
        catalog
            label
                divide
                      read
                          interpret
                              criticize

NO SEPARATION . . . Yeah, don't put me in no bag . . .
i'm open, may do anything
PUT ALL MY FOOD ON THE SAME PLATE!
AFRICAN concept of color . . . .
if it has light, it's yellow
NO SUBTLETIES

he must be colorblind
NO WAY . . . . . right, picasso?
read da music! play the music! create the music! read the music
                is there a chance of changing this notation?
Can u read music?
Naw, it's best jest to create it & play it
that's more   direct-t-t-t-t-t-t-t-t

—1979

Herbie Nichols

As a jazz composer, I've always felt that I should paint as clear a mental picture as possible of the foundation and the future of jazz music. That is why I draw freely, at times, from early New Orleans pianist Jelly Roll Morton, who witnessed and took part in the birth of this folk music. I have examined his cores and have had many happy moments listening to his Circle recordings from the Library of Congress Archives. Jelly was an honest extrovert who used the freedom of jazz piano to tell the story of his love of life and the historic times in which he lived.

I guess I've always had a burning desire and compulsion to compose. Ideas come from almost anywhere. Beethoven and Bach and Chopin are the strong musical pillars which I lean on whenever I find myself in a dark corner. Hector Villa-Lobos's many compositions under the title *Choros* and *Bachianas Brasileras* are infinite fantasies which bear repeated listening. Whenever I want to become astounded, there is always his great piano work, *Rude Poeme*. Among the jazz "greats" Duke Ellington and Art Tatum are unfailing giants to look up to in wonder. Dimitri Mitropoulos is another one of those calm musicians who intrigues me with his catholic taste and abilities. I listen repeatedly to Bartok's delightfully brooding *Sonata for Violin and Piano, No. 1*, also to the *Concerto for Violin and Orchestra*. Stravinsky's *Firebird Suite* and *Le Sacre du Printemps* just about wind up the basic core of music which I can never do without.

Sometimes I burst into laughter when I think of what the future jazzists will be able to accomplish. That is why I wrote in the February, 1956, issue of *Metronome:* "Think of what can be done with the sounds of the multiple counterpoint of Hindemith, the neo-classic polytonality of Shostakovitch and Piston and the melting of the vast musical devices which Bartok loved to use at random and which makes his kaleidoscopic style come closest to jazz."

But jazz has come a long way since "the stomp." A lot of myths have been dispelled and we find countless master jazzists who are masters of classical music as well. Time signatures are altered freely nowadays. For instance, I am beginning to learn that certain tunes that I write cannot become alive, even for one chorus, unless I score the drum part fittingly. Specific suspensions and inversions must be explicitly indicated or else I find that there is no "sound."

But there is nothing mystical about becoming a graduate jazzist. One should be willing to enjoy and study all of the great jazz musicians of the past and present. In addition, each one of these artists' limitations should be pinpointed and analyzed. As a lover of chess I would predict an easy and rewarding individuality as the outcome of these drudging moves.

There are reasons why the best jazz must "sound"—the same as it did in the beginning. I keep remembering that the overtones of "fifths" created by the beautiful tones of any ordinary tuned drum was surely the first music, the precursor of the historic major scale, no less, which was built on the same principles. That is why the cycle of "fifths" is so prevalent in elemental jazz. In other words, in a great desire to "sound," the beginner at improvisation grasps at easy and fundamental aural pleasures.

And so, after tracing this elementary history of "sound," we can readily understand why drummers started to "drop bombs" to usher in the new music of Charlie Parker, Dizzy Gillespie, and Bud Powell. Each "bomb" created a newly rich and wholly unexpected series of overtones beginning in the lower registers. These rich syncopations were fitting accompaniments to the supplemental overtones played by the horns in the higher registers. That is why pianists became so percussive with their left hands.

Among modern drummers, Art Blakey is considered invaluable. He astounds me when it comes to being in tune. I can hear overtones from his snare drum, cymbals, rimshots, everything he touches. Sometimes he "pounds" some of these recalcitrant instruments in tune when the atmosphere is unsteady. I've seen Denzil Best rub his bass drum head with a damp cloth at the start of a gig. He spoke of a *whooooosh* effect which he sought. This effect which he achieves plus his musical discipline makes him one of the best tubmen around today. I'm sure that this is also one of the prime reasons for Sonny Greer's great value to the Ellington orchestra for so many years.

The jazz "sound" is surely a living thing and as a piano player I find it mostly in old "uprights." Sometimes these faded pianos with muted strings, strange woodwork, and uneven "innards" have a way of giving up fast and resonant overtones. Each note shoots back at you like a bass drum. In such a situation, as soon as I find that I am not financially liable, I let myself go and use any kind of unorthodox touch needed to dig out the strange "sounds" which I know are in the instrument. The only respectable piano that gives up this sort of intimate "jazz sound" in any easy and copious manner is the Steinway upright.

———

In ending I would like to state that I am in a constant race to make my "classical theories" catch up to my "jazz theories." It used to be the other way around. But I am rather satisfied that I find no dearth of ideas when it comes to writing. At the piano I'm always sufficiently transported to new spiritual heights whenever I think of the beauties of any tuned drum.

—1956

Leon Forrest

Roland Kirk took on many roles as he tuned the surroundings into a kaleidoscopic-paradisio, or a most cooking, wildly electrical kitchen, and before the journey into the high and ennobling country of his art was climaxed, Kirk—who is a genius—had driven the patrons into the depths and ranges of their psychic night.

In that "Kitchen," wizard-chef-warlock Kirk, with the aid of the following mixing instruments: clarinet, manzello, stritch flute, tenor sax, celeste, thumb piano, invented up a mighty storm broth and served it up to the patrons.

As he floated his patrons out of The Apartment, Kirk devised his way through the surrealistic landscape, along the countryside of his Art, through the forest, through the Jobs' Tear grass; wisteria, cotton field; patches of maze; magnolia trees ... Then on through street car tracks, and rivers, screams of the Inferno-like city; back alleys; polluted avenues.

And all along the way, through the labyrinth-odyssey of Kirk's art, the vividness of his sound, the rich harvest of his tonality, the pictures that he draws through his horn hurl the audience into a new vision of the black condition. All of the old sounds, and familiar memories of today are hurled into stark relief, with "blinding sight."

Now Kirk appearing as a Giant behind the wheel suddenly brings the auto to a halt! He leaps from his car and scoops up the body of a little abandoned black girl under a tree. As he stands there he lyrically eulogizes her crumpled form, his sound, and his very own form seem to become transfixed and he appears to become a small child himself, bathed in blissful, lamb-like innocence. And he buried a golden horn inside the improvised coffin for the child that he shaped out of an oak tree; and he buried her high upon a hill.

At another junction, Kirk is a frantic lover, with a whale bone in his throat, and the sun on his spine.

At another burial site, he is the high-priest of the tribe extemporizing on a eulogy to Billie Holiday. (He apotheosized Lady Day's memory.)

Then he is a fairy-tale vulture chasing a lion; then he is Brer Rabbit, and Jack the Fox. Up the stream during a period of massive nostalgia, he becomes John-the-slave.

Heading north in a sudden rainstorm, he became an urban guerrilla fighter, blasting from the urban rooftops; then a looted brother in rags, jobless, weeping down his story to his woman in the thunder.

As the many canyons of Kirk's soul were revealed, he swept before our eyes the carved and bejeweled mountains, the erected temples out of his majestic soul searching sojourn.

Like Giants in the other arts, Kirk not only takes on many roles, he actually becomes all of the characters; stream-of-conscious voices; tears; rages and joy of his chaotic tower of babble that issue from his people, and his soul. He feels that he must deploy the many horns he employs to orchestrate the totality of his massive vision.

The strap yoking his neck leading to the instruments make Kirk appear as a kind of genie bogged down under the toil of discovering the nature of man's existence ... Like lacerations across his bowed-under body, Kirk seems strapped down to his craft, by a series of whips. But with his jump-diving space suit on, he captures the picture of modern man working through the burden of human problems.

In his attempts to carry everything he sees down the landscape of his

Art, Kirk must carry all that is present, all that is ever-green from past wars of survival of black people into today's larger war. All that can hear; and all that he can see with his "blinding sight."

Thus, you hear the foot-stomping from old-time revivals, and the slave field hollers, in his horns and sometimes in the actual howl from Mr. Kirk himself. Then in another "change" Kirk picks up the sounds of the urban scene, with all of the pathos, jagged-dreams, switchblade utterances; deep rock rhythms; haunting hyperbole. Kirk, for instance, could take a phrase like the following splattered across an urban building wall, MANIAC BOSS WOLF-LORDS, and turn it into a magical storm and a surrealistic dream of a black rebellion.

At the same time he takes phrases like this, and by running them through the ranges of his artistic sweep and memory, Kirk makes these phrases lynching ropes, and sometimes he captures up the memory and the impending terror of bloodhounds chasing an escaping slave through the high grass ... for in another way, that "Invisible Whip" that Kirk says drives his art also surges in our racial past.

An inspiring blind genius, Kirk hungers vastly to communicate the whole round mad circus world, that he envisions, and he does.*

*Roland Kirk died in 1976.

—1969

Cecil Taylor

It was earlier, in '51–'52, that I became aware of certain contrary ideas in my own playing which had to be resolved. Like, when Brubeck opened in 1951 in New York I was very impressed with the depth and texture of his harmony, which had more notes in it than anyone else's that I had ever heard. It also had a rhythmical movement that I found exciting. I went over and told him what I had heard, and he was amazed that anyone could see what he was doing. Remember, this is the Brubeck of the Tentet, when he was still serious. I don't think that that music is important now for what it made, but I still think that it was important then, for the gaps it filled. I was digging Stravinsky, and Brubeck had been studying with Milhaud. But because of my involvement with Stravinsky, and because I knew Milhaud I could hear what Brubeck was doing, which amazed Brubeck. Brubeck called [saxophonist Paul] Desmond over, but Desmond's attitude was standoffish. Reputedly during that show, Dizzy

Gillespie had thrown eggs up on the stage. Dizzy was working opposite Brubeck with a band that had Percy Heath, Milt Jackson, and John Lewis. That band of Dizzy's was so much more than Brubeck's band, but of course Brubeck had by then started to cop all the headlines in the magazines.

I found Brubeck's work interesting until I heard Tatum, Horace Silver, and Oscar Peterson within a period of six weeks. Of that crowd, I found Tatum the least interesting. He was like Hawkins in that he understands and respects musicianship, but I would rather hear, say, Fats Waller. At his best Tatum could get to anybody, including me, but his music lacked momentum. Fats Waller had a tone second to none, whereas Peterson had Bird's idea of swing but had a technique that was European. Then there's Tristano, whose ideas interested me because he was able to construct a solo on the piano, and I guess that has a lot to do with why I had dug Brubeck too. Brubeck was the other half of Tristano; Tristano had the line thing and Brubeck had the harmonic density that I was looking for, and that gave a balance.

But when I heard Horace, now that was a thing which turned me around and finally fixed my idea of piano playing. Horace was playing with Getz. Getz was all over the sax, and Horace was right on him. Listening to Horace that night I dug that there were two attitudes in jazz, one white and one black. The white idea is valid in that the cats playing it play the way their environment leads them, which is the only way they can play. But Horace is the Negro idea because he was playing the real thing of Bud, with all the physicality of it, with the filth of it, and the movement in the attack. Yet Horace supposedly had no technique, which again brings us to the idea of what technique is.

———

I'm digging the whole scene then. My consciousness was beginning to get to the decisive point. Then I went to Birdland one night to hear Brubeck playing opposite Horace Silver, and I noticed Brubeck imitating Horace. Then came Bird with Percy and Milt, and man, like they demolished Brubeck. Bird was acting grand that night. He would take a solo, step back, and Milt would tear the vibes up. Milt was one of the real forces on that early scene. Well, that ended Brubeck for me. And it ended my emotional involvement with his music and my intellectual involvement also.

—1966

Nina Simone

More and more of my life was spent away from the close confines of my home—at school, church, or Miz Mazzy's [piano teacher]—and as I became more independent and removed from the protection of my family I became aware that there were things going on all around me that I had never noticed before. Sometimes they were so obvious I couldn't understand why I'd gone for so long without remarking on them, like not being able to sit down at Owen's Pharmacy or not being able to use the bathroom at gas stations on the way back from backwoods revival meetings. Other times they were more puzzling: one day Mrs. Miller simply stopped bringing David around to play, and when I was at her house he was discouraged from playing with me; we had crossed an invisible boundary which neither of us understood. Somehow it had been decided that we were both now too old to play as if the color of our skins made no difference. One of John Irvine's friends left town overnight and the story went round that he'd been seeing a white girl. All the adults nodded wisely as if that was all right—they understood. Understood *what*, I wanted to know.

When I was eleven years old I was asked to give a recital in the town hall. I sat at the piano with my trained elegance while a white man introduced me, and when I looked up my parents, who were dressed in their best, were being thrown out of their front row seats in favor of a white family I had never seen before. And Daddy and Momma were allowing themselves to be moved. Nobody else said anything, but I wasn't going to see them treated like that and stood up in my starched dress and said if anyone expected to hear me play they'd better make sure my family was sitting right there in the front row where I could see them, and to hell with poise and elegance. So they moved back. But my parents were embarrassed and I saw some of the white folks laughing at me.

All of a sudden it seemed a different world, and nothing was easy any more. I really had thought that all white people were like Miz Mazzy and Mrs. Miller, all kind and elegant, all polite. I had no reason to think otherwise: they were the only white people I had ever talked to for any length of time. But now prejudice had been made real for me and it was like switching on a light.

I started to think about the way I felt when I walked over to Miz Mazzy's house and crossed the railtrack into the white district. I took to stopping in the drugstore to observe the mixture of indifference and disdain I provoked in the white customers. The day after the recital I walked around feeling as if I had been flayed and every slight, real or imagined, cut me raw. But the skin grew back again a little tougher, a little less innocent, and a little more black.

—1991

Linton Kwesi Johnson

BASS CULTURE / For Big Yout

muzik of blood
black reared
pain rooted
heart geared;

all tensed up
in the bubble and the bounce
an the leap an the weight-drop.

it is the beat of the heart,
this pulsing of blood
that is a bubblin bass,
a bad bad beat
pushin against the wall
whey bar black blood.

an is a whole heappa
passion a gather
like a frightful form
like a righteous harm
giving off wild like is madness.

—1975

Paul Gilroy

The contemporary musical forms of the African diaspora work within an aesthetic and political framework which demands that they ceaselessly reconstruct their own histories, folding back on themselves time and again to celebrate and validate the simple, unassailable fact of their survival. This is particularly evident in jazz, where quotes from and parody of earlier styles and performers make the pats actually audible in the present. This process of recovery should not be misunderstood. It does not

amount to either parody or pastiche. The stylistic voices of the past are
valued for the distinct register of address which each offers. The same
playful process is evident in the less abstract performances which define
Washington's "Go Go" dance funk. This style consists of a continuous
segue from one tune to the next. The popular black musics of different
eras and continents are wedded together by a heavy percussive rhythm
and an apparently instinctive antiphony. A recent concert in London by
Chuck Brown, the kingpin of the Go Go, saw him stitch together tunes
by Louis Jordan, Sly Stone, Lionel Hampton, Melle Mel, and T. Bone
Walker into a single epic statement. Reggae's endless repetition of "versions": and the tradition of answer records in rhythm and blues betray a
similar historical impulse. . . .

The anti-capitalist politics which animate the social movement against
racial subordination is not confined to the lyrical content of these musical cultures. The poetics involved recurrently deals with these themes but
the critique of capitalism is simultaneously revealed in the forms which
this expressive culture takes and in the performance aesthetic which gov-
erns them. There is here an imminent challenge to the commodity form
to which black expressive culture is reduced in order to be sold. It is a
challenge that is practiced rather than simply talked or sung about. The
artifacts of a pop industry premised on the individual act of purchase
and consumption are hijacked and taken over into the heart of collective
rituals of protest and affirmation which in turn define the boundaries of
the interpretive community. Music is heard socially and its deepest
meanings revealed only in the heat of this collective, affirmative consumption. Struggles over the commodification of black music are reflected in a dialectical conflict between the technology of reproduction
and the subcultural needs of its primary consumers in the "race market."
Here, the pioneering use of live recordings occupying the whole side of a
long-playing disc, issuing the same song in two parts on different sides of
a 45" and putting out various different mixes are all part of the story.
Musicians and producers for whom the "race market" is the primary
constituency are reluctant to compromise with the commercial formats
that the music business relies on. Where they are able to exercise control
over the form in which their music is issued, black artists anticipate this
specific mode of consumption and privilege it. Records are issued in an
open, participative form which invites further artistic input. The Toaster
or MC adds rhymes and comments to the wordless version of a tune
which is routinely issued on the reverse of the vocal version. Several different versions of the same piece are issued on a single record; 12" discs

which allow for extended playing time are favored. Thus the original arti-fact negotiates the supplementary input of other artists unseen and un-known yet anticipated by the original creator of the music.

The clubs, parties, and dances where these creative negotiations be-tween original and supplementary performances take place are governed by a dramaturgy which prizes the local, immediate, and seemingly spon-taneous input above all. Leaving behind the passive role of spectator to which they would be assigned by Western convention, these audiences instead become active participants. In this metaphysics of intimacy, "race" mediates the social relation between internal pain and its external-ization in cathartic performance. The audience's association with the performer dissolves Eurocentric notions of the disjunction between art and life, inside and outside, in the interplay of personal and public his-tories for which the traditions of the black church serve as a model and an inspiration. […]

It is interesting to note that, at the very moment when celebrated Euro-American cultural theorists have pronounced the collapse of "grand narratives," the expressive culture of Britain's black poor is domi-nated by the need to construct them as narratives of redemption and emancipation. This expressive culture, like others elsewhere in the African diaspora, produces a potent historical memory and an authorita-tive analytical and historical account of racial capitalism and its over-coming.

—1990

George Russell

As for the music … the jazz music of the future … the techniques are going to get more complex, and it will be a challenge for the composer to master the techniques and yet preserve his intuitive approach. And it will be a challenge for the improviser to master these techniques and also pre-serve the intuitive, earthy dignity of jazz.

Specifically, it's going to be a pan-rhythmic, pan-tonal age. I think jazz will bypass atonality because jazz actually has its roots in folk music, and folk music is scale-based music; and atonality negates the scale. I think jazz will be intensely chromatic; but you can be chromatic and not be atonal.

If you're atonal, you're not tonal. You're negating scales, and jazz is a scale-based music. So I think that atonality is technically just a means of expressing the chromatic scale without repeating any of the tones. It's an intellectual concept, in other words. It is terribly restricting in the sense that you must repeat, constantly, the tones of the chromatic scale, if you're a strict atonalist.

Even classical music is beginning to turn from that direction, because atonality is the extreme of tonality. It's the outer limb. It's as far as you can actually go in terms of extreme chromaticism.

But there is another realm between this and the very tonal music such as Mozart and the classicists wrote. This is called "pan-tonality," where the basic folk nature of the scales is preserved, and yet, because you can use any number of scales or you can be in any number of tonalities at once, and/or sequentially, it also crates a very chromatic kind of feeling, so that it's sort of like atonal with a Big Bill Broonzy sound. *You can retain the funk.*

As for jazz and classical music coming together, it depends on how you define classical. If you define it as meaning music which is art, music that is intellectually developed; music that is treated intellectually and thematically—if that's the way you define classical—then I'd say that jazz will become a classical music and that there will be writers who will write in the jazz idiom, using all the dowry that jazz has to bring to this new music. And there will also be writers who will not use the jazz idiom. But the two musics will certainly be equal. Equally good or equally bad ... that depends upon the composers.

There is no limit on human capacity for mastering mechanics, and this process goes on endlessly. No matter how complicated the techniques become, we can always master them and produce good art.

It's a precarious balance, but in that way art, I suppose, reflects life. An artist's very existence is precarious.

You can parallel it to life in this way: it reflects man's striving to over-come nature. And nature, I believe, has placed these musical elements, like rhythm and tonality, at our disposal to make beauty out of them. That's what we've been doing for centuries, trying to make beauty out of these elements—the sound system of nature—and in the meantime, we've built up some sort of musical know-how. We've always digested and produced good music, and we are still in the process of doing that now.

So, it just represents a continuance of man's struggle with nature to accept ever-more complex materials and subdue them, and build art or bridges or atomic bombs ...

—1960

Kristin Hunter Lattany

African culture has many flaws—we should beware of romanticizing a place that cooperated with slavery, worships snakes, and devalues women—but it is, mainly, life-affirming, spiritually aware, and integrated with, rather than antagonistic to, nature. As long as, and to the degree that, white America was Africanized by African Americans—as long as whites were dancing to the rags of Scott Joplin in the Jazz Age or to the music of Little Richard and Chuck Berry in the 1960s; absorbing some of the sermons of Martin Luther King; talking the talk of street folk and musicians—there was hope for America's redemption.

But now I no longer see that hope. White adaptations of black music have succumbed to the great white death urge, going from bland rock to suicidal punk and homicidal heavy metal in less than twenty years. Skinheads, the Klan, and other forms of naked fascism are emerging on the American political scene. We must pull back from white America, because it is now a great rush of lemmings toward the sea. We have passed the point of deciding, in Malcolm's phrase, whether to integrate into a burning house; what faces us now is a decision to leap, or not to leap, into a mass grave. And if it were possible to construct a great grappling hook to snatch back our young, I would volunteer to help build it. Sadly, too many of our youth have already joined the death march through drug addiction and armed drug wars.

The man's music is a triumphal military march to war and destruction, or a solemn dirge of death and despair. We can't afford to step to either one. We are about life. We must slip off his deadly beat to a rhythm of our own, and step right out of his gloomy cadence, sideways if necessary, into our joyous life-affirming dance.

Du Bois's generation and my parents', born respectively at the end of slavery and at the beginning of this century, did have a double- and perhaps even a triple-consciousness. They were proud of being black and of associating with black achievers; wary and watchful of whites, yet strictly disciplined so as to be acceptable to them, and scathing in their scorn for blacks who were not so minded and so disciplined. Products of the first Jazz Age, they taught us to off-time our private, subversive dances to the bewildering Afro-classical polyrhythms of progressive jazz.

I use off-timing as a metaphor for subversion, for code, for ironic attitudes toward mainstream beliefs and behavior, for choosing a vantage point of distance from the majority, for coolness, for sly commentary on the master race, for riffing and improvising off the man's tune and making fun of it.

The cakewalk was off-timing, mocking the airs of Massa and Missy, and making the antics of Philadelphia's New Year's mummers double, deliciously funny to blacks in the know. Louis Armstrong's mockery of minstrelsy was definitely off-timing, shored up by his strong talent, as it had to be; one needs a strong sense of self to play off the master and his stereotypes. Those Hampton students who cooly ignored George Bush's commencement speech in 1991 were off-timing. Haitians who adapt Catholic saints to voodoo rites are off-timing. No matter what she says, when Marian Anderson appeared on the Lincoln Memorial stage as a substitute for the DAR's—and opened her concert with "My Country 'Tis of Thee"—she was making dramatic and effective use of off-timing. The sister in Washington, D.C., who said, when asked her reaction to the Queen of England's visit, "Well, she's fascinating. But so am I," was definitely off-timing. Bill ("Bojangles") Robinson's tap routine to "Me and My Shadow" was a superbly elegant bit of off-timing, a mockery of the mocker that made a suave, ironic comment on racism.

Off-timing, I learned in my youth, was the subversive attitude we had to maintain if we were to survive in the man's society. It was Uncle Julius's sly devaluation of European values in "The Conjure Woman," and Larnie Bell's knowing jazz renditions of Bach fugues in "God Bless the Child," and was more a skewed, but single, ironic consciousness than a double one.

Later, when we reached our thirties, my generation, the Off-Timers, may also have been the first to develop a unified black consciousness, with the help of the fiery younger ones born in the 1940s who for a time became our teachers. Led by them, we moved from off-timing to rocking steady on straight doses of rhythm, blues, and Motown soul. I call the sixties radicals, with a nod to Amiri Baraka, the Soul People.

The ones who came after the Soul People, who were born in the 1950s and 1960s and came to maturity in the 1970s and 1980s, were the beneficiaries of the civil rights and integrationist struggles, which have been efficiently erased from their memories. They are as surely the products of the Reagan and Bush eras as any Yuppies. They are now between thirty and forty years old, with a five-year margin on either side of those boundaries. Some of them grew up in predominantly white suburbs and attended predominantly white schools, all of them were taught, primarily, by white teachers. They are the first African Americans—and, hopefully, the last—to have a purely white consciousness. With their pale contact lenses, permed hair, and bleached personalities, they are distressing to watch and even more distressing to listen to. They sound like tinny transistor radios. They aspire mainly to power positions in corporate America or in the drug economy, and to the possession of status objects. They think money, achievements, and possessions make their color invisible, and they think Bruce Springsteen can sing. They are, God help us, the Rock 'n' Roll Generation.

But take hope, and, maybe, take cover. The newer group, the Rap Generation, now under twenty-five, has come striding angrily on the scene in fade haircuts, kente, and beads. These youngsters are the first group of African Americans to have a purely black consciousness. They either do not know or do not care that if they are honest with the man he is likely to kill them, as is his historic habit. They do not believe, as I did in my youth, that subversion is necessary for survival, or perhaps they sense that their survival is at best tenuous, under the present conditions of race hatred, the failing economy, and the sick planet. Whatever the reasons, they are very open, and foolish, and vulnerable, and brave. Perhaps they sense that the millennium is at hand, and with it, the end of white power. But because I know that the powerful do not give up control easily, and because I love these young people, and want them to survive, I am afraid for them, even as I admire them. [...]

The only healthy double-consciousness, in my opinion, is that which I have labeled "off-timing"—a mockery of white folks and their madness, which is grounded in a secure and solid sense of who we are—the salt and greens eaters, the lovers and life affirmers, the ones who are at ease in our bodies and in nature and who move to an inner rhythm as familiar as the beating of our hearts. Yes, natural rhythm, if you will. Existing in nature rather than trying to control it. Revering God and life, protecting and preserving children, and keeping in touch with the kinfolk are all black traits. The rest of American culture, from singles bars to the hydrogen bomb, can be summed up in the off-timed pronunciation of the phrase "white folks." Properly timed, accompanied by a shrug and maybe an eye-roll if you can do it, this says, "Well, what can you expect?"

—1993

Sub-text

Racist culture dwells in easy polarities that assure its continuity; natural, continuous, a river running through its paces. It's not so much "separation anxiety" that fuels reactionary occlusion, it's inclusion, hybridization, creolization that electrify power's comic-book map of what is and isn't.

Three keywords insist and twist and shout through the Pre-Text: *white, power,* and *culture.*[6] If *white* is synonymous with power in American society, *black* is allowed its binary role as powerless necessity, host for white renewal and continuity. White culture is a black culture junkie, fixed and transfixed by African American art forms from the plantation through the minstrel shows through the Jazz Age through Rhythm 'n' Blues through Soul through Funk through Hip-Hop through whatever organic blending takes shape as the next new thing. Powerlessness is theory's soil, its fertilizer.

But what is "white," a blank page affording social privilege across class barricades, a passport for any body so skinned?

"An achromatic color of maximum lightness, the complement or antagonist of black ... Although typically a response to maximum stimulation, white appears always to depend on contrast."[7]

"Free from color ... being a member of a group or race characterized by reduced pigmentation."[8]

"White—presence of all colors—and its compounds occupy thirty-seven columns in OED."[9]

"The undifferentiated; transcendent perfection; simplicity; light; sun; air; illumination; purity; innocence; chastity; holiness; sacredness; redemption; spiritual authority."[10]

"The conception of black and white as diametrically opposed symbols of the positive and the negative, either in simultaneous, in successive, or alternating opposition, is very common. In our opinion it is of utmost importance. Like all dual formulae in symbolism, it is related to the number two and the great myth of Gemini. But some of its particular applications are of great interest ... In many primitive rites—medicinal dances, for example—the dancers dress up in white clothes and blacken their faces ... In Tibet, there are rites in which a man is chosen as the sacrificial victim, and his face is painted half white and half black ... Black, in fairly generalized terms, seems to represent the initial, germinal stage of all processes, as it does in alchemy ... Amongst primitive peoples, black is the color associated with inner or subterranean zones. Black also sometimes comes to symbolize time, in contrast to white, which represents timelessness and ecstasy ..."[11]

"White is the symbol of divinity or God;/Black is the symbol of the evil spirit or the demon./White is the symbol of light .../Black is the symbol of darkness and darkness expresses all evils./White is the emblem of harmony;/Black is the emblem of chaos./White signifies supreme beauty;/Black ugliness./White signifies perfection;/Black signifies vice./White is the symbol of innocence,/Black that of guilt, sin, and moral degradation./White, a positive color, indicates happiness./Black, a negative color, indicates misfortune./The battle between good an evil is symbolically expressed/By the opposition of white and black."[12]

"Though in many natural objects, whiteness refiningly enhances beauty, as if imparting some special virtue of its own, as in marbles, japonicas, and pearls; and through various nations have in some way recognized a certain royal preeminence in this hue; even the barbaric, grand old kings of Pegu placing the title "Lord of the White Elephants" above all their other magniloquent ascriptions of dominion; and the modern kings of Siam unfurling the same snow-white quadruped in the royal standard; and the Hanoverian flag bearing the one figure of a snow-white charger; and the great Austrian Empire, Caesarean heir to overlording Rome, having for the imperial color the same imperial hue; and though this preeminence in it applies to the human race itself, giving the white man ideal mastership over every dusky tribe; and though, besides all this, whiteness has been even made significant of gladness, for among the Romans a white stone marked a joyful day; and though in other mortal sympathies and symbolizings, this same hue is made the emblem of many touching, noble things—the innocence of brides, the benignity of age; though among the Red Men of America the giving of the white belt of wampum was the deepest pledge of honor; though in many climes, whiteness typifies the majesty of Justice in the ermine of the Judge, and contributes to the daily state of kings and queens drawn by milk-white steeds; though even in the highest mysteries of the most august religions it has been made the symbol of the divine spotlessness and power; by the Persian fire worshipers, the white forked flame being held the holiest on the altar; and in the Greek mythologies, Great Jove himself being made incarnate in a snow-white bull; and though the noble Iroquois, the mid-winter sacrifice of the sacred White Dog was by far the holiest festival in their theology, that spotless, faithful creature being held the purest envoy they could send to the Great Spirit with the annual tidings of their own fidelity; and though directly from the Latin word for white, all Christian priests derive the name of one part of their sacred vesture, the alb or tunic, worn beneath the cassock; and though among the holy pomps of the Roman faith, white is specially employed in the celebration of the Passion of our Lord; though in the Vision of St. John, white robes are given to the redeemed, and the four-and-twenty elders stand clothed in white before the great white throne, and the Holy One that sitteth there white like wool; yet for all these accumulated associations, with whatever is sweet, and honorable, and sublime, there yet lurks an elusive something in the innermost idea of this hue, which strikes more of panic to the soul than that redness that affrights in blood.

"This elusive quality it is, which causes the thought of whiteness, when divorced from more kindly associations, and coupled with any object terrible in itself, to heighten that terror to the furthest bounds. Witness the white bear of the poles, and the white shark of the tropics; what but their smooth, flaky whiteness makes them the transcendent horrors they are? That ghastly whiteness it is which imparts such an abhorrent mildness, even more loathsome than terrific, to the dumb gloating of their aspect. So that not the fierce-fanged tiger in his heraldic coat can so stagger courage as the white-shrouded bear or shark. [...]

"What is it that in the Albino man so peculiarly repels and often shocks the eye, as that sometimes he is loathed by his own kith and kin? It is that whiteness which invests him, a thing expressed by the name he bears. The Albino is as well made as other men—has no substantive deformity—and yet this mere aspect of all-pervading whiteness makes him more strangely hideous than the ugliest abortion. Why should this be so?"[13]

White culture wants everything blacks have to offer—music, clothes, moves, style, expressivity; it wants to be black but doesn't want to be black. (George Carlin reminiscing about childhood in Manhattan, hangs out with black kids, talks their talk, walks their walk, reminds his audience how he never saw any black kid who wanted to be white, walk the white walk, talk the white talk, no way. Or Richard Pryor doing whiteface and whitespeak in marionette stiff moves and joy-damping monotone.) Whites can escape into black culture with the privileged ease of plantation masters entering slave quarters for some kicks. For whites it's a two-way street; for blacks, a dead-end.

"The revolt of the Afro-American artist against specific literary or social conventions is, at bottom, a rebellion against authority and the memory of imposed systems. As trumpeter Clifford Thornton declared, true revolution of consciousness begins by a radical 'unlearning' of existent modes." Kimberly Bentson asserts that jazz engages Euro-American culture in a revolt and "a nearly total negation of Western history and civilization."[14]

Resistance through music creates and recreates identity and cause. A great underground railway of insubordinate cultural practices and pleasures runs twenty four hours, day and night. (Declaring identity is to voice a cause, a politic, a relation against.) In intercultural exchange there's a constant conflict between sharing and pilfering.

In 1935 Zora Neale Hurston wrote in *Men and Mules:* "The white man is always trying to know into somebody else's business. All right, I'll set something outside the door of my mind for him to play with and handle. He can read my writing but he can't read my mind. I'll put this play toy in his hand, and he will seize it and go away. Then I'll say my say and sing my song."[15]

Cornell West writes: "For me identity is fundamentally about desire and death. How you construct your identity is predicated on how you construct desire and how you conceive of death: desire for recognition; quest for visibility (Baldwin—no name in the streets; nobody knows my name); the sense of being acknowledged; a deep desire for association—what Edward Said would call affiliation. It's the longing to belong, a deep, visceral need that most linguistically conscious animals who transact with an environment (that's us) participate in. And then there is a profound desire for protection, for security, for safety, for surety. [...] But identity also has to do with death. [...] Persons who construct their identities and desires often do it in such a way that they're willing to die for it—soldiers in the Middle East, for example—or, under a national identity, that they're willing to kill others. [...] But if in fact identity has something to do with these various kinds of desires, these various conceptions of death (we are beings-toward-death), it's because we have, given our inevitable extinction, to come up with a way of endowing ourselves with significance."[16]

What do I mean by *culture?* What comes instantly to mind is yogurt, a continuously generating lactobacilli, "cultivation of living material in prepared nutrient media" (*Webster's Seventh New Collegiate*). "The totality of socially transmitted behavior patterns, arts, beliefs, institutions, and all other products of human work and thought characteristic of a community or population" (*American Heritage Illustrated Dictionary*). Raymond Williams calls it "the structure of feeling," Peter Burke writes: "*Culture* is an imprecise term, with many rival definitions; mine is 'a system of shared meanings, attitudes, and values, and the symbolic forms (performances, artifacts) in which they are expressed or embodied.'"[17] As fluid as "culture" is as a meaning system, "tradition" demands fixity, an essential conservatism. Culture reinvents, re-imagines it origins, puts tradition to new use. Despite arguments dreaming back to a "pure" state, uncontaminated by anything outside its own static perfection, culture-as-process is voraciously restless, predatory, and hungry. Anything and everything is fuel for its continuity. Despite the trench (and entrenched) warfares of current vocabulary wars, cultures (no matter how isolated) are various, predatory, and theft prone. Like bacilli on the move, cultures seek endless nourishment. "Tradition" assumes and upholds a pristine prelapsarian Past. It's an invention, a P.R. mirror of present tense tensions over turf and legitimacy. Righteous whistle-blowers can't stop the surge. What would be nailed-down as Culture, a singular topography, a precious and predictable entity, will always be a smashed vessel shattered by an ongoing influx of the creative forces of excluded others.

"*Culture* is one of the two or three most complicated words in the English language," writes Raymond Williams. It has a "range of meanings: inhabit, cultivate, protect, honor with worship. Some of these meanings eventually separated."[18] A quadernity of qualities that describe pop cult scholars, ecstatic fans, Bible-thumbing censors, agenda-advancing politicos, dreamers and schemers, cool operators and hot heads. We inhabit cultures as they inhabit us, cultivate them as we're "cultivated" by them, mulched in the mix, enculted to protect our chosen (and choosing) sounds as they protect us; our discernment is a commitment, an ongoing involvement; our music, our musicians. Ours as opposed to theirs, a rite for private fantasies of otherness that becomes exclusivity.

Cultures circulate the familiar, installs identity and a relationship to self through music explaining their particular world over and over again, long past the initial illumination.

"Often referred to as a 'freak of nature,' the freak, it must be emphasized, is a freak of culture. His or her anomalous status is articulated by the process of the spectacle as it distances the viewer, and thereby 'normalizes' the viewer as much as it marks the freak as an aberration,"[19] writes Susan Stewart in her essay on the imaginary body, suggesting another social process of racial division via whiteness enfreaking blackness, setting it apart in a store window, cage, or carnival midway, enabling dominion, and "normalcy" over and above the stigmatized black presence. White culture's privilege is the permission to watch, make visible the invisible man who remains, at once, seen and unseen.

In his study on nineteenth-century American blackface minstrelsy in the period leading up to and after the Civil War, Eric Lott could be writing about the white reception of jazz when he states, "Minstrelsy brought to public form racialized elements of thought and feeling, tone and impulse, residing at the very edge of semantic availability, which Americans only dimly realized they felt, let alone understood. The minstrel show was less the incarnation of an age-old racism than an emergent social semantic figure highly responsive to the emotional demands and troubled fantasies of its audiences … I depart from most other writers on minstrelsy, who have based their analyses on racial aversion, in seeing the vagaries of racial desire as fundamental to minstrel-show mimicry. It was cross-racial desire that coupled a nearly insupportable fascination and a self-protective derision with respect to black people and their cultural practices that made blackface minstrelsy less a sign of absolute white power and control than of panic, anxiety, terror, and pleasure."[20]

"Panic, anxiety, terror, pleasure" and "fascination" face another's unknowability, and withdraw into negation, erasure, or draw on internal amulets of "types," vis-aids typologies of closed selves in white's Rolodex of stereo-types rolled around in divinatory delirium: Black, Jew, Chinese, Mexican, Arab. Any other not white is not right; yet other needs its other, to wear its skin in an act of sympathetic magic. In panic, anxiety, terror, pleasure, fascination White imperials yearn for their dark others. Liberated from slave bodies by becoming them. An enigma, a masque, a mask.

Create and recreate the "savage," flee "civilization" whose tenants break faith daily, leave primary belief to engage in secondary doubt. Anything exciting and dangerous is savage; today it's gangsta rappers, yesterday it was beboppers, zootsuiters, JDs. (In nineteenth-century U.S.A. and U.K., "rappers" were primarily women, Spiritualists who tapped into the world beyond the world, challenging the priestly class with sassy demonstrations of how the dead and Eternity were reachable through a direct line without elaborate mediations of patriarchal hierarchy. In the age of telegraphy and electricity, metaphysical metaphors for technology and teleology flourished.)

Blacks as non-persons, a concept to amp-up white personhood (or hooded persons): The Dred Scott 1857 decision—two years after the first editions of Whitman's *Leaves of Grass* and P.T. Barnum's *My Life and Times*—stated blacks had no rights as "human beings"—"on the contrary, they were at that time considered as a subordinate and inferior class of beings, who had been subjugated by the dominant race, and, whether emancipated or not, yet remained subject to their authority, and had no rights or privileges but such as those who held the power and the Government might to grant them.

"Black slavery enriched the country's creative possibilities. For in that construction of blackness and enslavement could be found not only the not-free but also, with the dramatic polarity created by skin color, the projection of the not-me. The result was a playground for the imagination. What rose up out of collective needs to allay internal fears and to rationalize external exploitation was an American Africanism—a fabricated brew of darkness, otherness, alarm, and desire that is uniquely American," writes Toni Morrison.[21]

In his memoirs bassist Milt Hinton remembers working a gig in Texas with the Cab Calloway band where a rope divided the dance-hall to separate black dancers from white. Throughout *Writing Jazz* are memories of the divisive rope and its darker resonance as blunt emblem of lynching.

Resistance creates identity as identity creates resistance. The music functions as a diasporic intercultural underground railway, challenging through creation the forces of extermination. Everyone who listens to music refers to it personally, "my music," an element of personhood, identity, mine. Paraphrasing James H. Cone, music "affirms the somebodiness" of people, black or white, cuts across crunching class lines. Cone is speaking specifically of the blues, the ground of jazz and most pop music. "The blues is the transformation of black life through the sheer power of song. They symbolize the solidarity, the attitudes, and the identity of the black community ... [a] stoic feeling that recognizes the painfulness of the present but refuses to current to its historical contradictions."[22]

The blues evolved from transplanted African religious practice, worked out from spirituals and church hymns into a taproot of jazz. Linked as much to the West African griot tradition as to the white European/American nineteenth-century Romantic idea of artist as one who speaks for all, as soloist, virtuoso, voice, conscience, historian, critic, an ancient and modern figure. As all cultural production, Jazz is ancient and modern in its lineages.

James Baldwin, talking to Margaret Mead, said: "Everyone really knows how long the blacks have been here. Everyone knows on what levels blacks are involved with the American people and in the American life. These are not secrets. It is not a question even of the ignorance of white people. It is a question of the fears of white people … That's what makes it all so hysterical, so unwieldy, and so completely irretrievable. Reason cannot reach it. It is as though some great, great, great wound is in the whole body, and no one dares to operate: to close it, to examine it, to stitch it."[23]

Ida B. Wells-Barnett writes in 1892, "The Afro-American is not a bestial race … Brutality still continued. Negroes were whipped, scourged, exiled, shot, and hung whenever and wherever it pleased the white man so to treat them, and as the civilized world with increasing persistency held the white people of the South to account for its outlawry, the murderers invented the third excuse—that Negroes had to be killed to avenge their assaults upon women … Humanity abhors the assailant of womanhood, and this charge upon the Negro at once placed him beyond the pale of human sympathy. With such unanimity, earnestness, and apparent candor was this charge made and reiterated that the world has accepted the story that the Negro is a monster which the Southern white man has painted him."[24]

   Monster, beast, the animal within without, white skin turned inside out, tendons turn blood blue to blood red then blood black in the air and light of unfoldment and scrutiny. Pharmakoi, abject bodies chosen for seasonal sacrificial rites to expunge collective sins and guilt; scapegoats bear collective blame, remove it from spectators who cheer the ritual slaughter to its finale. We read how chosen bodies were mutilated, hanged, then burned; sometimes those with guns shot the body tied to a tree before it was burned; we read first-hand and fictional accounts of how participants took pieces of the black carcass as votive souvenirs, how parents with their children gathered around the ruined cadaver to pose for pictures. Corkscrews bit spiral hunks out of flesh tossed to ritualists. If it was a male (and it usually was), castration cut off a mystery deeply coiled in white imagination, a phantasm of phallic energy color-absent elites and underdogs brooded over. Genital trophies of the hunt and slaughter were coveted, put in lockers of desire and envy, opened on special occasions of racial renewal and affirmation.

"Some scientists now even believe that without impregnation, sexual intercourse with a black male leads to an infusion of the black sperm into the system of the White female which affects her body chemistry toward negroidal traits. Thus, in effect a White woman who engaged in sex with negroes should be considered no longer to be part of the White Race. We believe that such activity can even cause mental changes in the White female which would tend to make her pro-negro and pro-race mixing because she has in a chemical way become part of the black race even though she still has the appearance of a White person."[25]

Marx's early mentor, Georg Wilhelm Friedrich Hegel, writes: "The characteristic feature of the Negroes is that their consciousness has not yet reached an awareness of any substantial objectivity—for example, of God or the law—in which the will of man could participate and in which he could become aware of his own being. The African, in his undifferentiated and concentrated unity, has not yet succeeded in making this distinction between himself as an individual and his essential universality, so that he knows nothing of an absolute being which is other and higher than his own self." In his lectures on world history, Hegel describes the world beyond whiteness to his auditors: "All our observations of African man show him as living in state of savagery and barbarism, and he remains in this state to the present day. The Negro is an example of animal man in all his savagery and lawlessness, and if we wish to understand him at all, we must put aside all our European attitudes. We must not think of a spiritual God or of moral laws; to comprehend him correctly, we must abstract from all reverence and morality, and from everything we call feeling. All this is foreign to man in his immediate existence, and nothing consonant with humanity is to be found in his character." Though opposed philosophically to slavery—"Slavery ought not to exist, as it is by definition unjust in and for itself"—Hegel tells his congregation: "The distinguishing feature of the Negroes' contempt for humanity is not so much their contempt for death as their lack of respect for life. They set as little value on life as they do on human beings as such, for life is only valuable in so far as there is a higher value in man."[26] In *Phenomenologie des Geists* (Phenomenology of Spirit) Hegel proposes and analyzes the symbiotic interaction of the slave/master relationship: "It is for [consciousness] that it is and is not immediately the other consciousness; and even so, that this other is only for itself, in that it transcends itself in existing for itself; only for existing for the other is it for itself. Each is the medium for the other, through which each is mediated and united with itself; and each is for itself and the other an immediate being, existing for itself, which simultaneously is only for itself by virtue of this mediation. They recognize themselves as mutually recognizing one another."[27] Jessica Benjamin comments that "this abstract reciprocity is not really how the subject experiences things. Rather, the subject, first of all, experiences himself as an absolute, and then searches for affirmation of self through the other. The mutuality that is implied by the concept of recognition is a problem for the subject, whose goal is only to be certain of himself."[28]

How do we "recognize [ourselves] as mutually recognizing one another?"

In his book of fascinations, *Learned Pigs & Fireproof Women: A History of Unique, Eccentric & Amazing Entertainers*, Ricky Jay devotes a chapter to Blind Tom Bethune, an African-American musical prodigy of Victorian America. Blind Tom at four years old could play whatever he heard played on the piano. Born to slave parents, he was probably an idiot savant. Not only a musical mimic, Tom could recite in languages he did not understand, like German, French, Greek, and Latin; "he also did vocal imitations of the bagpipe, hurdy-gurdy, and fiddle. In Washington, D.C., he visited Congress and thereafter performed the speeches of the politicians with such accurate vocal inflections as to amuse and delight his audiences." Another facet of his talent was the ability to compose original music on the spot. "The inspiration for his novel work was often the wind, the trees, or the rain, which he thought 'spoke to him,' and he responded with improvisations on the piano." Exploited by his white owners, even though technically "freed" by the Emancipation Proclamation of 1863, the "natural musical curiosity" didn't own the copyrights to his own compositions "until after [an] 1887 court battle ... [yet] even after his death, legal battles over the disposition of his earnings continued."[29] It's said that Blind Tom ate too much, got uncomfortably bulky, hated bathing, and was regarded by his handlers as some kind of hybrid animal.

Blind black musicians—like Blind Lemon Jefferson, Art Tatum, Roland Kirk—are seen but cannot see. The ocular and occult nature of racial typing and stereotyping can't be known and practiced without sight; obviously, it has to be awakened through the oral folklore of racism.

Not to see difference but to be seen as different. How does a blind musician hear "black" or "white" in the music they hear and play? (Charlie Parker tells blind British jazz pianist George Shearing in postwar Fifty-second Street club, "You're really a Negro, you're a Negro!")

It's the other who's savage and uncivilized; the other one's a cannibal heart gobbler, tossing torn-off arms and legs of rite's victims to worshipers and dogs below the blood-slick platform of performance. The other is not the civilizer, builder of stores, museums, zoos, land leveler, culture poacher who turns spirit into stuff, who civilizes savagery into commodities, and guts social/sacred arts of their uncommodifiable meaning and purpose. White's dominion extends and ends in skin's surface, the nerve-ends and pores of its white mask covers destiny's skull that clothes death's unrelenting democracy.

Academic "white" discourse is busy explaining the pathos of whiteness as a condition of racialism, "skin privilege," which is, in principle, anti-racist while remaining safely insinuated inside white institutional castle culture power. The knowledge bureaucracies give permission for mea culpa choirs at self flagellating rituals (conferences, seminars, publications circulated and debated amongst themselves). Academicians share guilt and shame (and relief) for being directly or covertly involved in perpetuating racism. It is often elevated to a martyrdom that never transcends nor would it unlock those conceptual chains binding its adored others.

Double-bound multiculturalism is essentially a white discourse. While it benefits marginalized writers and performers elected by white supremacy's largesse, it's still just another minstrel show on the stages of white imperial cultural hegemony. "Whiteness" as academic discourse reflects its relation to color but in no way abandons its institutional authority of whiteness. Whiteness "allows" color but lives in an imaginary realm of its disappearance or visibility in commerce that counts between the privileged. Race is imagined then invented as real, consumed and digested within the white body politic as an essential foodstuff. White Euro-Ams invent race by announcing white skin's superiority making instantly inferior all other skins not white. "All this whiteness that burns me," wrote Frantz Fanon. "The white world, the only honorable one, barred me from all participation. A man was expected to behave like a man. I was expected to behave like a black man—or least like a nigger. I shouted a greeting to the world and the world slashed away my joy. I was told to stay within bounds, to go back where I belonged."[30]

"For such a common word—or rather two words, for 'people, population' and 'speed, competition' are unrelated—surprisingly little is known about the origin of [the word] *race.* The former comes via French from Italian *razza*, but the antecedents of razza are obscure."[31] Obscure magical origins of power enmeshed in economic boundary-making, a caste of a million slaves cast into the "colored" Darwinian dungeon of grotesquery. "Racism is not a biological but a discursive regime. The so-called bodily insignias—black skin, thick lips, curly hair, penises 'as big as cathedrals' and the rest—which appear to function as foundational, are not only constituted through and through in fantasy, but are really signifying elements in the discourse of racism," writes Stuart Hall.[32] "It was hate; I was hated, despised, detested, not by the neighbor across the street or my cousin on my mother's side, but by an entire race. I was up against something unreasoned," writes Fanon. The "unreason" of racism in the shadows of Enlightenment's white banners of triumph, universal humanism, is contradicted in planetary devourment via imperialism, colonialization, slave-making, rationalized through rewritten or obliterated histories, desecrated mysteries, and peoples eviscerated into empty husks, objects on display in a museum of abject and instructive otherness. "No attempt must be made to encase man, for it is his destiny to be set free."[33] "But Zombies are wanted for more uses beside field work. They are reputedly used as sneak thieves. The market women cry out continually that little Zombies are stealing their change and goods. Their invisible hands are believed to provide well for their owners."[34] Earlier I mentioned zombification, living dead automata, golems shaped from language and mud representing a kind of inhuman human. Golem was other and as other could not speak, a mute enforcer at the command of rabbis removed from the war zone. Golems were sent out to defend the beleaguered communities. Racism creates zombies and golems. Darwin's inadvertent master-plan, *Origin of Species* (1859), was subtitled "The Preservation of Favoured Races in the Struggle for Life." In *The Descent of Man* (1871) he prophesied: "At some future period, not very distant as measured by centuries, the civilized races of man will almost certainly exterminate and replace the savage races of the world."[35]

Whites still consider blacks as property. Objects of affection and rejection. Any other than white (and male) is property. Racism as metaphor can extend to include the battered-wife syndrome, the cycle of sexual abuse based on male ownership of woman as his subject and object, property. Property rites. "You're mine whether you want me or not," yowls Screamin' Jay Hawkins in his fifties' red alert, "I Put A Spell On You." Trance dance leads to danger's razored borders. "You do that hoodoo that you do so well." Power is the ability to oppress, suppress, repress; it comes with ownership and unfolds from above like a card-sharp's waterfall shuffle in tiers of descending demand on that which is below. Power is invariably visualized as "above," like the Judeo-Christian ineffable God now resymbolized as the CEO of a multinational corporation. "The Room at the Top" housing an absolute mystery refracted and reflected in the everyday mirroring of power-relations from below. As above, so below. Un-whites are believed to be "below" the imperious platform of white elevation. White shadows blanket faces and bodies of others, further darken them to make opposition clear and inevitable, to reinforce the distance between those on top and those below. It's a pathology, an amazing effort of denial, voluntary blindness, hysteria. Terminology scuttles down the pages of colonial sciences. In the Academy it's called "discourse."

One on the outside of that sightless site could easily say: "dis that course" where white is blind to itself professing "inclusiveness." White earnestly and duplicitously recognizes everyone else not white as "people of color," further diced into white-power affirming subdivisions of "African-American," "Chinese-American," "Japanese-American," "Jewish-American," "Zulu-American," "Miwok-American," "Mexican-American," and on in infinite permutations of "American" that, in the mouths of the namers, means subscribers to white supremacy segmenting otherness into a blitzkrieg of secondary identities all engulfed by "American," which has the implicit meaning of whiteness.

In her poem "The Unhappy Race," Aboriginal poet Oodgerroo Noonucaal writes: "White fellow, you are the unhappy race./You alone have left nature and made civilized laws./You have enslaved yourselves as you enslaved the horse and other wild things./Why, white man?/Your police lock up your tribe in houses with bars./We see poor women scrubbing floors of richer women./Why, white man, why?/You laugh at 'poor blackfellow,' you say we must be like you./You say we must leave the old freedom and leisure,/We must be civilized and work for you./Why, white fellow?/Leave us alone, we don't want your collars and ties,/We don't need your routines and compulsions./We want the old freedom and joy that all things have but you,/Poor white man of the unhappy race."[36]

As white's imagined so is black. We imagine each other, our absences and presences; what's seen is imagined, what's imagined is seen. The eyes have it. Aye, I. But what's my story, morning glory? Mourning false glory and unrealizable power is my story, the imperial branding race eye set against seeing, the I blinded within in order to reorder goods that appear magically in emporia of displacement. Blind eye, blind I, bound to the bondage of enslaving images whose surfaces thrive and survive, dazzle and blind, in a mirror hive of white entranced kingship. Ship of fools, delusional Titanic hits the impossible and passes into history as tragedy. Hubris as succubus, white vampirism of blackness. Sounds like a postmodern Gothic fiction whose terrors of desire for inclusion, fear of contamination, conflict with the master's need to be acknowledged as human by the slave he's made into an inhuman object. Not seen yet to oversee; expressive white body dances in a weave of blackness. In the rhythm's pulse yet apart and somehow in imiginary charge, as if participation meant domination. To be included in the excluded; included only as one imagines it, imagines them. It and them, animal, hopeless child, Sambo fool, Mammy cookie jar, castrated martyr Tom, all there to serve and please, amuse and terrorize, dis and rebel against mistress and master who command the anxious minstrelsy of "love and theft." It and them (never us) in white height's shadow tower of power; it appears as it disappears, an unwillingness to let go of the forked vision of race.

"There are two colors indicative of the Vessel itself: black and blue. Black indicates that there is no circuitry of energy, as black absorbs (or takes (-)) all of the rays of white light."[37] "I walk on white nails," writes Fanon. "And so it is not I who make a meaning for myself, but it is the meaning that was already there, pre-existing, waiting for me. It is not out of my bad nigger's misery, my bad nigger's teeth, my bad nigger's hunger that I will shape a torch with which to burn down the world, but it is the torch that was already there, waiting for that turn of history."[38] Langston Hughes writes, "But jazz to me is one of the inherent expressions of Negro life in America: the eternal tom-tom beating in the Negro soul—the tom-tom of revolt against weariness in a white world."[39] More compellingly poignant and stark than "Strange Fruit," the Popular Front song Billie Holiday sang at Café Society, was Fats Waller and Andy Razaf's "What Did I Do To Be So Black And Blue?"[40] ("Just 'cause you're black, folks think you lack,/They laugh at you and scorn you too,/What did I do to be so black and blue?")[41] "What do you mean I gotta do that? Ain't but two things I got to do—Be black and die." "Racism is always historically specific. Though it may draw on the cultural traces deposited by previous historical phases, it always takes on specific forms. It arises out of our present—not past—conditions. Its effects are specific to the present organization of society, to the present unfolding of its dynamic political and cultural processes—not simply to its repressed past," writes Stuart Hall.[42] The race, the human race, won't quit, despite millennial finish-line hysteria; running toward what and away from whom?

If racism is born in slavery, how does one explain freedom, what incubates there? Kant's inexplicable fact, the autonomy or self-determination of rational beings. Can I get a second opinion? Scanning a drybones sociology dictionary: "In a comparative perspective, it has also been argued that slavery in North America was far more repressive than in Latin America. There are a number of reasons for this: 1. The Protestants of North America regarded the slave as sinful and in need of sexual restraint, while Catholicism in South America was more tolerant. 2. The ethnic diversity of Latin America was extensive and therefore the divisions between black and white was less sharply drawn. 3. It was possible for slaves to purchase their freedom in South America, but this was uncommon in North America."[43] The purchase, the buy, keeps the flow of goods and products circulating, an economics that justifies turning beings into objects ranked by skin tone, slaves and wage-slaves producing goods for statewide and export manufacture, assemblyline cyborgs working in the inside of the margins of the disallowed, flash-frozen within a belief-system with its dark secret pockets of worry. In Hip hop, "free style" means to perform without a plan, a total improvisation, rapping on the spot to the beats, letting rhymes go, shaping their flow as fast as you can. On the other hand, the score: to slam bread down and slap the bag up in quick street Masonic handshake exchange; later, to go out and hustle cash for a stash to shoot the works but quickly get back to work as soon as utopia evaporates. No end to need; just a chainlink in the circle and recirculation of voluntary slavery. Dependency not independence is the death dance, the postmodern minstrelshow in late capital's disintegrating playgrounds and inner cities.

The inverted cornucopia, the void all the stuff absorbs but can't fill. The more it takes in, consumes, the emptier they become.

"Because it was so reliant on the institutionalization of their unfree labor, the slaves viewed the civilizing process with skepticism and its ethical claims with extreme suspicion," writes Paul Gilroy. "Their hermeneutic agency grounded a vernacular culture premised on the possibility that freedom should be pursued outside of the rules, codes, and expectations of color-coded civilization. The transgression of those codes was itself a sign that freedom was being claimed. It presented the possibility of an (anti)politics animated by the desire to violate—a negation of unjust, oppressive and therefore illegitimate authority. By breaking these rules in small, though ritualized ways it was possible to deface the clean edifice of white supremacy that fortified tainted and therefore inauthentic freedoms. Cultures of insubordination located more substantive and worthwhile freedoms [...] elaborated through the media of music and dance as well as through writing. Music expressed and confirmed unfreedom while evolving in complex patterns that pointed beyond misery towards reciprocity and prefigured the democracy yet to come in their antiphonic forms. Dance refined the exercise of autonomous powere in the body by claiming it back from the absolute sovereignity of work."[44]

Fanon writes, "I move slowly in the world, accustomed now to seek no longer for upheaval. I progress by crawling. And already I am being dissected under white eyes, the only real eyes. I am fixed ... I am laid bare. I feel, I see in those white faces that it is not a new man who has come in, but a new kind of man, a new genus. Why, it's a Negro!"[45] Freedom eludes, is rude, uncontainable, synonymous with culture, a constant struggle to stay unbroken and inventive.

"Canned jazz blared through the street with a monstrous high-strutting rhythm that pulled at the viscera. The board floor squeaked under my footsteps. I switched on the

light and looked into a cracked piece of mirror bradded with net nails to the wall. The
bald Negro stared back at me from its mottled sheen. I knew I was in hell. Hell could
be no more lonely or hopeless, no more agonizingly estranged from the world of order
and harmony.

"I heard my voice, as though it belonged to someone else, hollow in the empty
room, detached, say: 'Nigger, what you standing up there crying for?'

"I saw tears slick on his cheeks in the yellow light.

"Then I heard myself say what I have heard them say so many times, 'It's not right.
It's just not right.'

"Then the crush of revulsion, the momentary flush of blind hatred against the
whites who were somehow responsible for all of this, the old bewilderment of wondering, 'Why do they do it? Why do they keep us like this? What are they gaining? What
evil has taken them?' (The Negroes say, 'What sickness has taken them?') My revulsion
turned to grief that my own people could give the hate stare, could shrivel men's souls,
could deprive humans of rights they unhesitatingly accorded their livestock," wrote
John Howard Griffin in *Black Like Me.* Griffin, a white Texas novelist overdosed on injec-
tions of melanin in order to "pass" as a black, an experiment he begins as "a scientific
research study of the Negro in the South." In blackface undercover, he went into the
South to experience humiliation, hatred, segregation, objectification, desire, terror, and,
as in Virgilian tours, some kind of redemption. A Negro for six weeks and, as such,
Griffin at the book's conclusion hires a Negro youth to help clean his parents' home
after it's sold to new owners. "The youth knew me and had no reticence in talking since
he was sure I was 'one of them' so to speak. Both Negroes and whites have gained this
certainty from the experiment—because I was a Negro for six weeks, I remained partly
Negro or perhaps essentially Negro." Before he ends the book, Griffin fusses about
"the rise in racism among Negroes, justified to some extent, but a grave symptom nevertheless … The Negro who turns now, in the moment of near-realization of his liber-
ties, and bares his fangs at a man's whiteness, makes the same tragic error the white
racist has made. Too many of the more militant leaders are preaching Negro superiority. I pray that the Negro will not miss his chance to rise to greatness, to build from the
strength gained through his past suffering and, above all, to rise beyond vengeance."[46]
Be oppressed but have the fastidiousness not to rebel, nor riot, rage, destroy the hard-
line torments of abundance.

I read the book when I was twenty-three: married, a two-year-old daughter, living in
an apartment on one San Francisco's steepest hills. On TV, a filibuster against civil
rights initiated by eighteen Southern senators. Felton Turner, a black Houston resident,
was beaten with a tire iron, suspended upside down in an oak tree. The initials KKK
were carved on his chest.[47]

Black is what white imagines.

Racism is underwritten in fear: at any moment, white privilege will be wrested away by
the oppressed, toppled, viciously redeemed. This tidal wave of panic justifies further
blind objectification in the mass mediated demonology of our post-Willie Horton,
Rodney King, O. J. Simpson sound-bitten epoch.

"The discovery of personal whiteness among the world's peoples is a very modern
thing,—a nineteenth- and twentieth-century matter, indeed. The ancient world would
have laughed at such a distinction. The Middle Ages regarded skin color with mild cu-

riosity; and even up into the eighteenth century we were hammering our national manikins into one, great, Universal Man, with fine frenzy which ignored color and race even more than birth. Today we have changed all that, and the world in a sudden, emotional conversion has discovered that it is white and by that token, wonderful!" DuBois writes in 1920.[48]

"The attitude we normals have toward a person with a stigma, and the actions that we take in regard to him, are well known, since these responses are what benevolent social action is designed to soften and ameliorate. By definition, of course, we believe the person with a stigma is not quite human. On this assumption we exercise varieties of discrimination, through which we effectively, if often unthinkingly, reduce his life chances. We construct a stigma-theory, an ideology to explain his inferiority and account for the danger he presents, sometimes rationalizing an animosity based on other differences, such as those of social class," writes sociologist Erving Goffman in 1963.[49]

"Race, as a social question, exists only for the ideologists of the bourgeoisie and in the minds of those deluded by them," writes black Red Harry Haywood in 1930. "With these the purely biological category race, based upon differences within the human species, such as color of skin, texture of hair, etc., acquires a social meaning, i.e., race becomes an explanation of social phenomena. Upon this false premise are reared equally false theories which claim the existence in nature of master and slave races, the former by their 'inherent' qualities destined to rule, while the latter because of the absence of these qualities are fitted only for a menial position. The existence of a different level of advancement among peoples, the fact that European nations have reached a higher economic and political stage of development than say, the Africans or Asiatics, is not considered accidental, i.e. as the result of objective natural and social causes, but is attributed to the 'natural' superiority of the Europeans. The purely physical concept 'race' is identified by these theoreticians with intellectual, moral, and cultural traits. White skin becomes the symbol of civilization, high culture, and intellectual prowess, while black skin symbolizes barbarity, low morals, dependency, etc. The struggle between the two is regarded as the result of 'instinctive,' racial antagonisms. It is perfectly logical therefore that in the 'interests' of humanity it becomes the duty of the master races to watch over these incapables, to shoulder the 'white man's burden' and to see to it that they serve society in that capacity, which by virtue of their 'natural' shortcomings they are best fitted."[50]

> What is the thing that we are dreaming? I was thinking last night about the ecstasy of ideas and wanting to be in this world without flesh; where the flesh has fallen away and there is no skin. Part of the failure of the imagination on all our parts in terms of a liberatory vision is that we don't know what we seek.[51]
>
> —*bell hooks*

Notes

PRE-TEXT

1. Using oral as-told-to interviews and autobiographies of African-American musicians makes me aware of how their primary scribes are white like those who took dictation for many nineteenth-century slave narratives.

2. The anthropological voyeuristic approach was epitomized in British jazz buff Spike Hughes's "Day by Day in New York," published in *The Melody Maker*, April 1933: "When I eventually did my Columbus act and set foot on American soil, I found myself completely unable to realize that the Negro porters were not all trumpet players or drummers doing a spot of spare-time portering. John Hammond assured me that they probably did no more than hum rather out of tune when they were not pushing trunks around.... How shall I describe that first visit to Harlem? Perhaps I was filled with the same feeling that accompanied my first visit, as a child, to the house where Mozart was born; or my first view of Hobbs batting. It was a feeling of visiting for the first time a place which had been so distant and legendary hitherto that one had almost doubted its very existence. Much has been said about 'spiritual homes,' but for my first hour of time in Harlem I found myself not intruding so much as doubting that I was really there.... To cross over 125th Street into Harlem is to enter an entirely foreign country. Everybody on the streets, including the police, is Negro, but what a contrast these people's faces present with those of the whites down-town. Whereas south of Central Park the streets are filled with scurrying, glum, characterless people, Harlem is populated by leisurely, cheerful, laughing folk—the men with shoulders to their overcoats that reach heavenwards, the women clad in every color of the rainbow ..."

3. "Tin Pan Alley" was the name given to the New York music songwriting and publishing zone from the teens through the forties.

4. Bret Primack, "Tony Williams" in *JazzTimes* (February 1997): 44.

5. *Electronic Civil Disobedience and Other Unpopular Ideas by the Critical Art Ensemble* (New York: Autonomedia, 1996), 114–15.

SUB-TEXT

6. *White Power*, the neologism and title of George Lincoln Rockwell's 1967 U.S. *Mein Kampf* update: "To all White Men of courage/who from the beginning created Western Civilization/and in the present sustain and/in the future fulfill human destiny/this book is dedicated"—is no doubt a source text for generations of disempowered racist true believers. Rockwell finds the sixties an aberration and abomination, leveling his funhouse zoom lens on Hippies, Homosexuals, Jews, and Negroes. "Millions and millions of these primitive misfits and incompetents forced into urban, crowded living conditions, forced to compete with intelligent White people, forced to give up their natural pleasures in voodoo, uninhibited sex, etc., forced to try to pretend what they are not—forced to FAIL, day after day, week after week, month after month—finally get so frustrated and desperate that they are ready for any kind of violence and horror, since nothing could be much worse that the agonizing frustration they face every moment of their miserable lives."

7. *The American Heritage Illustrated Dictionary of the English Language* (Boston: Houghton Mifflin Company, 1979), 1481.

8. *Webster's Seventh New Collegiate Dictionary* (Springfield, AZ: G. & C. Merriam Company, 1967), 1017.

9. Joseph T. Shipley, *The Origins of English Words: A Discursive Dictionary of Indo-European Roots* (Baltimore: The John Hopkins University Press, 1984), 166.

10. J.C. Cooper, *An Illustrated Encyclopaedia of Traditional Symbols* (London: Thames & Hudson, 1978), 41.

11. J.E. Cirlot, *A Dictionary of Symbols* (New York: Philosophical Library, 1962), 54-55.

12. J. M. Paillot de Montabert, "Du caractere symbolique des principales soulerus employees dans les peintures chretiennes: Question empruntee au savant ouvrage de M. Frederic Portal, et simplifiee et disposee a l'usage des artistes," *Memoires de la societtte d'agriculture, science, arts et belles lettres des department de l'Aube 17* (1838): 19, quoted in Albert Boime, *The Art of Exclusion: Representing Blacks in the Nineteenth Century* (London: Thames & Hudson, 1990), 2.

13. Herman Melville, *Moby Dick; or, The Whale* (1851), from *Redburn, White-Jacket, Moby-Dick* (New York: The Library of America, 1983), 993-97.

14. Kimberly Bentson, *Late Coltrane: A Re-membering of Orpheus' in Chant of Saints*, ed. by Michael S. Harper and Robert B. Steptoe (Urbana: University of Illinois Press, 1979), 414.

15. Zora Neale Hurston, *Men and Mules* [1935] (New York: Harper Perennial, 1990), 1-2.

16. Cornell West, "A Matter of Life and Death" in *October 61* (Summer 1992): 20-21.

17. Peter Burke, *Popular Culture in Early Modern Europe* (New York: Harper Torchbooks/ Harper & Row, Publishers, 1978), i.

18. Raymond Williams, *Keywords: A Vocabulary of Culture and Society* (Revised Edition) (New York: Oxford University Press, 1983), 87.

19. Susan Stewart, *On Longing: Narratives of the Miniature, the Gigantic, the Souvenir, the Collection* (Durham: Duke University Press, 1993), 109.

20. Eric Lott, *Love and Theft: Blackface Minstrelsy and the American Working Class* (New York: Oxford University Press, 1993), 6.

21. Toni Morrison, *Playing in the Dark: Whiteness and the Literary Imagination* (Cambridge: Harvard University Press, 1992), 38.

22. James H. Cone, *The Spiritual and the Blues* (New York: Seabury Press, 1972), 117.

23. Margaret Mead and James Baldwin, *A Rap on Race* (Philadelphia/New York: J.B. Lippincott Company, 1971), 3.

24. Ida B. Wells-Barnett, *On Lynchings: Southern Horrors; A Red Record; Mob Rule in New Orleans* (1892) (Salem: Ayer Company Publishers, Inc., 1991), 60-61.

25. Quoted from white supremacist periodical, *Thunderbolt 274* (1982): 9, in Jessie Daniels, *White Lies: Race, Class, Gender and Sexuality in White Supremacist Discourse* (New York/London: Routledge, 1997), 80.

26. Georg Wilhelm Friedrich Hegel, "Geographical Basis of World History" in *Race and the Enlightenment: A Reader*, ed. by Emmanuel Chukwudi Eze (Oxford: Blackwell Publishers Ltd., 1997), 127-36.

27. Translated by Jessica Benjamin in *The Bonds of Love: Psychoanalysis, Feminism, and the Problem of Domination* (New York: Pantheon Books, 1988), 255-56. Compare this with W.E.B. DuBois's concept of "double consciousness," and bear in mind that DuBois was an ardent Germanist.

28. Ibid., 32-33.

29. Ricky Jay, *Learned Pigs & Fireproof Women: A History of Unique, Eccentric & Amazing Entertainers* (London: Guild Publishing, 1986), 78, 80.

30. Frantz Fanon, *Black Skin, White Masks*, trans. by Charles Lam Markmann (New York: Grove Press, Inc., 1967), 114–115.

31. John Ayto, *Dictionary of Word Origins* (New York: Arcade Publishing/Little, Brown and Company, 1990), 428.

32. Stuart Hall, "The After-life of Frantz Fanon: Why Fanon? Why Now? Why Black Skin, White Masks ?" in *The Facts of Blackness: Frantz Fanon and Visual Representation*, ed.

by Alan Read (London/Seattle: Institute of Contemporary Arts/Bay Press, 1996), 21.

33. Fanon, *Black Skin,* 118, 230.

34. Zora Neale Hurston, "Tell My Horse" (1938) in *Zora Neale Hurston: Folklore, Memoirs, and Other Writings* (New York: The Library of America, 1995), 473.

35. Charles Darwin quoted in George Fredrickson, *The Black Image in the White Mind* (New York, Harper's, 1971), 230.

36. Oodgerroo Noonucaal, *Inside Black Australia: An Anthology of Aboriginal Poetry,* ed. by Kevin Gilbert (Ringwood, Victoria: Penguin Books Australia Ltd., 1988), 98.

37. Nekhama Schoenburg, *The Unifying Factor: A Review of Kabbalah* (Northvale: Jason Aronson, Inc., 1996), 70-71.

38. Fanon, *Black Skin,* 134.

39. Langston Hughes, "The Negro Artist and the Racial Mountain," in *Nation* (23 June 1926).

40. Compare Fats Waller's surprisingly low-key singing of it to Louis Armstrong's upbeat snarl.

41. Singer, Barry, *Black and Blue: The Life and Lyrics of Andy Razaf* (New York: Schirmer Books, 1992).

42. Stuart Hall, "Racism and Moral Panics in Post-War Britain," in *Five Views of Multi-Racial Britain* (London: Commission For Racial Equality, 1978).

43. *The Penguin Dictionary of Sociology* (Second Edition), ed. by Nicholas Abercrombie, Stephen Hill, and Bryan S. Turner (London: Penguin Books, 1988), 223.

44. Paul Gilroy, "'After Love Has Gone': Bio-politics and Etho-poetics in the Black Public Sphere" in *The Black Public Sphere: A Public Culture Book,* ed. by the Black Public Sphere Collective (Chicago: University of Chicago Press, 1995), 74–75.

45. Fanon, *Black Skin,* 117.

46. John Howard Griffin, *Black Like Me* (New York: New American Library, 1960), 67, 156.

47. Years later, SCTV presented *Black Like Vic,* a complex satire on the Griffin book, and the TV gumshoe series *Johnny Stacatto,* starring John Cassavetes. Joe Flahrety played Vic, a PI jazz saxophonist who corks up, to be "undercover," and takes the Greyhound down South to solve a murder. His first mistake is sitting in the front of the bus. SCTV also dismantled *The Jazz Singer,* both the Jolson and Neil Diamond versions. Featuring "real life" black jazz singer Al Jarreau, who only wants to be a cantor, a chazzan, not jazz singer, despite the unrelenting pressure to sing jazz enforced by his glitz-stunned rabbi father played by Eugene Levy, decked in dreads, disco high-heel shoes, speaking a weird patois of Yiddish Ebonics.

Cassavetes's first film as indepedent director was *Shadows,* whose 1960 verite style focused on the hipster/jazz subculture and racism.

48. W.E.B. DuBois, "The Souls of White Folk" in *W.E.B. DuBois: Writings,* ed. by Nathan Hale Huggins (New York: The Library of America, 1986), 923.

49. Erving Goffman, *Stigma: Notes on the Management of Spoiled Identity* (Englewood Cliffs: Prentice-Hall, Inc., 1963), 5.

50. Harry Haywood, "Against Bourgeois-Liberal Distortions of Leninism on the Negro Question in the United States" in *The Communist IX* (August 1930), in *American Communism and Black Americans: A Documentary History, 1930-1934,* ed. by Philip S. Foner and Herbert Shapiro (Philadelphia: Temple University Press, 1991), 18-19.

51. *The Fact of Blackness: Frantz Fanon and Visual Representation,* ed. by Alan Read (London/Seattle, Institute of Contemporary Arts/Bay Press, 1996), 136.

Con-text

BOOKS ON PARADE

General Surveys, Sweeps, and Ideological Scans

Alkyer, Frank, ed. *Down Beat: Sixty Years of Jazz* (Milwaukee: Hal Leonard Corporation, 1995).

Attali, Jacques. *Noise: The Political Economy of Music* (Minneapolis: University of Minnesota Press, 1985).

Baraka, Amiri and Amina Baraka. *The Music: Reflections on Jazz and Blues* (New York: William Morrow & Co., Inc., 1987).

Bayles, Martha. *Hole in Our Soul: The Loss of Beauty and Meaning in American Popular Music* (New York: The Free Press, 1994).

Berendt, Joachim E. *The Jazz Book: From Ragtime to Fusion and Beyond*, translated by H. and B. Bredigkeit, with Dan Morgenstern (Westport, CT: Lawrence Hill, 1982).

Blacking, John. *How Musical is Man?* (Seattle: University of Washington Press, 1973).

Bogle, Donald. *Toms, Coons, Mulattos, Mammies and Blacks: An Interpretive History of Blacks in American Films* (New York: Viking Press, 1973).

Boskin, Joseph. *Sambo: The Rise and Demise of an American Jester* (New York: Oxford University Press, 1986).

Brown, Sterling A., Arthur P. Davis, and Ulysses Lee, ed. *The Negro Caravan* (1941). (New York: Arno Press/NY Times, 1969).

Burke, Peter. *Popular Culture in Early Modern Europe* (London: Maurice Temple Smith Ltd., 1978).

Burrett, Robert. *The Global Jukebox: The International Music Industry* (London/New York: Routledge, 1996).

Chanan, Michael. *Repeated Takes: A Short History of Recording and its Effects on Music* (London/New York: Verso, 1995).

Cooper, Ralph, with Steve Dougherty. *Amateur Night at the Apollo: Ralph Cooper Presents Five Decades of Great Entertainment* (New York: HarperCollins, 1990).

Cripps, Thomas. *Slow Fade to Black: The Negro in American Film, 1900-1942* (Oxford/New York: Oxford University Press, 1977).

Cruse, Harold. *The Crisis of the Negro Intellectual* (New York: William Morrow & Co., 1967).

Cunard, Nancy, ed. *Negro: An Anthology* (1934), edited and abridged with an introduction by Hugh Ford (New York: Continuum, 1996).

Dahl, Linda. *Stormy Weather: The Music and Lives of a Century of Jazz Women* (New York: William Morrow & Co., 1984).

de Barros, Paul. *Jackson Street After Hours: The Roots of Jazz in Seattle* (Seattle: Sasquatch Books, 1993).

Dennison, Sam. *Scandalize My Name: Black Imagery in American Popular Music* (New York: Garland Publishing, 1982).

Early, Gerald. *Tuxedo Junction: Essays on American Culture* (New York: Ecco Press, 1989).

Ellison, Ralph. *Going to the Territory* (New York: Random House, 1986).

——. *Shadow and Act* (New York: Random House, 1964).

Ely, Melvin Patrick. *The Adventures of Amos 'n' Andy: A Social Hisory of an American Phemomenon*

(New York: The Free Press, 1991).

Erenberg, Lewis A. *Steppin' Out: New York Nightlife and the Transformation of American Culture, 1890-1930* (Westport, CT: Greenwood Press, 1981).

Fanon, Frantz. *Black Skin, White Masks* (New York: Grove Press, 1967).

Fletcher, Tom. *100 Years of the Negro in Show Business* (New York: Burdge, 1954).

Floyd, Jr., Samuel A. *The Power of Black Music: Interpreting its History from Africa to the United States* (New York: Oxford University Press, 1995).

Frederickson, George. *The Black Image in the White Mind: The Debate on Afro-American Character and Destiny, 1817-1914* (New York: Harper & Row, 1971).

———. *White Supremacy: A Comparative A Study in American and South African History* (New York: Oxford University Press, 1981).

Gabbard, Krin. *Jammin' at the Margins: Jazz and the American Cinema* (Chicago: University of Chicago Press, 1996).

———, ed. *Jazz Among the Discourses* (Durham; Duke University Press, 1995).

———, ed. *Representing Jazz* (Durham: Duke University Press, 1995).

Gates, Jr., Henry Louis. *The Signifying Monkey: A Theory of Afro-American Literary Criticism* (New York: Oxford University Press, 1988).

———, ed. *"Race," Writing, and Difference* (Chicago: University of Chicago Press, 1986).

George, Nelson. *The Death of Rhythm and Blues* (New York: E.P. Dutton/Obelisk, 1988).

Goffman, Ervin. *Stigma: Notes on the Management of Spoiled Identity* (Englewood Cliffs, NJ: Prentice-Hall, Inc., 1963).

Gossett, Thomas F. *Race: A History of an Idea in America* (Dallas: Southern Methodist University Press, 1963).

Henderson, Stephen. *Understanding the New Black Poetry: Black Speech and Black Music as Poetic References* (New York: William Morrow & Co., 1973).

Hennessey, Thomas J. *From Jazz to Swing: African-American Jazz Musicians and Their Music, 1890-1935* (Detroit: Wayne State University Press, 1994).

Hughes, Langston and Arna Bontemps, eds. *Book of Negro Folklore* (New York: Dodd, Mead & Company, 1959).

Hughes, Langston and Milton Meltzer. *Black Magic: A Pictorial History of the Negro in American Entertainment* (Englewood Cliffs, NJ: Prentice-Hall, 1967).

Jones, LeRoi. *Blues People: Negro Music in White America* (New York: William Morrow & Co., Inc., 1963).

———. *Black Music* (New York: William Morrow & Co., Inc., 1967).

Jordan, Winthrop D. *White over Black: American Attitudes Toward the Negro, 1550-1812* (Chapel Hill: University of North Carolina Press, 1968).

Keil, Charles and Stephen Feldman. *Musical Grooves* (Chicago: University of Chicago Press, 1996).

Kernfeld, Barry, ed. *The New Grove Dictionary of Jazz* (London: Macmillan, 1988, 2 vol.).

Kochman, Thomas, ed. *Rappin' and Stylin' Out: Communications in Urban Black America* (Chicago: University of Illinois Press, 1972).

Kovel, Joel. *White Racism: A Psychohistory* (New York: Pantheon Books, 1970).

Lees, Gene. *Cats of Any Color: Jazz Black and White* (New York: Oxford University Press, 1994).

Leonard, Neil. *Jazz and the White Americans: The Acceptance of a New Art Form* (Chicago: University of Chicago Press, 1962).

———. *Jazz: Myth and Religion* (New York: Oxford University Press, 1987).

Levine, Lawrence W. *Black Culture and Black Consciousness* (New York: Oxford University Press, 1977).

Lipsitz, George. *Time Passages: Collective Memory and American Popular Culture* (Minneapolis:

University of Minnesota Press, 1990).

Locke, Alain Leroy, ed. *The New Negro* (1925), with a new preface by Robert Hayden (New York: Atheneum, 1974).

Lott, Eric. *Love and Theft: Blackface Minstrelsy and the American Working Class* (New York: Oxford University Press, 1993).

Lowe, Allen. *American Pop From Minstrel to Mojo: On Record 1893-1965* (Redwood, NY: Cadence Books, 1997).

Mills, Charles W. *The Racial Contract* (Ithaca: Cornell University Press, 1997).

Neal, Jr., Larry. *Visions of a Liberated Future: Black Arts Movement Writing*, edited by Michael Schwartz (New York: Thunder's Mouth. 1989).

Ostrovsky, Leroy. *Jazz City: The Impact of Our Cities on the Development of Jazz* (Englewood Cliffs, NJ: Prentice-Hall, 1978).

Peretti, Burton W. *Jazz in American Culture* (Chicago: Ivan R. Dee, 1997).

Pieterse, Jan Nederveen. *White on Black: Images of Africa and Blacks in Western Popular Culture* (New Haven: Yale University Press, 1992).

Placksin, Sally. *American Women in Jazz, 1900 to the Present: Their Words, Lives, and Music* (New York: Putnam, 1982).

Porter, Lewis. *Jazz: From Its Origins to the Present* (Englewood Cliffs: Prentice-Hall, 1992).

Roediger, David. *The Wages of Whiteness: Race and the Making of the American Working Class* (London: Verso, 1988).

Rogin, Michael. *Blackface, White Noise* (Berkeley: University of California Press, 1996).

Rowland, Mark and Tony Seterman, eds. *The Jazz Musician: Fifteen Years of Interviews* (New York: St. Martin's Press, 1994).

Sanjek, Russell. *American Popular Music and Its Business: The First Four Hundred Years* (New York: Oxford University Press, 1988).

Santoro, Gene. *Dancing In Your Head: Jazz, Blues, Rock and Beyond* (New York: Oxford University Press, 1994).

Saxton, Alexander. *The Rise and Fall of the White Republic* (London: Verso, 1990).

Small, Christopher. *Music of the Common Tongue: Survival and Celebration in Afro-American Music* (London: John Calder, 1987).

Southern, Eileen. *The Music of Black Americans* (1971) (New York: W.W. Norton & Co., Inc., third updated edition, 1997).

Spencer, Jon Michael. *The Rhythms of Black Folk: Race, Religion and Pan-Africanism* (Trenton: Africa World Press, Inc., 1995).

Stearns, Marshall and Jean. *Jazz Dance: The Story of American Vernacular Dance* (New York: Macmillan, 1968).

Tate, Greg. *Flyboy in The Buttermilk: Essays on Contemporary America* (New York: Simon & Schuster, 1992).

Taylor, Arthur. *Notes and Tones: Musician-to-Musician Interviews* (New York: Perigree Books, 1982).

Thompson, Robert Farris. *Flash of the Spirit: African and Afro-American Art and Philosophy* (New York: Random House, 1983).

Toll, Robert C. *Blacking Up: The Minstrel Show in Nineteenth-Century America* (New York: Oxford University Press, 1974).

Travis, Dempsey J. *An Autobiography of Black Jazz* (Chicago: The Urban Research Institute, 1983).

Walton, Ortiz M. *Music: Black, White, and Blue* (New York: William Morrow & Co., 1972).

Ward, Brian. *Just My Soul Responding: Rhythm and Blues, Black Consciousness, and Race Relations* (Berkeley: University of California Press, 1998).

Watkins, Mel. *On the Real Side: Laughing, Lying, and Signifying—The Underground Tradition of*

African-American Humor That Transformed American Culture, from Slavery to Richard Pryor (New York: Simon & Schuster, 1994).

Wayne, Enstice and Paul Rubin. *Jazz Spoken Here: Conversations with Twenty-Two Musicians* (Baton Rouge: Lousiana State University Press, 1992).

Williams, Patricia J. *The Alchemy of Race and Rights: Diary of a Law Professor* (Cambridge: Harvard University Press, 1991).

Young, Al. *Bodies and Soul: Musical Memoirs* (Berkeley: Creative Arts Book Company, 1981).

———. *Kinds of Blue: Musical Memoirs* (Berkeley: Creative Arts Book Company, 1985).

———. *Things Ain't What They Used To Be: Musical Memoirs* (Berkeley: Creative Arts Book Company, 1987).

Blues, Roots

Barlow, William. *"Looking Up At Down": The Emergence of Blues Culture* (Philadelphia: Temple University Press, 1989).

Bradford, Perry. *Born With the Blues.* New York: Oak Publishing, Inc., 1965).

Broonzy, "Big Bill," with Yannick Bruynoghe. *Big Bill's Blues* (1955) (New York: Oak Publications, Inc., 1964).

Charters, Samuel. *The Roots of the Blues: An African Search* (Boston: Marion Boyars, 1981).

———. *The Country Blues* (New York: Rinehart: 1959).

———. *Poetry of the Blues*, with photographs by Ann Charters (New York: Oak Publishing, Inc. 1963).

Cone, James H. *The Spirituals and the Blues: An Interpretation* (1972) (Maryknoll: Orbis Books, 1991).

Dance, Helen Oakley. *Stormy Monday: The T-Bone Walker Story* (Baton Rouge: Louisana State University Press, 1987).

Davis, Angela. *Blues Legacies and Black Feminism: Gertrude "Ma" Rainey, Bessie Smith, and Billie Holiday* (New York: Pantheon Books, 1998).

Dixon, Robert and John Goodrich. *Recording the Blues* (London: Studio Vista, 1970).

Evans, David. *Big Road Blues: Tradition and Creativity in the Folk Blues* (Berkeley: University of California Press, 1982).

Fahey, John. *Charley Patton* (London: Studio Vista, 1970).

Ferris, Jr., William. *Blues From The Delta* (London: Studio Vista, 1970).

Garon, Paul. *The Devil's Son-in-Law: The Story of Peetie Wheatstraw and His Songs* (London: Studio Vista, 1971).

Guralnik, Peter. *The Listener's Guide to the Blues* (New York: Facts on File, Inc., 1982).

———. *Searching for Robert Johnson* (New York: E.P. Dutton, 1989).

Harris, Michael W. *The Rise of the Gospel Blues: The Music of Thomas Andrew Dorsey in the Urban Church* (New York: Oxford University Press, 1994).

Harrison, Daphne Duval. *Black Pearls: Blues Queens of the 1920s* (New Brunswick: Rutgers University Press, 1988).

Lieb, Sandra. *Mother of the Blues: A Study of Ma Rainey* (Amherst: University of Mass. Press, 1981).

Keil, Charles. *Urban Blues* (Chicago: University of Chicago Press, 1966).

Lipscomb, Mance, as told to Glen Alyn. *I Say Me for a Parable: The Oral Autobiography of Mance Lipscomb* (New York: W.W. Norton and Company, 1993).

Murray, Albert. *Stomping the Blues* (New York: Alfred A. Knopf, 1967).

Oakley, Giles. *The Devil's Music: A History of the Blues* (New York: Taplinger, 1977).

Oliver, Paul. *Songsters and Saints: Vocal Traditions on Race Records.* (New York: Cambridge University Press, 1984).

Olsson, Bengt. *Memphis Blues* (London: Studio Vista, 1970).

Russell, Tony. *Blacks, Whites and Blues* (London: Studio Vista, 1970).

Sackheim, Eric. *The Blues Line: A Collection of Blues Lyrics from Leadbelly to Muddy Waters* (New York: Schirmer Books, 1975).

Spencer, Jon Michael. *Blues and Evil* (Knoxville: University of Tennessee Press, 1993).

Stewart-Baxter, Derrick. *Ma Rainey and the Classic Blues Singers* (London: Studio Vista, 1970).

Taylor, Frank C., with Gerald Cook. *Alberta Hunter: A Celebration in Blues* (New York: Mc-Graw-Hill Company, 1987).

Titon, Jeff Todd. *Early Downhome Blues* (Chicago: University of Illinois Press, 1977).

Welding, Pete and Toby Byron, eds. *Bluesland: Portraits of Twelve Major American Blues Masters.* (New York: Dutton, 1991).

Early Jazz

Armstrong, Louis. *Satchmo: My Life in New Orleans* (1954) (New York: Da Capo, 1986).

Collier, James Lincoln. *Louis Armstrong: An American Success Story* (New York: Macmillan, 1985).

Foster, Pops, with Tom Stoddard. *The Autobiography of a New Orleans Jazzman* (Berkeley: University of California Press, 1971).

Handy, W.C. *Father of the Blues: An Autobiography* (New York: Da Capo Press, 1961).

Marquis, Donald. *In Search of Buddy Bolden: First Man of Jazz* (New York: Da Capo, 1980).

Jazz Age

Baker, Houston A. *Modernism and the Harlem Renaissance* (Chicago: University of Chicago Press, 1987).

Bechet, Sidney. *Treat It Gentle: An Autobiography* (New York: Hill & Wang, 1960).

Bernhardt, Clyde E.B., as told to Sheldon Harris. *I Remember: Eighty Years of Black Entertainment, Big Bands, and the Blues: An Autobiography by Jazz Trombonist and Blues Singer* (Philadelphia: University of Pennsylvania Press, 1986).

Bontemps, Arna, ed. *The Harlem Renaissance Remembered* (New York: Dodd, Mead & Company, 1972).

Bricktop (Ada Smith) and James Haskins. *Bricktop* (New York: Atheneum, 1983).

Chilton, John. *Sidney Bechet: The Wizard of Jazz* (New York: Oxford University Press, 1987).

Douglas, Ann. *Terrible Honesty: Mongrel Manhattan in the 1920s* (New York: Alfred A. Knopf, 1995).

Fairbain, Ann. *Call Him George: A Biography of George Lewis, The Man, His Faith and His Music* (New York: Crown Publishers Inc., 1969).

Giddins, Gary. *Satchmo* (New York: Doubleday and Company, Inc., 1988).

Huggins, Nathan Irvin. *Harlem Renaissance* (New York: Oxford University Press, 1971).

Hutchinson, George. *The Harlem Renaissance in Black and White* (Cambridge: The Belknap Press of Harvard University Press, 1995).

Johnson, James Weldon. *Black Manhattan* (1930) (New York: Atheneum, 1968).

Jones, Max and John Chilton. *Louis: The Louis Armstrong Story, 1900-1971* (Boston: Little, Brown and Company, 1971).

Kennedy, Rick. *Jelly Roll, Bix, and Hoagy: Gennett Studios and the Birth of Recorded Jazz* (Bloomington: Indiana University Press, 1994).

Kimball, Robert and William Bolcom. *Reminiscing With Sissle and Blake* (New York: Viking Press, 1973).

Lomax, Alan. *Mr. Jelly Roll: The Fortunes of Jelly Roll Morton, New Orleans Creole and "Inventor of Jazz"* (1950) (Berkeley: University of California Press, revised edition, 1973).

Morris, Ronald L. *Wait Until Dark: Jazz and the Underworld, 1880-1940* (Bowling Green: Bowling Green University Popular Press, 1980).

Ogren, Kathy J. *The Jazz Revolution: Twenties America and the Meaning of Jazz* (New York: Oxford University Press, 1989).

Peretti, Burton W. *The Creation of Jazz: Music, Race and Culture in Urban America* (Urbana: University of Illinois Press, 1992).

Reed, Ishmael. *Mumbo Jumbo* (New York: Doubleday and Co., Inc., 1972).

Rose, Al. *Eubie Blake* (New York: Schirmer Books, 1979).

Tucker, Mark. *Ellington: The Early Years* (Urbana: University of Illinois Press, 1992).

Vincent, Ted. *Keep Cool: The Black Activists Who Built the Jazz Age* (London: Pluto Press, 1995).

The Thirties and Forties

Allen, Walter C. *Hendersonia: The Music of Fletcher Henderson and His Musicians* (Jazz Monographs 4) (Highland Park, IL: Walter C. Allen, 1973).

Basie, Count, as told to Albert Murray. *Good Mornin' Blues: The Autobiography of Count Basie* (New York: Random House, 1985).

Berger, Morroe, Edward Berger, and James Patrick. *Benny Carter: A Life in American Music* (Metuchen, NJ: Scarecrow Press and the Institute of Jazz Studies, Rutgers University, 2 vols. 1982).

Bigard, Barney. *With Louis and Duke,* ed. Barry Martyn (New York: Oxford University Press, 1986).

Buchmann-Moller, Frank. *You Just Fight For Your Life: The Story of Lester Young* (New York: Praeger, 1990).

Bushell, Garvin, as told to Mark Tucker. *Jazz From The Beginning* (Ann Arbor: University of Michigan Press, 1988).

Calloway, Cab and Bryant Rollins. *Of Minnie the Moocher and Me* (New York: Thomas Y. Crowell Company, 1976).

Chilton, John. *Billie's Blues: The Billie Holiday Story* (New York: Da Capo Press, 1989).

———. *The Song of the Hawk: The Life an Recordings of Coleman Hawkins* (Ann Arbor: University of Michigan Press, 1991).

Coleman, Bill. *Trumpet Story* (Boston: Northeastern University Press, 1990).

Dance, Stanley. *The World of Duke Ellington* (New York: Charles Scribner's Sons, 1970).

———. *The World of Count Basie* (New York: Charles Scribner's Sons, 1980).

———. *The World of Earl Hines* (New York: Charles Scribner's Sons, 1977).

Delannoy, Luc. *Pres: The Story of Lester Young, translated by Elena B. Odio* (Fayetville: University of Arkansas Press, 1993).

DeVeaux, Alexis. *Don't Explain: A Song of Billie Holiday* (New York: Harper and Row, 1994).

Ellington, Edward Kennedy. *Music is My Mistress* (Garden City: Doubleday and Company, Inc., 1973).

Ellington, Mercer, with Stanley Dance. *Duke In Person: An Intimate Memoir* (Boston: Houghton Mifflin Company, 1979).

Hajdu, David. *Lush Life: A Biography of Billy Strayhorn* (New York: Farrar, Straus & Giroux, 1996).

Hampton, Lionel, with James Haskins. *Hamp: An Autobiography* (New York: Warner Books/Amistad Books, 1990).

Hasse, John Edward. *Beyond Category: The Life and Genius of Duke Ellington* (New York: Simon and Schuster, 1995).

Hinton, Milt and David G. Berger. *Bass Lines: The Stories and Photographs of Milt Hinton* (Philadelphia: Temple University Press, 1988).

Holiday, Billie, and William Dufty. *Lady Sings the Blues* (1956) (Hammondsworth: Penguin, 1984).

Lester, James. *Too Marvelous For Words: The Life and Genius of Art Tatum* (New York: Oxford University Press, 1994).

O'Meally, Robert. *Lady Day: The Many Faces of Billie Holiday* (New York: Arcade, 1991).

Pearson, Jr., Nathan W. *Goin' To Kansas City* (Urbana: University of Illinois, 1987).

Porter, Lewis. *Lester Young* (Boston: Twayne Publishers, 1985).

——, ed. *A Lester Young Reader* (Washington: The Smithsonian Institute Press, 1996).

Stewart, Rex. *Jazz Masters of the 30s* (New York: Macmillan, 1972).

——. *Boy Meets Horn*, ed. Claire P. Gordon (Ann Arbor: University of Michigan Press, 1991).

Stowe, David W. *Swing Changes: Big Band Jazz in New Deal America* (Cambridge: Harvard University Press, 1994).

Vance, Joel. *Fats Waller: His Life and Times* (New York: Berkeley Medallion Books, 1979).

Wells, Dicky, as told to Stanley Dance. *The Night People: The Jazz Life of Dicky Wells* (Washington/London: Smithsonian Institute Press, 1991).

Bebop

Bergerot, Franck, and Arnaud Merlin. *The Story of Jazz: Bop and Beyond* (New York: Harry N. Abrams, Inc., 1993).

Bryan, Cora et al, eds. *Central Avenue Sounds: Jazz in Los Angeles* (Berkeley: University of California Press, 1998).

Callender, Red and Elaine Cohen. *Unfinished Dream: The Musical World of Red Callender* (London: Quartet Books, 1985).

Cox, Bette Yarbrough. *Central Avenue—Its Rise and Fall, 1800-c.1955* (Los Angeles: BEEM Publications, 1989).

DeVeaux, Scott. *The Birth of Bebop: A Social and Musical History* (Berkeley: University of California Press, 1997).

Gillespie, Dizzy and Al Fraser. *To Be, or Not . . . To Bop: Memoirs* (Garden City: Doubleday & Company, Inc., 1979).

Gitler, Ira. *Swing to Bop: An Oral History of the Transition of Jazz in the 1940s* (New York: Oxford University Press, 1985).

Gourse, Leslie. *Sassy: The Life of Sarah Vaughan* (New York: Charles Scribner's Sons, 1993).

Mingus, Charles. *Beneath The Underdog* (New York: Alfred A. Knopf, 1971).

Owens, Thomas. *Bebop: The Music and its Players* (New York: Oxford University Press, 1995).

Reisner, Robert G. *Bird: The Legend of Charlie Parker* (New York: Bonanza, 1962).

Russell, Ross. *Bird Lives! The High Life and Hard Times of Charlie Parker* (New York: Charterhouse, 1973).

Vail, Ken. *Bird's Diary: The Life of Charlie Parker, 1945-1955* (Surrey: Castle Communications, 1996).

Woideck, Carl. *Charlie Parker: His Music and Life* (Ann Arbor: University of Michigan Press, 1996).

Postbop, Free Jazz, and Onward

Backus, Rob. *Fire Music: A Political History of Jazz* (Chicago: Vanguard Books, 1976).

Blancq, Charles. *Sonny Rollins: The Journey of a Jazzman* (Boston: Twanye Publishers, 1983).

Brown, Marion. *Recollections: Essays, Drawings, Miscellanea* (Frankfurt: Juergen A. Schmitt, 1984).

Chambers, Jack. *Milestones, Volumes 1 and 2* (Toronto: University of Toronto Press, 1983 and 1985).

Charles, Phillipe and Jean-Louis Comolli. *Free Jazz/Black Power* (Paris: Editions Champ Libre, 1971).

Corbett, John. *Extended Play: Sounding Off From John Cage to Dr. Funkenstein* (Durham: Duke University Press, 1994).

Coleman, Janet and Al Young. *Mingus/Mingus: Two Memoirs* (Berkeley: Creative Arts Book Company, 1989).

Coryell, Julie and Laura Friedman. *Jazz-Rock Fusion: The People, the Music* (New York: Delacorte Press, 1978).

Crouch, Stanley. *Notes of a Hanging Judge* (New York: Oxford University Press, 1990).

Davis, Miles, with Quincy Troupe. *Autobiography* (New York: Simon & Schuster, 1989).

Gray, John. *Fire Music: A Bibliography of the New Jazz, 1959-1990* (New York: Greenwood Press, 1991).

Haskins, Jim. *Queen of the Blues: A Biography of Dinah Washington* (New York: William Morrow & Co., Inc., 1987).

Hawes, Hampton and Don Asher. *Raise Up Off Me: A Portrait of Hampton Hawes* (New York: Coward, McCann and Geoghegan, Inc., 1974).

Horricks, Raymond. *The Importance of Being Eric Dolphy* (Tunbridge Wells, UK: D.J. Costell, Ltd., 1989).

Kofsky, Frank. *Black Nationalism and the Revolution in Music* (New York: Pathfinder, 1970).

Litweiler, John. *The Freedom Principle: Jazz After 1958* (New York: William Morrow & Co., 1984).

———. *Ornette Coleman: A Harmolodic Life* (New York: William Morrow & Co., Inc., 1992).

Nisenson, Eric. *Ascension: John Coltrane and His Quest* (New York: St. Martins Press, 1993).

Rivelli, Pauline and Robert Levin, eds. *Black Giants* (New York/Cleveland: The World Publishing Company, 1970).

Rosenthal, David H. *Hard Bop: Jazz and Black Music, 1955-1966* (New York: Oxford University Press, 1992).

Ruff, Willie. *A Call to Assembly: An American Success Story* (New York: Viking Penguin, 1991).

Sakolsky, Ron and Fred Wei-Man Ho, eds. *Sounding Off! Music as Subversion/Resistance/Revolution* (New York: Autonomedia, 1995).

Sidran, Ben. *Talking Jazz: An Illustrated Oral History* (San Francisco: Pomegranate Books, 1992).

Simosko, Vladimir and Barry Tepperman. *Eric Dolphy: A Musical Biography and Discography* (Washington, DC: Smithsonian Institution Press, 1974).

Sinclair, John and Robert Levin. *Music and Politics* (New York/Cleveland: The World Publishing Company, 1971).

Such, David G. *Avant-Garde Jazz Musicians: Performing "Out There"* (Iowa City: University of Iowa Press, 1993).

Spellman, A.B. *Black Music: Four Lives in the Bebop Business* (New York: Pantheon Books, 1970).

Bey, Faruq Z. From page 39 of *Solid Ground: A New World Journal*, Volume 1, Number 1, Fall 1981, edited by Kofi Natambu. Copyright © by Faruq Z. Bey. Published by Go-For-What-You-Know, Inc., Detroit.

Bey, Faruq Z. From "Interview: Faruq Z. Bey at the Belcrest Hotel" [p. 47] in *Solid Ground: A New World Journal*, Volume 1, number 3/4, Winter/Spring 1983. Copyright © 1983. Go-For-What-You-Know, Inc., Detroit.

Brathwaite, Edward Kamau. From *Black + Blues*. Copyright © 1976 by Edward Kamau Brathwaite. Published by Oxford University Press, Havana.

Braxton, Anthony. From "Conversation With Anthony Braxton, 3/31/76," by Peter Kostakis and Art Lange [pp. 57-85] in *Brilliant Corners: A Magazine of the Arts*, #4, Fall 1976, Art Lange, ed. Copyright © 1976 by Art Lange/Brilliant Corners. Reprinted by permission of the publisher.

Broonzy, William "Big Bill." From "Baby, I Done Got Wise" [pp. 57-59] in *Selections from the Gutter: Portraits from "The Jazz Record,"* Art Hodes and Chadwick Hansen, eds. Copyright © 1977 by Regents of the University of California. Reprinted by permission of Regents of the University of California Press.

Brown, Arthur. From pages 17-42 of *A Trumpet in the Morning*. Copyright © 1985 by Arthur Ray Brown. Reprinted by permission of James Brown.

Brown, Sterling. From *The Collected Poems of Sterling Brown*. Copyright © 1980 by Sterling Brown. Reprinted by permission of Northwestern University Press.

Broyard, Anatole. From pages 69-71 of *Kafka Was The Rage: A Greenwich Village Memoir* by Anatole Broyard. Copyright © 1993 by Anatole Broyard. Reprinted by permission of Crown Publishers, Inc.

Callender, Red. From pages 76-79, 118-19 of *Unfinished Dream: The Musical World of Red Callender* by Red Callender and Elaine Cohen. Copyright © 1985 by Red Callender. Published by Quartet Books, London.

Campbell, E. Simms. Originally published in *Esquire* c. mid 1930s. Reprinted [pp. 983-89] in *The Negro Caravan*, edited by Sterling A. Brown, Arthur P. David, and Ulysses Lee. Citadel Press/Dryden Press, New York.

Coleman, Ornette. From "Ornette Coleman: Interview at the Power Center, Eclipse Jazz Concert, February 18, 1982," [p. 44] in *Solid Ground: A New World Journal*, Volume 1, number 3/4, Winter/Spring 1983, edited by Kofi Natambu. Copyright © 1983. Published by Go-For-What-You-Know, Inc., Detroit.

Coleman, Wanda. From page 97 of *Heavy Daughter Blues: Poems and Stories, 1968-86*. Copyright © 1987 by Wanda Coleman. Reprinted by permission of Black Sparrow Press.

Cone, James H. From pages 114-18, 129-30 of *The Spirituals and the Blues* by James H. Cone. Copyright © 1972, 1991 by James H. Cone. Published in 1991 by Orbis Books, Maryknoll, New York 10545. Used by permission.

Crowder, Henry. From pages 36-40 of *As Wonderful as All That? Henry Crowder's Memoir of His Affair with Nancy Cunard, 1928-1935* by Henry Crowder with Hugo Speck. Copyright © 1987 by Wild Trees Press, Navarro, CA.

Cruse, Harold. Text of pages 104-105 from *The Crisis of the Negro Intellectual* by Harold Cruse. Copyright © 1967 by Harold Cruse. Reprinted by permission of William Morrow & Company, Inc.

Cruse, Harold. Text of pages 115-16 from *Rebellion or Revolution* by Harold Cruse. Copyright © 1968 by Harold Cruse. Reprinted by permission of William Morrow & Company, Inc.

Davenport, Charles "Cow Cow." "Cow Cow and the Boogie-Woogie," [pp. 41-42] from *Selections from the Gutter: Portraits from the Jazz Record*, Art Hodes and Chadwick Hansen,

Lipscomb, Mance. From pages 207-210, 465-466 of *I Say Me for a Parable: The Oral Autobiography of Mance Lipscomb, Texas Bluesman* by Glen Alyn, ed. Copyright © 1993 by A. Glenn Myers. Reprinted by permission of W.W. Norton & Company, Inc.

Locke, Alain Leroy. From pages 68-74 of *The Negro In American Culture* by Margaret Just Butcher. Copyright © 1956 by Margaret Just Butcher. Reprinted by permission of Alfred A. Knopf, Inc.

Lynch, Acklyn. From "Black Culture in the Early Forties" [pp. 64-70] in *Nightmare Overhanging Darkly: Essays on Black Culture and Resistance.* Copyright © 1992 by Acklyn Lynch. Reprinted by permission of Third World Press.

Malcolm X. From pages 74-76, 129-30 of *The Autobiography of Malcolm X* by Malcom X and Alex Haley. Copyright © 1964 by Alex Haley and Malcolm X. Copyright © 1965 by Alex Haley and Betty Shabazz. Reprinted by permission of Random House, Inc.

McKay, Claude. From pages 29-31 of *Harlem Glory: A Fragment of Aframerican Life.* Copyright © 1990 by Charles H. Kerr Co. Reprinted by permission of Charles H. Kerr Co., Chicago.

Mingus, Charles. From pages 185-192 of *Beneath The Underdog: His World as Composed by Mingus.* Copyright © 1971 by Jazz Workshop, Inc. Reprinted by permission of Jazz Workshop, Inc.

Morgan, Thomas L., and William Barlow. From pages 95-101 of *From Cakewallks to Concert Halls: An Illustrated History of African American Popular Music from 1895 to 1930.* Copyright © 1992 by Elliott & Clark of Black Belt Communications Group. Reprinted by permission of Black Belt Communications Group.

Murray, Albert. Reprinted from pages 83-85 of *The Hero and the Blues* by Albert Murray, by permission of the University of Missouri Press. Copyright © 1973 by the Curators of the University of Missouri.

Neal, Larry. From pages 79-80 of *Visions of a Liberated Future: Black Arts Movement Writings* by Larry Neal, Michael Schwartz, ed. Copyright © 1989 by Evelyn Neal. Reprinted by permission of Thunder's Mouth Press.

Nichols, Herbie. From liner notes for Blue Note BLP 1519 [1956], reprinted in album booklet for *The Complete Blue Note Recordings of Herbie Nichols,* Roswell Rudd, ed. Published by Mosaic Records, Stamford, CT.

Pasteur, Alfred B., Ph.D., and Ivory L. Toldson, Ed.D. From page 63 of *Roots of Soul: The Psychology of Black Expressiveness.* Copyright © 1982 by Alfred B Pasteur, Ph.D. Anchor Press/Doubleday, Garden City.

Peery, Nelson. From pages 182-85 of *Black Fire: The Making of an American Revolutionary.* Copyright © 1994 by Nelson Peery. Reprinted by permission of The New Press.

Porter, Thomas J. From "The Social Roots of Afro-American Music: 1950-1970" [pp. 40-49] in *A Freedomways Reader: Afro-America in the Seventies,* Ernest Kaiser, ed. Copyright © 1976 by Freedomways Associates Inc. Reprinted by permission of International Publishers Co., NY.

Reed, Ishmael. From pages 64-66 of *Shrovetide in Old New Orleans,* published by Atheneum. Copyright © 1978 by Ishmael Reed and reprinted by permission of the author.

Rogers, J.A. From "Jazz at Home" [pp. 216-224] in *The New Negro,* Alain Locke, ed. Copyright © 1925 by J.A. Rogers. Albert & Boni, Inc., New York.

Russell, George. From pages 190-91 of *The Jazz Word,* Dom Cerulli, Burt Korall, and Mort Nasatir, eds. Copyright © 1960. Published by Ballantine Books, New York.

Sanchez, Sonia. From *We A BaddDD People.* Copyright © 1970 by Sonia Sanchez. Reprinted by permission of Sonia Sanchez.

Shepp, Archie. From "Archie Shepp: We Must Move Toward a Critique of American Culture" [pages 20-21] in *Solid Ground: A New World Journal,* Volume 1 Number 2, Win-

INDEX OF ANTHOLOGIZED MATERIAL

About the Editor

DAVID MELTZER began his literary career during the Beat heyday in San Francisco, reading poetry to jazz accompaniment at the famous Jazz Cellar. He is the author of *The Secret Garden: The Classical Kabbalah; Birth: Hymns, Prayers, Documents, Myths, Amulets; Death: An Anthology of Ancient Texts, Songs, Prayers, and Stories;* and *Reading Jazz* (Mercury House, 1994), as well as many books of poetry, including *Arrows: Selected Poetry 1982–1992*. He teaches in the Humanities and graduate Poetics programs at the New College of California. He lives in the Bay Area.

About the Artist

Out of his studio in San Francisco's beat-historic North Beach, WARD SCHUMAKER draws for clients around the globe, from Japan's *Esquire* and *Playboy* magazines to *Macworld* and *The New Yorker.* He has created two children's books, *Dance!* and *Sing a Song of Circus,* as well as illustrated volumes as diverse in subject matter as Julia Child's *Baking* and Véronique Vienne's *French Style.* He lives on Potrero Hill with his whining twenty-four-year-old cat, Sylvester.